Shotokan Legends

Jose M. Fraguas

Disclaimer
Please note that the author and publisher of this book are NOT RESPONSIBLE in any manner whatsoever for any injury that may result from practicing the techniques and/or following the instructions given within. Since the physical activities described herein may be too strenuous in nature for some readers to engage in safely, it is essential that a physician be consulted prior to training.

First publish in 2015 by AWP LLC/Empire Books.
Copyright (c) 2015 by Jose M. Fraguas.

All rights reserved. No part of this publication may be reproduced or utilized in any form or by any means, electronic or mechanical, including photocopying, recording, or by any information storage and retrieval system, without prior written permission from AWP LLC/Empire Books.

EMPIRE BOOKS
P.O. Box 491788
Los Angeles, CA 90049

First edition
Library of Congress Catalog Number:
ISBN-13: 978-1-933901-54-1

15 14 13 12 11 10 09 08 07 06 05 04 03 02 01 00

Library of Congress Cataloging-in-Publication Data
Fraguas, Jose M.
Shotokan Legends / by Jose M. Fraguas. -- 1st ed.
p. cm.
Includes index.
ISBN 1-933901-54-1 (pbk. : alk. paper)
1. Karate. 5. Martial artists--Interviews. 3. Large type books. I. Title.
GV1114.3.F715 2014
796.815'3--dc22

2006012535.
Printed in the United States of America.

"Even a life-long prosperity is but one cup of sake;
A life of fifty-two years is passed in a dream;
I know not what life is, nor death.
Year in year out-all but a dream.
Both Heaven and Hell are left behind;
I stand in the moonlit dawn,
Free from clouds of attachment."

- Uesugi Kenshin (1530-1578)

Dedication

I dedicate this book to the memory of Grandmaster Gichin Funakoshi.

Acknowledgments

Many people were responsible for making this book possible, some more directly than others. I want to extend my gratitude to all those whom so generously contributed their assistance to the preparation of this work. Assistance is an inadequate term for all the patience, time and knowledge that they so generously provided.

A special thanks to Lois Luzi, whose flights of guidance in the idea of this book were always on the wings of excitement. I also want to thank France's Thierry Plee, long-time friend and president of Sedirep and Budo Editions; Mr. Schlatt, kind friend and founder of Schlatt-Books in Germany; John Cheetham, editor of *"Shotokan Karate"* magazine in England, your knowledge and friendship has been always greatly appreciated; Harold E. Sharp, a true legend in the world of martial arts who kindly supplied great photos of his personal archives; Glenn Stoddard and Bill Bly, ong-time friends and martial artists; Shaun Banfield, director of *www.theshotokanway.com* and passionate Shotokan karateka and writer; dear friend Oleg Larinov, a great karateka, impecable filmmaker and better human being; I truly admire your passion for karate-do, and finally to Teruyuki Okazaki Sensei, who not only accepted to write the Foreword to this work but who was the "origin" of the idea for this book.

A word of appreciation is also due to my good friend Masahiro Ide, president of *JK Fan* and *Champ* videos, for his generosity and cooperation in this project; I also want to thank the publishers of *Gekkan Karate-do* magazine (Fukushodo, Ltd., Japan), for their assistance, kindness and supply of great photographic material for some of the chapters. Without their support, kindness and commitment to preserve the art of karate-do, this book would not exist.

I would further like to give my heartfelt gratitude to all the masters appearing in this book. They not only generously gave me an enormous amount of personal time for the long interviews, but also provided wonderful personal photographs to illustrate the book.

And last but not least, to all my instructors, past and present, for giving me the understanding and knowledge to undertake all the karate-do projects I've done during my life. My understanding of the art has grown over the years, thanks, in great part, to the questions they made me ask myself. These questions — both perceptive and practical — have sent me further and deeper in search for answers in my life.

You all have my enduring thanks.

— Jose M. Fraguas

About the Author

Born and raised in Madrid, Spain, Jose M. Fraguas began his martial arts studies with judo, in grade school, at age 9. From there he moved to taekwon-do and then to kenpo-karate, earning black belts in these three styles. During this same period, he also studied karate-do under Japanese Master Masahiro Okada, eventually receiving a seventh-degree black belt and the title of Shihan from Soke K. Mabuni. He began his career as a writer at age 16 as a regular contributor to martial arts magazines in Great Britain, France, Spain, Italy, Germany, Portugal, Holland and Australia. In 1980, he moved to Los Angeles, California, where his open-minded mentality helped him to develop a realistic approach to the martial arts. Seeking to supplement his previous training, he researched other disciplines such as Gracie jiu-jitsu, and muay Thai.

In 1986, Fraguas founded his first publishing company in Europe, authoring dozens of books and distributing his magazines to 35 countries in three different languages. His reputation and credibility as a martial artist and publisher became well known to the top masters around the world. Considering himself a martial artist first and a writer and publisher second, Fraguas feels fortunate to have had the opportunity to interview many legendary martial artists. He recognizes that much of the information given in the interviews helped him to discover new dimensions in the martial arts. "I was constantly absorbing knowledge from the great masters," he recalls. "I only trained with a few of them, but intellectually, academically and spiritually all of them have made very important contributions to my growth as a complete martial artist."

Steeped in tradition yet looking to the future, Fraguas understands and appreciates martial arts history and philosophy and feels this rich heritage is a necessary steppingstone to personal growth and spiritual evolution. His desire to promote both ancient philosophy and modern thinking provided the motivation for writing this book. "If the motivation is just money, a book cannot be of good quality," Fraguas says. "If the book is written to just make people happy, it cannot be deep. I want to write books so I can learn as well as teach. Karate-do, like human life itself, is filled with experiences that seem quite ordinary at the time and assume a fabled stature only with the passage of the years. I hope this work will be appreciated by future practitioners not only of the art of Shotokan but karate in general, regardless of the style."

It is clear that every one of us will some kind of leave a legacy behind when we die. The challenge is the same for all of us. For Fraguas, who has authored more than 30 books, the important question is what kind of legacy will I leave? "I believe our main legacy as writers is to educate or even just re-echo those things that we believe are worthwhile - a subjective matter. Even if the idea is obvious or simple, we believe it deserves to be kept alive, and we do that using different ways current with the times; we broadcast our worldview with our family, friends, co-workers, and so on, "he says. "Ideally we live by our beliefs so as to lend them credence; the "unfollowing adherent" is just a meaningless mouthpiece - a preacher not following his own sermon. A legacy of values proven out by the bearer's own life would be a very good legacy for anyone. Life is motion, and the real goal of a writer should be to arrest that motion [which is life] and preserve knowledge [the words of these masters in this book] by artificial means, and hold it fixed so that a hundred years later, when a stranger opens a book and reads it, it moves again since it is life. Since man is mortal, the only immortality possible for a writer is to leave something behind him that is immortal since it will always move. This is the writer's way of scribbling "I was here" on the wall of the final and irrevocable oblivion through which we all must someday pass."

Jose M. Fraguas lives in Los Angeles, California.

Foreword

When Jose M. Fraguas initially asked me to write the forward for this book – "Shotokan Legends", I thought to myself, why me? What can I say to contribute to a fine collection of interviews with the some of the premium karate masters in Shotokan? My decision to agree to write it was twofold. One, because I have considerable respect for the work Mr. Fraguas has done over the years. He has brought information about martial arts to many people worldwide while doing his best to keep it traditional and maintain the true spirit of karate-do. This is a characteristic rarely seen these days. Mr. Fraguas has gone out of his way to give to readers an insight into history with a personal viewpoint directly from the masters. The second reason I have agreed to do this, is I feel very strongly that is the responsibility of all martial arts instructors to pass on not just the physical technique, but more importantly the legacy of our sensei.

When I was a young man training with Master Gichin Funakoshi, founder of Shotokan Karate, my intention was to be the strongest and fastest. It was all I could think about. However, Master Funakoshi kept telling me I had to change my way of thinking. I had to think more about the Dojo Kun and Shoto Niju Kun. It took me many years to understand this aspect of his advice and teaching. As I grew older and my physical training was not the same as a young man, I began to understand what he meant. It was also under the guidance of Master Masatoshi Nakayama that he showed to me that when we become instructors, we are accountable to our students. We must teach them what a real martial artist is and he, Master Nakayama reminded me of that and how Master Funakoshi would always teach us that a true martial artist is one that is a good human being and follows the Dojo Kun. That was why I wrote the book "Perfection of Character". It was my way of translating Master Gichin Funakoshi's Dojo Kun and Shoto Niju Kun so that I could pass on what Master Funakoshi's intention was. His basic intention was to help people become good human beings so that they would be the best martial artists and contribute to bring peace to the world.

I am proud of the collection of interviews in this book that Mr. Fraguas has assembled. I am personally familiar with most of these men, and I am happy to say those who are still on this earth continue to contribute to the rich essence of true karate-do. And those who are not are always contributing through the fine quality of students and instructors they have left behind.

Teruyuki Okazaki
Chairman & Chief Instructor
International Shotokan Karate Federation.

Introduction

Some of my best days were spent interviewing and meeting the shotokan masters in this book. There is little I enjoy more than reading a great interview while time slows and sometimes even seems to stop. Having the opportunity to meet and interview the most prestigious shotokan icons of the past five decades is something that every karateka doesn't have the chance to do. Hopefully, in some small way, this will help make up for that. Meeting the masters and having long conversations with them allowed me to do more than simply scratch the surface of the technical aspects of the art; it also allowed me to understand the human beings behind the teachers. Some of the dialogues and interviews began by simply commenting about the superficial techniques of fighting, and ended up turning into a spiritual conversation about the philosophical aspects of karate-do. Although these masters are all very different, they share a common thread of traditional values such as discipline, respect, positive attitude, dedication and etiquette.

For more than 35 years I've interviewed great karate-do masters, one-on-one, face-to-face, with no place to run if I asked a stupid question. Many times it was a real challenge to not just talk to them, but to make the questions interesting enough to bring out their deepest knowledge. I tried to absorb as much knowledge as I could, ranging from their training methods, to their system, to their philosophies about life itself. Their personal cultural backgrounds never prevented them from analyzing, researching or modifying anything they considered important. They always kept their minds open to improving the art and themselves. From a formal philosophical point of view, many of them followed classical philosophies and religions—but they all tempered that with vast amounts of common sense.

They devoted themselves to the art of karate-do, often in solitude, to the exclusion of other "normal" pursuits. They worked themselves into extraordinary physical condition. They ignored distractions and diversions and concentrated on their mental and physical training. They got as good as they could possibly get at performing and teaching the art while the rest of us watched them, leading our "balanced lives," and wondering how good we might have gotten at something had we devoted ourselves to it as ferociously as these masters embraced their journey. In that respect, they bear our dreams.

If you read carefully between the lines, you'll see that none of these men were trying to become a fighting machine, or create the most devastating martial arts system known to man. They focused, rather, on how to use karate-do to become a better person. There are many principles that once discovered open a wide spectrum of possibilities, not only to karate, but to a better existence as individuals.

The interviews often lasted as long as three or four hours. I would begin at their school and finish the conversation at a restaurant or coffee shop. Much of this information had never been published before and some had to be trimmed either at the master's request or edited to avoid misunderstandings. It is not the questions that make an interview. An interview is either good or bad depending on the answers. Considering the masters in this book, I had an easy job. My goal was to make them comfortable talking about life and karate training.

"The great old masters are gone," many like to say. But as long as we keep their teachings in our heart, they will live forever. To understand karate-do properly, it is necessary to take into account its philosophical methods as well as its physical techniques. There is a deep distinction between a fighting system and a martial art. Unfortunately, the roots of karate-do have been de-emphasized, neglected or totally abandoned today.

Karate-do is not a sport, although it can be useful as such in our modern society. Someone who chooses to devote himself to a sport such as basketball, tennis, soccer or football—which is based on youth, strength, and speed—chooses to die twice. When you can no longer do that sport, due to the lack of their required attributes, waking up in the morning without the activity that has been the center of your life for 35 years is troubling and unsettling. In contrast, karate-do can and should be practiced for life—it never leaves you.

All the masters have expressed similar ideas in very different ways. Regardless of the words they used, there must be truth in the philosophies and principles that so many different people have believed in and lived by — and in some cases — died for. The more I interviewed them, the more I realized that those great masters are more like you and me than they are different. They had difficult days and seemingly impossible hurdles, yet they endured and prevailed. Most of what passed as human wisdom is merely the post-examination gabble of excited individuals trying to guess how the new lessons will explain the old questions of life and karate-do training. Anything is fresh on the first hearing ... even though others may have heard it a thousand times through a score of generations.

A true karate-do practitioner is like a musician, painter, writer or actor—theirart is an expression of themselves. The need to discover who they are becomes the reason for an endless search for the perfect technique, great melody, inspiring poetry, amazing painting or Academy Award performance. It is this motivation to reach that impossible dream that allows a simple individual to become an exceptional artist and master of his craft. Many of the greatest teachers share a commonly misunderstood teaching methodology. They know the words they could use to teach their students have little or no meaning. They know that to try "self-discovery" in quantitative or empirical terms is a useless task. A great deal of knowledge and wisdom comes from oral traditions, which karate-do, like every other cultural expression, has. These oral traditions have always been reserved for a certain kind of student and considered "secrets," given only to a special few who have the minds and attitudes to fully grasp them. Alexandra David-Neel wrote: "It is not on the master that the secret depends but on the hearer. Truth learned from others is of no value, the only truth which is effective and of value is self-discovered ... the teacher can only guide to the point of discovery." In the end, "the only secret is that there is no secret." As Kato Tokuro, arguably the finest potter of the last century, a great art scholar, and the teacher of Pablo Picasso said: "The sole cause of secrets in craftsmanship is the student's inability to learn." To find out what karate-do means to you, what it does for you, and what it holds for you, is a deeply personal process. Each path is different and we all have to find a personal rhythm that fit us individually, according to what surround us.

As human beings, we are always tempted to follow linear logic towards ultimate self-improvement—but the truth is that there are no absolute truths. You have to find your own way in life whether it be in martial arts, business or cherry picking. Whatever path you pursue, you have to distill the personal truths that are right for you, according to your own nature. The quest for perfection is very imperfect, and not in tune with human nature or experience. To have any hope of attaining even a single perfection, you have to concentrate on a single pursuit and direct all your energy towards it. In this sense, perfection comes from appreciating endeavors for their own sake—not to impress anyone—but for your own inner satisfaction and sense of accomplishment. It is important to have a feeling of responsibility; and putting yourself into an art as genuinely as you can, without any sense that you are going to get something back in return, reverberates throughout time and space. We need to honor those who came before us, as well as nurture those who will come after, so the art can grow and expand—you've got to send the elevator back down.

Karate is a large part of my life and I draw inspiration from it. I really don't know the "how" or the "why" of its effect on me, but I feel its influence in even my most mundane activities. All human beings have sources or principles that keep them grounded, and karate is mine. That is when the term "way of life" becomes real. In bushido, the self-discipline required to pursue mastery is more important than mastery itself—the struggle is more important than the reward. A common thread throughout the lives of all the masters appearing in this book is their constant struggle towards self-mastery. They realized that life is an ongoing process, and once you achieve all your goals you are as good as dead. But this process is not all driven by action. Often the greatest action is inaction, and the hardest voice to hear is the sound of your own thoughts. You need to sit alone and collect yourself, free from technology and distraction, and just think. This is perhaps the only way to achieve mental and spiritual clarity.

I don't believe that books are meant to be read fast. I've always thought that writing is timeless and that reading is not a detraction. So take your time. Books are an essential part of our existence and they open new and exciting avenues of life. My goal is to share these interviews with as many people as possible. I hope this collection provides comfort and inspiration for the karate practitioner, the martial artist — regardless of style — and for the casual reader. If you, the reader, find this work useful as both a guide and a reference work and discover some unexpected thoughts and philosphies, the book will have served its purpose.

Approach this book with the Zen "beginner's mind" and "empty cup" mentality and soak up the words of these great shotokan karate teachers. They will help you to not only grow as a karateka but as a human being as well.

Contents

XVII
Gichin Funakoshi
THE FATHER OF SHOTOKAN KARATE

1
Tetsuhiko Asai
MASTER OF THE UNEXPECTED

13
Keinosuke Enoeda
THE TIGER

23
Hirokazu Kanazawa
MASTER OF THE KARATE SPIRIT

39
Taiji Kase
KARATE'S TIMELESS MASTER

49
Shojiro Koyama
THE PERFECT BALANCE

83
Takayuki Mikami
THE ESSENCE OF PERSEVERANCE

93
Masaru Miura
SLICES OF BUDO

101
Masatoshi Nakayama
A LEGACY OF EXCELLENCE

115
Hidetaka Nishiyama
KARATE'S DRIVING FORCE

127
Hideo Ochi
WISDOM OF AGE

135
Teruyuki Okazaki
HEART OF FIRE

157
Tsutomu Ohshima
STRICT EYES

171
Yoshiharu Osaka
KARATE'S PERFECT FORM

183
Osamu Ozawa
TEMPERED BY FIRE

189
Hiroshi Shirai
BUDO WITHIN

195
Shunsuke Takahashi
UNDIVIDED PAST

203
Masahiko Tanaka
THE LEGEND

213
Katsuhiro Tsuyama
CHANGING LIVES

221
Yutaka Yaguchi
A CUT ABOVE

229
Mikio Yahara
THE UNCONQUERABLE SPIRIT

GICHIN FUNAKOSHI

THE FATHER OF SHOTOKAN KARATE

"It is important that Karate can be practiced by the young and old, men and women alike. That is, since there is no need for a special training place, equipment, or an opponent, a flexibility in training is provided such that the physically and spiritually weak individual can develop his body and mind so gradually and naturally that he himself may not even realize his own great progress."

"Karate-Do strives internally to train the mind to develop a clear conscience, enabling one to face the world honestly, while externally developing strength to the point where one may overcome even ferocious wild animals. Mind and technique become one in true Karate."

"When you look at life think in terms of Karate. But remember that Karate is not only Karate - it is life."

"You may train for a long time, but if you merely move your hands and feet and jump up and down like a puppet, learning Karate is not very different from learning a dance. You will never have reached the heart of the matter; you will have failed to grasp the quintessence of Karate-do."

"To search for the old is to understand the new. The old, the new, this is a matter of time. In all things man must have a clear mind. The Way: Who will pass it on straight and well?"

⇒

"Karate is a technique that permits one to defend himself with his bare hands and fists without weapons."

⇒

"Just as it is the clear mirror that reflects without distortion, or the quiet valley that echoes a sound, so must one who would study Karate-Do purge himself of selfish and evil thoughts, for only with a clear mind and conscience can he understand that which he receives."

⇒

"Karate is like boiling water: without heat, it returns to its tepid state"

⇒

"He who would study Karate-Do must always strive to be inwardly humble and outwardly gentle. However, once he has decided to stand up for the cause of justice, then he must have the courage expressed in the saying, "Even if it must be ten million foes, I go!" Thus, he is like the green bamboo stalk: hollow (kara) inside, straight, and with knots, that is, unselfish, gentle, and moderate."

⇒

"When two tigers fight, one is certain to be maimed, and one to die."

⇒

"There are many kinds of martial arts, ...at a fundamental level these arts rest on the same basis. It is no exaggeration to say that the original sense of Karate-Do is at one with the basis of all martial arts. Form is emptiness, emptiness is form itself. The kara of Karate-Do means this."

"The correct understanding of Karate and its proper use is Karate-do. One who truly trains in this do [way] and actually understands Karate-do is never easily drawn into a fight."

"Students of any art, including Karate-do must never forget the cultivation of the mind and the body."

"Any man will be able, after sufficient practice, to accomplish remarkable feats of strength, but he may go only so far and no farther. There is a limit to human physical strength that no one can exceed."

"To win one hundred victories in one hundred battles is not the highest skill. To subdue the enemy with out fighting is the highest skill."

"The ultimate aim of the art of Karate lies not in victory or defeat, but in the perfection of the characters of its participants."

Tetsuhiko Asai

MASTER OF THE UNEXPECTED

A MAN WHO PRACTICED WHAT HE PREACHED, TETSUHIKO ASAI SENSEI WAS ONE OF THE MOST SOUGHT-AFTER KARATE INSTRUCTORS IN THE WORLD AND ONE OF THE FIRST KARATEKA TO EVER COMPLETE THE LEGENDARY JAPANESE KARATE ASSOCIATION INSTRUCTOR'S COURSE. IN SEARCH OF A FUNCTIONAL APPROACH THAT WOULD BE PRACTICAL AND RELEVANT IN THEORY AS WELL AS IN AN ACTUAL SELF-DEFENSE SITUATION, HE COMPLETED AN IN-DEPTH STUDY OF ALL THE MAJOR STYLES. HIS GREAT PERSONALITY MADE HIM A TRUE MASTER OF THE ART IN EVERY SENSE. HE RECOMMENDED HIS STUDENTS TO LISTEN AND RECOGNIZE THE TRUTH CONCERNING KARATE. "ASK YOURSELF: 'IF IT CAME DOWN TO A SITUATION DEMANDING FIGHTING ABILITY IN THE NAME OF HONOR OR LIFE, WOULD I HAVE IT ... HERE AND NOW?'"

ALTHOUGH HE WAS AN EXCEPTIONAL MASTER OF THE PHYSICAL ASPECTS OF KARATE, HE WAS A STRONG PROPONENT OF THE IDEA THAT THE GREATEST VALUE OF TRAINING IS THE REFINEMENT OF CHARACTER THAT IT PRODUCES. "A SOUND BODY MAKES A SOUND MIND." ASAI SENSEI WAS ONE OF THE LEADING VOICES IN THE WORLD OF JAPANESE KARATE AND WORKED QUIETLY IN AN EFFORT TO SHARE HIS KNOWLEDGE AND EXPERIENCE WITH A THE YOUNGER GENERATION OF PRACTITIONERS AROUND THE WORLD.

Q: Tell us a little bit about yourself.

A: I was born in Shikoku in 1935. I studied judo and kendo before getting involved in karate at Takushoku University. This is where Grandmaster Funakoshi, Nakayama Sensei and Okazaki Sensei were in charge of the

training. I entered the JKA instructor's course. After I graduated, I was sent to Hawaii and Taiwan to teach the art. It was in Taiwan where I had the opportunity to meet several Chinese kung-fu masters with whom I shared training and knowledge. Some people approached me to learn and others challenged me, so I had to fight. I still keep in touch with some of my friends from my time in China.

Q: Your father played an important influence in your life. What can you say about him?

A: He was a very strong man and many people consider him an eccentric. He was very strict with me, and he had an ironclad code of ethics. He always said that once you begin something you can't stop. You must finish it. I respect my father very highly and this sense of commitment has been the guiding principle of my life.

Q: Sensei, in your classes you always stress the importance of relaxation. Would you elaborate on that?

A: This is a mistake that many practitioners make, regardless if they are Japanese, European or American. The problem is everywhere ... West and East. Students come to class with the excitement of [participating in] hard training. Due to their passion and youth, they are too tense in [virtually] every action they make. In order to practice karate properly, you need to learn how to relax the muscles and use them properly to generate speed. If your muscles are not relaxed, they simply can't be fast [and you can't] produce power. It is necessary to know how to relax the muscles and use the natural energy of your body. Karate is good for health, so students need to find out how to do it right. Unfortunately, many instructors around the world never learnt the right way and always practiced with tension and hard movements. This is one of the reasons why people think karate is a hard style while the truth is that it is not. It is important to look at the art from a softer point of view. For instance, men should try to emulate the way women do karate. Women are not built like men, so they use more technique and more subtle ways of doing the movements instead of relying on muscle and strength. If a man tries to use this approach, he will discover that the techniques will flow more naturally. Then he can add the natural power he has in his body to accentuate the action.

Q: What is the key factor in becoming a good karateka?

A: There are many factors, and all of them must work together to bring the best out of the practitioner. Hard training is important. You have to put your mind into it. Strive to find a good instructor; learn the right technique, timing, kime and the proper use of the body; and use your natural energy. If you do these things, everything else will fall into place. You should strive to control every part of your body at will. This is a true sign of mastery, and it goes beyond any style. It doesn't matter if you practice shotokan, shito-ryu, goju-ryu, et cetera. If you control your body at will, you'll be one of a few people who can do that. If you take a tsuki, as an example, you'll see that anatomically there are no great differences between a shito-ryu exponent and a shotokan practitioner. The important thing is to perform the technique with a certain spirit in a certain atmosphere. This is one of the main principles we were trying to develop at the old JKA. We wanted to use the human body in the most efficient way for the martial arts. Once you follow this rule, you'll see an infinite amount of possibilities, although the human body is limited. In fact, the only limit in martial arts training is the limit of the human body.

Q: What are the main aspects of your teaching?

A: My teaching is for health but my karate is for real fighting, and that's the reason why I emphasize relaxation all the time. Making the muscles tense is not good for your body and can cause many injuries during training. I want the students to learn and understand how to use the body properly and how to produce the right kime without using useless movements or unnecessary tension. Proper kime involves going through the target and not stopping your technique short. Of course, having control over your techniques is very important. But, in order to be effective, you need to be able to generate devastating power in your punches and kicks without holding back any energy. To do this, you must use the principle of snapping your body. Try to use it like a whip. This is a difficult concept to master, but it is extremely important and should be practiced from the very beginning.

Karate has five different aspects that should be developed. First, there is the martial side of it or the combative and self-preservation of the individ-

ual. Second, the health benefits derived from its practice. Third, is the physical activity, which is always good. Fourth, the sportive element that brings people together. Last but not least is the development of character and spirit. My approach to teaching includes all of these elements because I consider them all necessary. Nowadays, we don't need karate like we did after the war; it is a completely different approach. Karate needs to be useful for modern society. I want to return to the roots and to the original essence and reason of karate ... a time in which there are no limitations. Karate is not only for young people. Real fight karate is for everybody and in that type of karate is not a game Bujutsu is everything to me. In combat, you die or I die.

Q: Do you think modern training methods like weightlifting are responsible for this?

A: Maybe a little. The martial arts have been around for a long time, and the ancestors based their styles on natural movement and relaxation. Today, people don't want to use the old traditional methods to use both physical and inner strength because it is easier to lift weights. There is no reason why the old and new methods can't work together, but it is important to understand how both work and the direction you want to take in your training. Weightlifting creates muscle mass and a rapid increase in strength, but this kind of training works against the relaxation necessary for karateka to generate internal power, which is more important than muscle power. Tense muscles come from the incorrect use of the body during training. You can do two training session with weights everyday and still be relaxed, and you can punch 1,000 gyaku-tsuki and be tense for a week! It is a matter of knowing how to use your body properly when executing a karate technique. You need to understand how your body works and how to correctly use the training methods. I recommend focusing more on speed than developing strength with weights.

Q: What should a student look for if he is interested in karate for self-defense?

A: First, you must study the vital points and attack those. Forget about your powerful reverse punch to the stomach. Self-defense is a whole different situation. Attack the eyes, the throat, the groin, the knee and all the vital areas where you can infringe a lot of pain with simple natural weapons. If you train with this concept in mind, you'll always have real karate in your hands. You will also have an effective karate, and this will bring self-confidence to you. It is not about muscle; it is about knowing what tool to use and

what targets to hit. The art of karate is practiced barehanded and its essence is to render an opponent unable to fight by using a single technique. If you want to put a nail all the way into a piece of wood, you don't use a screwdriver. You use a hammer. Learn what weapons are more appropriate to hit certain parts of the human body, especially when you have to protect yourself against a much bigger aggressor. In that case, you want to hit the targets that really hurt him. Attacks to vital points require speed and accuracy. Otherwise, all you get is an aggressive opponent!

Q: How is your personal training?

A: I train everyday for more than two hours. I have a routine of exercises that I practice daily. These are a very important part of my training. They keep my body flexible and limber. Flexibility is an open door for relaxation, and I make this principle my main objective. It is important to try to keep all joints loose and supple. I have tried everything, and I am constantly learning and absorbing. I am not an expert in every style I practice, but I have picked up the ones I could do well and that suited my personal style. Also, I recommend [that you should] use your imagination when training and think about karate. Look at the things and the live creatures around you. Study them and try to absorb the knowledge they have. You may think that this is crazy, but you would be amazed at the amount of important knowledge surrounding us.

Q: How would you describe yourself?

A: I try to be honest and stick to my principles. I'm very demanding on myself, and that allows me to judge myself first. I have to live with myself — not with my critics — so I try to be at peace. I don't really spend time talking about others. Life is very short, and I have a lot of things I want to do and accomplish. I'm a martial artist, not a politician. I always welcome anyone who wants to train with me, regardless of his association with other karate groups. I like to do karate and not waste time talking and arguing. I have nothing to hide. From the technical point of view, I am a researcher. I may study a technique for 10 years because there is a period of study, of trial, for any new technique before I can really accept it as useful. Then I must make sure it is teachable. If I am the only one who can do it, then there is no point [in pursuing it]. My goal is to become a total martial artist and do research just for myself.

Q: Sensei, when you were part of the old unified JKA, your way of physically expressing karate was substantially different from the rest of the top instructors. Why?

A: As I said before, I can't talk about others. My karate has always been the product of my personal training and experiences. And I had many experiences in other martial arts systems that some of my old peers in the JKA never had. Japanese karate has been very closed-minded for many years. [Contrary to what they believe], the karate way is not the only way. There are many other good ways and approaches that can be beneficial to all karateka, if they know and learn how to use them to complement their karate. Shotokan sometimes is too straight-lined. It was like a horse with blinkers on. You have to study hard, see what is missing and then try to compensate for this. Before I started getting older, I always thought that shotokan should have a soft side because it is natural to the body. For many years, the JKA tried to create hard and strong people. And that's good, but it is not the only way to do it. I have always looked at Chinese chuan-fa [kung-fu], kendo, aikido, judo and any other art that could make my karate more versatile and adaptable. I tried to develop a shotokan that would be practiced by people of all ages ... not only young and strong people.

Q: You are using two words — versatility and adaptability — that fit into the Chinese way of combat.

A: Well, that's the way I have always thought. Some may think this is new, but I have always believed in this and practiced my karate based on these premises. That's probably the reason why my karate has always had a very different flavor when compared to other JKA head instructors. Adaptability and versatility are concepts not only found in the Chinese arts. True karate is capable of adapting to the situation and changing accordingly. That is the essence of life. Change is simply the product of education. The more you learn, the more you realize other things. Therefore, it is natural for you to change and adapt to that knowledge. Some people may say that my karate is always changing. Although that is not completely correct, it is not incorrect either. In my approach to karate, I have been strongly influenced by the Chinese styles I have studied. The Chinese seem to be more natural and casual when doing things, and that affects the way they train and conceive the martial arts. In karate, we have the same movements and principles, but you have to look closely to discover them.

Q: Based on your comments, what is missing in the hard approach to shotokan that the JKA used for so long?

A: A soft side and — instead of using force — the use of more circular and evasive defensive actions using body angling and techniques to re-direct an opponent's energy. You block softer but you hit as hard as always.

The basics and essential aspects of karate are the same Nakayama Sensei developed. I haven't changed any of those. Because I have studied other methods and systems, it is logical to think that I included my own point of view and flavor to the art. The late Grandmaster Funakoshi established the roots, Nakayama Sensei developed the foundation and now it is up to us to expand the art in different ways to meet the current needs of students and society. Many people may think that my style of teaching is very strange, but this is only because I emphasize aspects that we usually don't see in regular karate. I am now researching ways of training for life. I'm trying to develop techniques and training methods that we can use until we die. It's an unlimited world, and we must try to expand. It is like a telescope. Don't look down the wrong end at a little circle; look through the wide end so you can see more.

Q: Do you still believe in thousands and thousands of repetitions of the same technique as a good training method?

A: It depends on your age and your goal. However, the answer is yes. I do believe in this kind of training because it builds a strong spirit and determination to keep going no matter what. People need this kind of training, but they [also] need to learn how to relax and take care of their bodies. Otherwise, they will have problems and injures later on. Don't forget to stretch and massage the muscles. Remember what we said about tension. Relaxing and contracting the muscles improperly can cause many injures.

Q: Are you against the sport aspect of karate?

A: Not at all, but karate is a martial art — not a sport. The sport aspect of karate has allowed the art to spread greatly. In itself, that is not particularly bad, but it sure brings consequences if you do not watch out. I was one of the first competitors in karate history, but karate for me has always been a martial art. The problem arises because the competitions standardize the way instructors teach and students practice. Basically a "competition style" has been created, and all of the fighters look the same. The participants lose their own identity because the sport approach has been taken to the extreme.

Competition has changed a lot throughout the years. In the old days, it was more of a one-punch, one-kill [mentality]. We really were aware of any possibility and making a single mistake meant defeat. That is the true spirit of Budo, and this spirit can be maintained in modern competition. That's why I like the idea of shobu-ippon. It represents what true Budo is. The system for shobu-ippon set the fighter's mind in a different direction, than, for instance, the six-wazari format. The training methods changed according to this. Today, competitors simply jump and throw techniques without real kime or meaning behind them. If they are losing by three wazari, they think, "It's alright. I can still catch up!" Competition karate is only a very small part of karate. I have great students who are tournament champions, but this doesn't prevent them from training real Budo karate. In sport or competition karate, you can always find shortcuts to win. In traditional karate, there are no shortcuts of any kind. Shiai-kumite is not even a complete form of kumite.

Q: What do you mean by a complete form of kumite?

A: I mean that you can only use certain techniques allowed in sport competition. I truly enjoy dojo kumite because you can use anything you want ... headbutts, elbows, knees, throws and even locks. In short, all the real tools of true karate. Karate is a complete package; you simply need to understand how to bring it to life and make it work for yourself.

Q: Are there some other important differences when fighting under the mentality of shobu-ippon?

A: I wouldn't say that it is because this one-blow, one-kill concept, but when I was competing the use of ma-ai [distance] was different. We tried to bring the opponent into our distance so we could strike with a decisive blow. The distance was longer than in modern competition. Now, it seems the proper distance doesn't matter anymore. The competitors know that — even if they are hit — they won't die from it [the strike]! The real dimensions of danger and menace have disappeared.

Q: What should be done to improve the current situation of the art?

A: We have to be able to look at what is happening without any kind of preconception or prejudices. There is traditional karate, modern karate and contact karate. These are the facts, and they are here to stay. We must be able to accept these different trends, try to find unity and assimilate them, but there are some limitations to this because there are things that cannot be called karate, like an excessively sport approach, because that doesn't deserve to be called karate. It is important that the public has a clear idea of what is and is not the art of karate.

Q: You don't make your living teaching karate. Does this situation make things easier for you?

A: Yes it does, because I can teach whomever I want, and I don't rely on memberships to put food on my plate. I can be honest with myself and everybody else, but the love of my life is karate.

Q: Let's talk about kata. Has the format of kata changed throughout the years?

A: Yes, and I think it is natural. All of the head instructors of the old JKA trained and practiced the same kata. However, when one [of them] left Japan and lived for 30 years in another country, it was logical that some changes (his feelings and teaching methods) were going to occur. This is natural, and there is nothing wrong with that. The essence of the form is still there and nothing has changed, but the personal flavor the instructor put into it [changed] because of his evolution as a martial artist.

Q: How important is the bunkai of kata in karate and does it have any real value of self-defense in modern society?

A: Kata represents the history of the art. All the tradition in these forms [has been] passed down from masters to students throughout the generations. The kata were structured and formatted by the old masters to preserve realistic knowledge of self-defense. It is very important to study the form and to understand what you are doing and why are you doing it. It's occasionally difficult to completely decipher the bunkai and realistic applications of kata movements because they are not so obvious at first. The variations in the use and study of the forms bring new perspectives and ideas to the kata, and this is always good for the art. The main idea is to use the kata as a training method and the bunkai as the actual application in combat. It is very important to link the actual form with the application against an opponent. This is practiced in yakusoku kumite, and it brings the movements from kata alive in a combat situation. It is here in which you use your own ideas and imagination to create and develop [concepts] while maintaining the original flavor of the specific kata. You can also use different kata to develop different attributes and qualities. Not all kata are designed for the same thing.

Q: Explain this concept, please.

A: For example, let's say that a student needs to develop hip rotation. Well, there are specific kata that put a strong emphasis on this principle. Another student may need to develop bodyweight shifting. He uses other kata to improve this particular aspect of his karate. Different kata help to

develop different attributes. Not all kata were created for the same purpose. You need to know what your weak points are and choose the kata that will help you to improve those. That's when kata becomes a training method for specific purposes.

Don't forget that kata is a training tool to practice the basic fighting principles. It is not about this or that kata, the secret lies in the body movement. The body action is the key factor. Many people look at kata too much and miss the main point; body action.

Q: You have studied several Chinese styles of chuan-fa [kung-fu]. What are the differences you see between Chinese and Japanese forms?

A: Well, as we talked about previously, the Chinese always stress the relaxation aspect of it. The stances are very fluid, and the transition between positions is always done in a very natural way. Karate should be the same … because it is natural. Natural is always the answer to any question. I know about more than 100 forms, and each and every one of them teaches me something different, but I am Japanese and my karate is Japanese. A shotokan practitioner shouldn't be fixated on only training the 26 standard kata of the style.

Q: Therefore, is it better to keep your stances high in karate because that is more natural than making them low?

A: In the beginning and for training purposes, the student must work techniques from low stances. This builds muscle and strengthens the practitioner's hips. Everyone needs this kind of training in the beginning. Don't forget that strong leg muscles will prevent knee injuries later on. After years of training and experience, when the student knows how to use the hips properly, it is OK to use higher stances. Students can use deep stances for specific techniques and higher stances for something else. It doesn't really matter as long as the student knows what he is doing. But this is pretty much up to the individual. There is not a set rule that everybody must follow.

Q: It is sad to see how organizations separate practitioners…

A: Organizations does not separate karatekas, only karateka separate karateka. It is the individual who makes that decision. Organizations are not really important as long as the karate taught is good and solid. There is no best organization. No karate group is better than any other. Find a good teacher, a solid organization and…train. That is all.

Q: You have created the Japan Karate Shotokai. Why?

A: I simply wanted to express karate in my own way. Karate has taught me to overcome my fears and myself and to get along with and work with others. I am an engineer of the art … not a politician. I want to train and teach people ... not argue about things. I don't have time for that. I want to create collaboration and support among the students. This organization is a martial arts organization, not a group for politics. Division in the world of karate is not good, but it is a fact. The reason for this is very simple; ego. Everybody wants to be the boss, but nobody wants to be the Indian.

Q: What advice would you give to karate practitioners?

A: To truly understand what Budo means, I would tell them to put their hearts into it and never stop training. Budo is Japanese culture, and sometimes it is hard for non-Japanese to understand. That's why it is important that students first understand their own culture and then absorb what Budo can offer. Make karate training part of your life and set realistic goals that you can achieve. Set a goal and work hard to accomplish it. Define where you are going. Study new ways and develop new ideas that can improve what you are doing. Be creative. Time is essential because it allows us to look at the same thing differently. Karate — like a human being — needs time to grow. There is no end to expanding. Consider yourself always a student and never think that you are already there. Never give up.

Keinosuke Enoeda

THE TIGER

Keinosuke Enoeda was a true celebrity in the world of karate. He graduated from Takushoku University where his main instructor was the late Master Nakayama. Sensei Enoeda mastered all karate techniques through his total dedication to the art - but even more importantly he captured and understood the philosophy and spirit of karate-do as laid down by Master Gichin Funakoshi. As a former All-Japan Champion, he was respected and feared as a fighter. Such prowess has earned him a reputation of high standing and made him one of the most famous and respected karate-do instructors in the world. He was one of the fittest, most powerful karate technicians - but he had another, less definable quality. His aura of energy and charisma was something special. He had that ability to bring out the best in a student, forcing them to perform better karate. Living in the United Kingdom since 1966, he developed countless number of fine karate-ka and many leading champions in the art. Master Enoeda was instrumental in making Great Britain one of the strongest karate nations in the world. He found time, over the years, to coach many celebrities for fight scenes in films, including Lee Marvin, Michael Caine, and Sean Connery. Sensei Enoeda taught regularly at his famous London dojo and traveled the world teaching his unique brand of dynamic[1] karate. Simply said, he was "The Tiger" of Shotokan.

Shotokan Legends

Q: Would you tell us about your beginning days in karate?

A: I was born in Fukuoka on the island of Kyushu in southern Japan on July 4, 1935, and practiced martial arts from an early age. While my brother and sister played games, at the age of 7 I began judo. I continued my training through high school, where I regularly entered judo competitions and was runner-up in the All-Japan High School Championships. At the age of 17, shortly after I gained my second degree black belt, I watched a demonstration given by two members of the Takushoku University Karate Club in Tokyo. I was won over. Aside from any academic merits, Takushoku University was well known for its strong martial arts, particularly its tough karate team, and this was my main reason for enrolling at the university.

After two years training I passed my shodan examination, and then two years later, at age 21, I was made captain of the karate club. It was during my university training that I received instruction from the great master, Funakoshi Gichin. Master Funakoshi was very old when I met him, but one thing that I still recall is that once he put the gi on, his whole attitude and body movement changed immediately. It was like he received some kind of external energy by wearing the karate gi. The transformation in his physical movements was amazing.

After graduating in 1957 with a degree in Commerce, I was invited to take the special instructors course at JKA headquarters. I accepted and for the next three years studied long and hard on a daily basis under Masatoshi Nakayama, the chief instructor of the JKA, and Hidetaka Nishiyama, a leading senior. I regularly entered various tournaments and achieved several victories, including the East University Karate Championships. Then in 1961 I won third place in the kumite division of the JKA All-Japan Championships and also finished high in the kata event. The following year I repeated my kata placing and moved another step up in the kumite by finishing second - losing to Hiroshi Shirai, a fellow JKA instructor. Then in 1963, after another year's hard preparation, I turned the tables on Shirai in the kumite finals and became the All-Japan Champion, and again placed as a kata finalist.

Q: When you began to travel abroad to teach?

A: Up until my 1963 triumph, I had only taught locally at the Tokyo Art College and a military university. Among the spectators at that year's championships was President Sukarno of Indonesia and he negotiated for my services. Together with Master Nakayama, I spent four months in Indonesia teaching the his personal bodyguards and also at various police and military establishments. Following the JKA's policy of sending its best instructors out from Japan to spread shotokan karate, I began my worldwide travels that were to culminate in my settling in Great Britain as the shotokan chief instructor.

Q: Who gave you the nickname "The Tiger"?

A: Nakayama sensei watched one of my fights and he mentioned that I fought like a tiger. So after that moment everybody started to use the term when referring to me and my attitude in kumite.

Q: Did you include the makiwara in your training sessions?

A: Of course! In those days the training was very intense. Every morning I would do 500 punches on the makiwara. It was not something I did to impress anyone. It was simply a single-minded attitude necessary to develop power and kime in my techniques.

Q: You always emphasize the importance of kata in the art of karate. Why?

A: The importance attached to kata makes it one of the most recognizable features in all of martial arts. Kata was the creation of the most important teachers of each style of karate in the past. They formalized their knowledge and made a set of practical techniques to pass to their students. They systematized this huge amount of knowledge in forms that have been preserved throughout the years. They recorded for posterity the physical movements they came as a result of them risking their lives in actual contests.

When studying kata, we can see a model for a particular method of certain techniques. There is a formalized way of doing things but kata also offers freedom of expression. Not only the techniques of the creator, but

also the acquisition of the right state of mind called kokoro. Kata must be memorized, incorporated into one's own being and then mastered to perfection. It is essential to break into areas of techniques that are original. Kata training offers a way of understand other aspects of human existence, that's why is so important not to study the form from a strictly structural point of view. All traditional katas are greatly respected in the martial arts, and you can search your entire life to find the deeper meanings of a particular form. Moreover, the beauty of refinement (kohga) and the elegant simplicity (sabi) are also important kata training elements.

If we simply focus on training the external movements (waza), without also analyzing the state of mind behind the form, it will be impossible to practice the true art of karate-do. Kata has dignity in its severity and is extreme in its beauty. Simply said, kata is physical movements by each individual. Due to this fact, it is possible to continue to train for the acquisition of technique and mind even when we are old. People tend to be really attracted to sparring, but a true karate-ka must stop and look very careful about the role kata plays in the art.

Q: What is your personal approach to kata?

A: When doing kata you must live the form. Each kata must be done full-out. If done correctly, the karate-ka will reach his physical limits and not be able to continue. He'll be near his end. You shouldn't endlessly repeat a kata. To do so is to show that one is not living the kata. Only on certain occasion will one repeat a kata a number of times - and that is for mental and spiritual purposes – to force you to go beyond the body, the mind and the art. You have to live the kata. Use all your power as if in life or death. This is something that sport karate does not have. This is why kata is important. The body is trained, the mind is trained, and the understanding of the technique deepens.

Q: What about bunkai?

A: Bunaki is the practical application of the kata. It is very important that the student understands the application of the technique. Many times students do not understand kata because they cannot see the meaning of the movement they are doing. They see slow, broad movements and tend to think that kata has no purpose. Bunkai shows them the purpose. As the student advances in his study, his understanding of the techniques becomes deeper and more profound. Each technique improves his precision and kime. Kata helps karate-ka to understand the many uses the techniques and how to apply them. Without kata training, one is not following the way of martial arts. Profound technique is one of the main benefits of kata training. Other important facets are the artistic aspects and the individual self-expression.

Q: Do you have a favorite kata?

A: Yes. My favorite kata is jitte. Sensei Nakayama suggested that I should practice this kata. It translates as "ten hands" and is the kata I enjoy the most. It is heavier and more solid that some other forms derived from the shorei style of Okinawa. The name means that one who is proficient in this kata can fight with the strength of ten men.

Q: How does sport sparring relate to self-defense?

A: Sport sparring is not self-defense and has very little to do with it. Sparring is a test of ability, but ability of a different kind. It is in kata again, where we can find the answer. The kata keeps the meaning of the technique deep. It makes one fresh to respond. Knowledge of the art increases because self-defense is found in kata. Without kata training, the body cannot properly understand the technique There will be no calm and no confidence. With kata training, one is capable at all times - and calm and confident of their ability. With the self-assurance gained from kata, there is little need to ever use karate for self-defense.

Q: Is karate-do a composition of many different elements?

A: A long time ago, karate-do was an art practiced by a select few under the founder of a particular style. In those days, the art had a great deal of morality and dignity. A good karate-do student would never show off - and even in combat was expected to not use the art unless completely necessary. Of course, things have changed today but the essence and heart of the art should still be the same. To many people today tend to train simply for competition. Winning competitions is not the true meaning karate - it is not enough just to do the techniques correctly. Those whose execute the techniques without true heart cannot call themselves true karate-ka. Karate-do is many things at once. It is budo. It is being fit and calm. It develops good

character and confidence. It is crisp and powerful physical movements. It can be a sport and at the same time be a complete self-defense method. Karate competition has become increasingly popular, and gradually the true heart of karate has almost been forgotten. Modern karate-ka must think about the true root of the art and try to understand the essence of it deeply. Without this deep understanding, it will be difficult for future generations to know what the real art is about.

Q: Why do so many quit karate after few years?

A: If you train hard and consistently, one day you are going to come face-to-face with what is called a "brick wall." This stage is also known as "hitting the wall," or reaching a "plateau." In order to progress and follow real karate-do, you must be able to break through the wall - one step at a time and brick by brick. Only by destroying this obstacle will you succeed. Only then can you reach a higher level of technical mastery. Unfortunately, many reach this wall and do not succeed in breaking through. Thus, they limit themselves. This not only happens in martial arts, but in many other aspects of life. After you have succeeded in conquering your 'brick wall' in any field, you will have a feeling of true achievement. This is because you met a challenge and broke out of a difficult period. This will build confidence and bring about great results. This is when karate-do becomes a practical way of life and not a mere physical exercise.

Q: Is sport competition bad for karate?

A: Sport karate is a definite aspect of karate-do. Competition is not bad. It is good for the spirit. It is specifically good for the spirit when the proper etiquette – win or lose - is present. Sport karate is also a demanding test of one's individual ability. It is also a good test of the mind and one's control of power. And if etiquette and sportsmanship is present, it is always good for the spirit.

Q: Are there any drawbacks?

A: There are some. Technique, because of the tournament training, can become weak. The practitioner's techniques can becomes shallow because certain moves work best in sport karate. This means that one can devote all his time to practicing these techniques. This works against the true spirit of karate and all martial arts. There are many techniques in karate-do. In budo karate-do, not sport karate, one must know and develop all these techniques - not just two or three. The way to avoid this is intensive kata training. This is how I trained in my youth in Japan. Before competition we would train kata, kata and more kata. Only at the end of the session would there be one-step sparring. Don't focus excessively on sparring before a tournament; train kata. Then immediately before

the tournament, move to one-step kumite, and then just few days before the tournament day, concentrate on free-sparring. You'll be amazed by the results - especially when you win the kata division the same day!

Q: How much contact should be allowed in sport competition?

A: The important concept here is control. Good karate-ka should have good control, so there is no need for excessive contact. If there is too much contact, then there is a chance of injury if the technique is delivered with power. It is necessary to develop good control so that you can control the amount of body contact when you reach the target. The problem appears when the competing karate-ka doesn't have control due to insufficient training at the dojo. Then as a referee, you have to deal with the problem in the competition. What the teachers should do is train students correctly and don't allow them to compete until they have the proper skill to control their punches and kicks.

Q: How is kata related to budo?

A: True budo is many things. Sport karate is OK, but you must practice kata as well. Kata training is very necessary for taking part in sport karate. This keeps techniques fresh and it is also important because it develops the body properly. It is necessary to keep fit for the art. Kata teaches how each technique is to be performed in terms of body movements. It conditions the body and the mind. With kata training you reach a higher level of fitness. All you techniques are sharp and fresh. You have been drilling and exercising the body, extending your knowledge of tactics, techniques, and applications. This keeps one fresh and also insures that all the techniques will have the right amount of power and precision.

Q: What do you look for when refereeing a sport karate match?

A: I must always see a clean and powerful technique to award a point. This is the danger in practicing only sport karate. Punches end up looking weak and without proper kime.

Q: Should a fighter compromise karate-do principles in order to win?

A: In every karate match, victory is of prime importance; however, since a karate match is based on budo, you cannot use any means to defeat your opponent. In a karate match you must fight strictly under the true spirit of budo and play fair in order to be victorious. This is the right way to win.

Appropriate rules for karate match-play are currently being developed in hopes of karate being accepted as an Olympic sport. A great amount of research and study has been done for this. The ideals of rules development are that mind, body and waza will be naturally perfected and combined for all styles - and consequently the karate match itself will be improved. A karate match is not only a place for testing your daily training, but also the culmination of numerous fights and experiences that have helped each practitioner progress in the art of karate-do - this is the true essence of a karate match.

Taking part in a match is a big responsibility as well as a great opportunity for both yourself as an individual and the organization to which you belong. In your journey through life, it is important to study and learn how to seize an opportunity and gain victory by displaying your own powerful ability. Composure, courage, sharpness, precision and courtesy must all be present in your waza when you move your entire body – not merely your hands and feet. In an instant every part of you moves in unison.

In order to win the match it is of great value to know your opponent and to know yourself. If your opponent is unknown to you, you should get to know him before your fight - paying attention to his strong points and favorite techniques. Then, after accumulating vast experience in the course of many matches, you will become very sharp in your observations and be able to recognize your opponent's strong and weak points at first sight.

When the time comes to fight, you must not think in terms of simply winning, but you should feel delighted that you have attained your long-cherished chance to compete. This will help you to focus and to defeat fear. When you have vanquished your own fear, then you will be ready to fight against your opponent – whoever he may be.

When you stand face-to-face with your opponent, the first thing you want is to make him feel that your energy will overwhelm him. The second thing is not to miss any of his movement - even slight ones - and at the same time act as if you were engulfing the opponent's whole body with the inside of your hands and feet. Even if your opponent is a strong and experienced practitioner you must not fear him. By the same token, if your opponent is weak and inexperienced you must not underestimate him. Always fight every match with your maximum power.

When you attack, do not forget to protect yourself with defensive maneuvers, but just remember that defense alone won't win the fight. Attack with right posture, correct spirit and precise techniques. Strive to be the one who always takes the initiative. If you act before your opponent moves, you will go on to victory. This is, I think, the most important point of all.

Q: What do you think about your own journey in karate-do?

A: I come from a very traditional background and karate is part of my nature. It affects the way I look at things and how I lead my life. Karate taught me discipline, and with discipline a person can continue karate practice for many years. My objective was and still is, to train everyday regardless of the weather or the condition I'm in. I never neglect my daily training. I haven't missed a day's training since a very young age. I believe my everyday effort, plus my judo and kendo practice when I was very young, helped to develop my mental and physical strength. This strength as a human being has helped me to achieve my goals throughout my life.

All practitioners should remember to train in true budo karate-do. Do sport karate if you like, but always focus your mind and body on the perfection of yourself as a human being. This is true karate-do. And no matter where your interests lead you, remember that kata is the vehicle that will allow you to reach a true understanding of real karate.

Hirokazu Kanazawa

MASTER OF THE KARATE SPIRIT

ONE OF MARTIAL ARTS MOST REVERED TEACHERS, SENSEI KANAZAWA'S JOURNEY FROM SCHOLARSHIP TO KARATE MASTERY IS A STORY OF PHYSICAL SKILL AND SPIRITUAL ACHIEVEMENT.

SENSEI KANAZAWA WAS THE SECOND PERSON TO GRADUATE FROM THE JKA INSTRUCTOR TRAINING PROGRAM, AND IS CONSIDERED BY MANY TO BE ONE OF THE MOST SKILLFUL FIGHTERS OF ALL TIME. TEMPERED BY YEARS OF STRICT AND DIFFICULT PRACTICE, HIS BODY REFLECTS THE DECADES OF GRUELING KARATE TRAINING AND CONDITIONING. USED BY MASATOSHI NAKAYAMA AS A MODEL FOR KARATE TECHNIQUES IN THE CLASSIC BOOK DYNAMIC KARATE, KANAZAWA IS AN LIVING EXAMPLE OF THE POWER OF KARATE-DO AT ITS HIGHEST LEVEL.

AN ORIGINAL THINKER, KANAZAWA CREATED HIS OWN ORGANIZATION, SHOTOKAN KARATE INTERNATIONAL, IN 1975 AFTER TEACHING IN HAWAII AND BEING THE JKA'S CHIEF INSTRUCTOR IN GREAT BRITAIN UNTIL THE MID-70S. IT IS SAID THAT TRAINING WITH A TRUE MASTER IS THE ONLY WAY TO FULLY UNDERSTAND KARATE DO. HIROKAZU KANAZAWA IS ONE OF THOSE RARE TEACHERS WHO POSSESSES THE ABILITY TO PASS BOTH THE SPIRITUAL AND PHYSICAL ESSENCE OF THE ART TO YOUNGER INITIATES.

Q: Many karate practitioners consider you a rebel. Why?

A: I don't know. The karate that I teach is a product of more than thirty years of spiritual and physical research into the true meaning of martial

Shotokan Legends

arts. Perhaps because of my training in tai chi and kobudo, some karateka look at me differently. Also, it may be due to my very personal perception of karate – I teach for everybody, not only for the young and the strong. For me, karate is unlimited. I always said that karate is a form of self-administered therapeutic massage. It is not just a sport.

Q: How did you begin in tai chi?

A: I began when I went to Hawaii, but it was not regular training. Later on, I met Mr. Yang, who is a member of the family tree of the Yang family style of tai chi. He is very famous and his organization is probably the best in Japan. I met him when he came to the JKA to learn karate. I had the feeling that he was already practicing another martial art but he didn't say anything. Later on, I discovered that he was a master in tai chi. I began training under him around 1957 and I haven't stopped since.

Q: Do you have any rank in tai chi?

A: In Yang tai chi there are only seven degrees and I hold the highest. I received my certification many years ago.

Q: Has tai chi helped you to improve and understand your karate?

A: I don't practice tai chi for tai chi, but for my karate. After I started training in tai chi, I began to really understand how to keep and develop a healthy body, mind, and spirit. In the beginning, tai chi was very difficult, I couldn't use any tension at all and had to force myself to relax all my muscles. You see, I was trying to do tai chi with karate power, and it was painful trying to move with no force at all. My body felt really uncomfortable but after a couple of years of training I began to understand and developed a natural softness that still retained the real strength in the technique.

Q: Were you initially frustrated with tai chi?

A: Of course. During my first year of training even my stomach used to make weird noises. Mr. Yang told me once that the reason was that I had no internal power and my body was protesting! You see, the human body changes and your martial art has to change with it. And I think this has to be done using internal power because it strengthens the internal organs. There is a point in every karate practitioner's life where the punch's unify-

ing force must no longer be rooted in the muscles but in the internal organs.

I am much older and I will honestly tell you that my body is not as supple as it used to be and does not respond as quickly as it once did. This is a physiological reality and is perfectly normal – that's why I adapted my karate to the needs of my body and why tai chi has been of a great benefit to me. I have many students who did not start karate until they were fifty years old and they all get do quite well. They could not fight the young men with hard contact, of course, but then that is not their approach. By the same token, young men need to train differently.

Q: Have you attempted to combine karate and tai chi?

A: I don't think that is a good idea. I feel it is better to study them separately. But even although they are opposites, the study of both brings a more balanced view. Tai chi has allowed me to step outside of karate in much the same way as you need to step outside your house to fully appreciate it. From the inside, you do not have a complete view of it. This act of stepping outside afforded me a chance to see karate from an entirely different point of view and to appreciate it even more.

Q: You also train in Okinawa kobudo, correct?

A: I train in bo, sai and nunchaku. I have always said that tai chi is very much like the nunchaku movement. When you're using the nunchaku, your arms must be relaxed and soft – "empty" is the right word – no tense muscles. In nunchaku training if you move the weapon with tension, then you lose power. The same is true in tai chi.

Q: How did you start your kobudo training?

A: I started in Okinawa, and when I returned to Japan I tried it for myself. At that time I knew the basics only. My teacher told me that there was no kubudo kata. So I devised some kata myself. Many people twirl the nunchaku, but this doesn't allow real power to develop. In kata training one learns concentration and how to develop smoothness in motion in order to create devastating striking power.

Q: Was kobudo ever practiced at the old Japan Karate Association?

A: No, never. But it is interesting that there is some evidence of Master Funakoshi Gichin using the sai for training.

Q: Do you think weapons training should be a part of every karateka training?

A: Maybe it is not important for everyone, but it is for me. I truly consider karate and kobudo part of the same family. Therefore, if I learn kobudo I will better understand the history of karate.

Q: Do you like the direction karate is currently taking?

A: I believe it is quite a confusing period for students. They really don't know if they are practicing a sport or a martial art. Sport is an aspect of karate but it is not everything. Unfortunately, karate today is neither a sport nor a martial art, and that's very confusing for the students. I think it would be better if sport karate evolved separately from the martial art side.

Q: Why did you split from the JKA and create Shotokan Karate International?

A: I never wanted to create my own organization. That was never my goal. When I was in Europe, making plans to go to Montreal University in Canada to teach for a few months, I sent a letter of resignation to the JKA – not as a JKA instructor – but as the director of a section of the JKA. I just didn't feel I could function in that capacity while I was out of the country. Three months later, when I returned to Europe, I received a letter from the JKA informing me that I was summarily dismissed.

Q: How did you feel?

A: I was completely shocked. But I said to myself that I wouldn't go back to Canada but would struggle on in Europe. Giving up would have been against the budo spirit of everything I had been taught. So I decided that if the JKA was against me, I had to defend myself.

Q: Did you think Shotokan Karate International would last?

A: In the beginning, many people said that it would only last a couple of months. Fortunately, as you can see, we are still going strong! But I want to emphasize that I never wanted to leave the JKA. Some people said that I deserted Nakayama Sensei, but the truth is that I never wanted to be independent – that's not in my spirit. But I had to defend myself. A samurai must not be frightened – even of death.

Q: What was your purpose in developing the SKIF system as it exists today?

A; For teaching kihon, it was to make it precise, like teaching kata, and for discipline. For the kumite system, it was for the same reasons but also to develop a number system for the different types of kumite, so when the student would hear the number, for example "kihon ippon kumite number one," the student automatically would remember the movements and be able to do them with his or hr partner. So it is also to train the mind for memory and the body for response. In addition, the kumite system is for training the body and spirit together.

Q: You always mention that kumite it is very important to "harmonize oneself with the opponent." What does this mean?

A: I know this is a very difficult concept to understand until the practitioner is able to experience by himself. The basic idea is to establish harmony within yourself – harmonize your breathing, your movements, and your power. This will lead you to harmonize with the opponent. With this kind of harmony your opponent will be unable to find a good moment to attack you and it will be very difficult for him to beat you. Only then will you be able to use and combine sen no sen, and go no sen. You must work in harmony with your opponent and not against him.

Q: How many different types of defenses are there in the SKIF system for each type of prearranged (yakusoku) kumite?

A: For each type, there actually are eight different defenses. However, I only have five in my books, because that is enough for most people to learn. Also, number six is more difficult and performing numbers seven and eight can be dangerous. But I have developed the higher ones for myself as part of the philosophy of the SKIF system.

Q: When you say they are part of the philosophy of the system, what do you mean?

A: In the system, I have eight defenses and I also use eight different angles of defense. This is because eight is an important number in the philosophy of Budo historically. Also, using rotation on eight angles (tenshin), we can evade many different attacks using stepping and shifting (tai sabaki). This makes it possible for a smaller, weaker person to be able to defend against a larger, stronger person by using the different movements, techniques, and angles.

Q: Is there more to the philosophy behind the SKIF kumite system?

A: Yes, a major idea behind the kumite system is the philosophy that karate-do and kumite training is for everyone, not just competitors. It is to develop body, mind, and spirit. Thus, it helps develop inner harmony and harmony with your training partner. If there are 100 people training, all 100 can improve their karate, including their timing, distance, and techniques by training in the kumite system. Also, it is important to be able to train for life. Free sparring (jyu kumite) is not so safe or good for older people, but prearranged (yaku-soku) kumite can be done like kata and kihon for a person's whole life. This is consistent with Funakoshi Sensei's precept number fourteen that "karate is for your whole life."

Q: There are some minor differences in some of the Shotokan kata in the SKIF from the way the JKA generally practices the kata today. Why are there differences between the schools?

A: Actually, most of the SKIF kata are taught and practiced the original way, as they were taught by Funakoshi Sensei when the JKA was first organized. However, since then, the JKA has made many changes. In SKIF, I have made only some very small changes to some kata in order to make the application work correctly or for another reason. Kata is not just self-defense. It also is art and, therefore, each kata has its own meaning or philosophy behind it, so it is important for the movements in the kata to reflect the kata's own philosophy or meaning.

Q: In addition to the 26 Shotokan kata, you have included four more kata in the SKIF system, including Seienchin, Seipai, Gankaku-sho, and Nijuhachiho. Why did you decide to include these four kata in the SKIF system?

A: I added the four kata to give SKIF more history, and for technical reasons. For example, Seienchin is from Shito-ryu and Seipai is from Goju-ryu. These two kata include the shiko-dachi (square stance), which we don't have in our 26 Shotokan kata. In the Shotokan kata, we have kiba-dachi but not shiko-dachi. But both stances are very important and complement each other. Kiba-dachi is very strong but rigid. It is like a house make of bricks and cement. Shiko-dachi is also strong but a little more flexible. It is like a house made of wood. It also is the stance used by Sumo wrestlers. For older people who have knee problems, shiko-dachi can be easier and better for them. Kiba-dachi is very good for younger people and people with strong knees. These kata have different timing and a different meaning or philosophy from our other Shotokan kata, so this helps Shotokan people learn more and have a broader understanding of karate-do.

Q: Why did you include Gankaku-sho and Nijuhachiho in the SKIF system?

A: Both Gankaku-sho and Nijuhachiho are very old kata, so I included them in the SKIF system partly for history and partly for their techniques. For example, Gankaku-sho is the old version of our Shotokan Gankaku kata. So it gives us this history. But it also includes many different stances, and it is very good for stance training and for changing from one stance to another. This is very important for more advanced students. Likewise, Nijuhachiho is a very original kata. It gives us history and also many different techniques that we do not have in our 26 Shotokan kata.

Q: What is the origin of the Gankaku-sho and Nijuhachiho?

A: Both are from the crane style, which mostly was practiced in the village of Tomari in Okinawa. So, they sometimes are called Tomari-te kata. The Shito-ryu style largely originated from there, whereas the Goju-ryu style largely originated from the village of Naha in Okinawa. Shotokan, however, is mostly from Shorin-ryu.

Q: Where did you first learn the Nijuhachiho kata?

A: I learned this kata and Gankaku-sho from Master Inoue who used to live in the countryside of Japan near Gifu. He did not teach other people but he practiced a very original style of karate-do and I had a friend who knew him. He just wanted to keep his karate for his own practice. But through my friend, I asked him if he would teach me. At first, he said no but when my friend said my name he agreed. But he said he would only teach me the kata three times. If I did not learn it by then, he would not teach anymore. Fortunately, I learned the kata. I also learned Gankaku-sho from him. After he taught me, I found out that he had not even taught Nijuhachiho to his own son, so I felt very lucky. I think his son became upset and maybe later he taught the kata to his son. I have not seen him in several years and I am not sure if he is still alive.

Q: In your classes, you sometimes have taught about the different types of kiai ("yell" or "shout") in the kata. Would you explain this further?

A: In each kata, there usually is a positive kiai and a negative kiai. A positive kiai usually sounds like "yah." With a positive kiai, the feeling of the technique is to send the power outward to the opponent. Therefore, for punching, striking, and kicking, we do a positive kiai. But a negative kiai is different. A negative kiai usually sounds like "eh." With a negative kiai, the feeling of the technique is more to bring energy in to yourself. Therefore, when we do blocking or jumping, we do a negative kiai.

Q: Is there any other type of kiai?

A: Actually, Funakoshi Sensei used to do a kiai that sound like "tooh." This was a little different and I think it was more like a middle type of kiai. This is the kind of kiai we sometimes do when we do two techniques at the same time, like a block and a counter punch at the same time.

Q: In SKIF, there are certain ways in which we break down the techniques, for example doing punches in two or sometimes three counts. Also, doing blocks and kicks and strikes in the same manner. Why do you teach the kihon this way?

A: For kihon and for all of karate, form is very important. This is not only for the art but for balance and power in the techniques. In particular, moving from the center of gravity, using correct breathing, and having the right spirit all are very important and good form helps to achieve these things. It is especially important to concentrate on the Hara (center of abdomen) and breathe from there when doing karate techniques, and especially in kihon training. This helps improve mental concentration, as well as circulation and the health of the internal organs like the lungs and heart. This is good especially for juniors (children) because it helps them learn to concentrate their minds. The other thing about training from the Hara is that it is good for safety because it improves balance. So, it is very important in all kihon training for the instructor to check to make sure the students are doing the techniques from their Hara. Actually, kumite and kata should be trained in the same way.

Shotokan Legends

Q: How would you describe the different purposes of kihon, kata and kumite training in karate-do?

A: Kihon training is for yourself, to develop harmony with yourself. Kata training is for developing harmony with nature and, therefore, the image in your own mind of what you are doing and of your feeling is very important. Kumite training is to develop harmony between you and your opponent. This means it is not to beat your opponent but, instead, to find harmony with your opponent and to show each other mutual respect. It is important to move at the same time as your opponent and to have the same breathing pattern. This way you do not become frightened. Also, in kihon-ippon-kumite (basic one step sparring), for example, it is important to always see your opponent's eyes. This is true for other types of kumite also.

Q: During training, and especially after doing a series of kihon techniques or a kata, you practice and teach your students to do a special breathing exercise with their arms. How did you develop this breathing exercise and what is its purpose?

A: I developed this exercise after studying Tai Chi Chuan. The purpose is to develop and invigorate the brain, the chest, and the Hara. First, you breathe in and have the feeling of the air coming to your head and brain. This improves intelligence. Second, you push the air out and down and contract the Hara and lower abdominal muscles. This develops your power and fighting spirit. Finally, you straighten up and let your chest come back to a natural and relaxed position with good posture. This develops good character and a feeling of kindness toward others. The words for this are "ten," "chi," "jin," meaning head, Hara, chest or "sky," "ground," "human."

Q: Do you think there is something like "pure" shotokan?

A: No. Pure shotokan does not exists. The JKA practices a type of shotokan – but it is the shotokan of the JKA. Oshima sensei practices a shotokan but again it is his shotokan. Each master has a different view, a different brain, a different comprehension of things. This is normal.

Q: Do you train actively in any karate styles besides shotokan?

A: I have been fortunate of study different ryu under other great teachers. I sometimes invite instructors of different styles to teach at my dojo.

Likewise, I visit other ryu's dojos and occasionally teach. I've been lucky! I researched shorin ryu, uechi ryu, goju ryu, and others, because I really believe that no karate style is complete. We must look to the different roots. That's why I decided train in Okinawan styles. After all, they are the root of karate. Unfortunately, some organizations forbid this. This close-minded thinking is driven by politics, not karate.

Q: Do you recommend makiwara training?

A: Yes, I do but with conditions. As a yound student, I used to punch the makiwara more than 1,000 times daily, which is not correct. This kind of training is very important for karate but only with 50 or 60 full-powered blows per hand. It's important to develop power, speed and kime. I remember my knuckles were split open to the bone during my early training sessions. Once I went to see a doctor who cleaned the wounds and wrapped my hands! My senpai almost kicked me out of the dojo!

Q: Did you modify the karate you were taught?

A: Not really, but I did try to go back to its roots. Not to kung fu but to kong fu. Kong fu was a healthy exercise for mind and body. Daruma developed Zen exercises for internal power. This is very hard training and the students should never stop or they will never understand. In history, there was always a trend to improve health exercises for self-defense techniques. I haven't changed karate, I just kept it within the historical tradition.

Q: Why do so many karatekas develop problems in the lower back?

A: The main reason is the lack of adequate self-care. Most practitioners limit their self care to karate training. But you must take the proper pre-

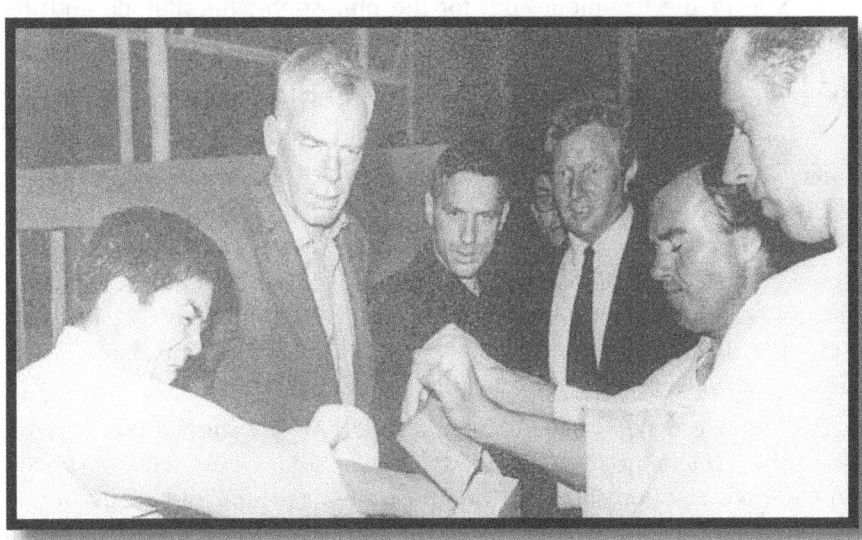

Shotokan Legends

cautions before a problem arises. Performing karate like a machine, without the proper relaxation, correct posture and breathing, will cause problems. That's the reason why I make my karate "self-chiropractic." Karate should improve health, not cause injuries.

Q: What do you think about karate going into the Olympic Games?

A: Sport is good as long as it is regarded as a recreation that you can leave and then go back to karate budo. Competition by itself is bad for the art, because you will understand nothing. Sport is open and enjoyable. Karate is not always enjoyable, because it is never easy to do the right thing. Karate is for the self. In sport we win over an opponent – in karate, we win over the self. In budo, a good kata performer must be a good fighter and vice versa. To realize the spirit of budo, one must be good at both kata and kumite – both sides have to be taught. The positive and the negative balance is very important. Good things always come in twos. In sport karate, one is only good at kata or kumite. Kata must look good for the referees, but at the same time must not be changed for aesthetics to create an extra flourish.

Q: Do you believe that it is important to go to Japan to study karate?

A: Not for the technique, but for the philosophy, the attitude and the spirit.

Q: In general, what are your most important teaching points?

A: Breathing, movement and timing – but breathing is first. The very first thing we do in this world is to breathe – but 90 percent of the population do not know how to breath correctly. If your breathing is wrong, your body will be wrong and your mind will be wrong also. There is a very strong connection. You control your spirit with your breathing and should always be thinking and trying to learn more about this most vital aspect, since it is the very core of life. I always stress the philosophical and health aspects of karate and try to explain the reason behind the techniques.

For instance, when I'm teaching the tsuki I do not show a punch to hit someone, I relate the movement to the person's hara – his center. I explain in the tsuki, that you should always push the head straight because it will promote good health by sending blood and oxygen into the head, which nourishes the cells. Utilizing the correct breathing, the hara, the concentration, and the impact produces a slight vibration on the vertebral column, which communicates to the brain and produces a sort of massaging effect. Remember that basic movements must be good for health; if not, then they are not good for human life. I can give you an example. Performing the fumikomi in the "tekki" kata flexes the base of the spine which uses the whole correctly. The base of the spine is a nerve center which stimulates the internal organs.

Two hundred years ago, bushi was OK. It was a matter of being strong without caring about health or anything else because there was a continuous life and death struggle. One had to be strong and have no fear in order to face daily life. Now, things have changed in society, and it is more important to be healthy in body and mind. Our character must be more peaceful but still having the same bushido spirit.

Q: Did your understanding of breathing change your physical techniques?

A: Yes. In the beginning I did not teach so much about breathing, but I adhered to a power style – quite a natural thing when I was young because at that age you favor strength. But with time and thought, I have come to a realization that winning can be done using only 60 percent of your power – 100 percent is not necessary if you have good technique. If I use 60 percent correctly and then use 40 percent of my opponent's power against him, the total is still 100 percent and the combination will result in more damage to him. This approach is the result of my tai chi studies.

Q: Have you modified any of the basic karate techniques?

A: Not really, but my tsuki has developed considerably since my younger days – but it happened subconsciously. I was not thinking about it, it just developed. I now have a double kime – a physical focus first, and then a speed focus, which delivers more shock. I did not realize what I was doing until it was pointed out to me by Matsuda Ryuchi, a very famous authority on Chinese martial arts. He mentioned that my punch was from Chinese kempo – but I was unaware of that. The same happened in other aspects. For instance, some people think that I have changed kata, but I never did. After five years of kata training, two people can practice the same movement and look identical – but after ten years differences emerge. They may think that they are doing the same movement, but since the body, character, and thoughts are different it is only natural that the kata will be different.

Q: How do you feel about full-contact sports?

A: There are schools where the students start free-sparring almost immediately. With this way it might be possible to improve quickly, but you will never reach the higher levels. The bottom line is that if you don't train extensively in the basics, you cannot reach the higher stages of martial arts. Some people misunderstand the meaning and use of the basics. You see, full contact karate, like Western oxing, is both good and not good. If you are young and strong it is very good but, of course, for older people and children it is not good. The kihon are just the basic techniques, but a thorough grounding in those will teach your body to instantly understand what is required in combat. The idea is to merge the body and mind. You should be able to perform any movement without thinking. This is the real meaning and purpose of the kihon.

Q: You always have been in a great physical condition. How do you train?

A: If I could train as I like, I'd be in even better condition, but sometimes is impossible due to meetings, visitors, business, et cetera. I believe a good karateka must use his body and his mind, so I study and read also. This gives a practitioner a much stronger quality – a balanced personality. As far as food, I think a lot depends on the mental attitude. If you eat something and think, "This is not good for me," then your body won't make proper use of it. But even if you eat curry, for example, and think, "This is good! It's great for my body," then you'll derive something positive from it.

I also think that control of the hara helps your body to use the food properly.

Q: Do you weight train?

A: No, but it might be beneficial for other people. There is good training equipment for the martial artist if they know how to use them properly. It is important to understand that the body changes and one loses the power of the muscles as you age. You cannot retain physical power forever. At some point you must develop the power of the internal organs. When you're older, the power of the spirit is what shapes your karate.

Q: What's your advice to practitioners?

A: I would like to see them work to understand the real spirit of karate – the breathing control and the cultivation of hara. They are difficult to put into words but can be found and experienced with thought and by applying oneself. My philosophy is to always be true to myself and to others. I can honestly say that I fear nothing, not even death – and I do not mean this in a big-headed or conceited way. I simply always try my best in everything I do, so I will be satisfied when I die. I think the reason that people fear death is because they want to accomplish so many things that are left undone – they feel their life is unfinished.

Tournaments are OK, but the practitioner has to understand more than only sport. Usually the practitioner is disappointed when the point goes against him because winning is everything, and he understands nothing else. A person like this is very dangerous to society because he respects only himself. If you respect your opponent, you'll never start a war. Everything connects to karate. True budo is good for society.

Q: Do you have any karate secrets?

A: There is no secret other than hard training. When I started karate training, the first year included a lot of running. The dojo at Takushoku University was so small that the loser of the race were eliminated from karate class! This built spirit. You must never forget that your the purpose of training is to master the art of karate, and to do so one has to develop perseverance, patience, and imagination to survive the ups and downs of being in the dojo. This is the real spirit of karate.

Q: Are there any other issues you would like to mention before closing this interview?

A: Yes. I think it is important to respect sports but it is very important to remember that competition is only a small part of karate-do.

Taiji Kase

Karate's Timeless Master

TAIJI KASE WAS ONE OF THE TOP KARATE-DO INSTRUCTORS IN THE WORLD. BORN IN TOKYO ON FEBRUARY 9, 1929, AND A DIRECT STUDENT OF MASTER FUNAKOSHI, SENSEI KASE DISPLAYED A VERY PERSONAL EXPRESSION OF THE ART. HIS PERFORMANCE IN TRADITIONAL KATA WAS FLAWLESS AND HIS SKILL IN KUMITE WAS SECOND TO NONE. YEARS OF PRACTICE AND HARD TRAINING FORGED THIS ICON OF JAPANESE KARATE INTO A LIVING EMBODIMENT OF KIME OR FIGHTING SPIRIT.

HE WAS CONSTANTLY TRAVELING ALL OVER THE WORLD AND WAS ONE OF THE FIRST INSTRUCTORS SENT TO THE WEST WHEN THE JAPAN KARATE ASSOCIATION DECIDED TO SPREAD THE ART OF THE EMPTY HAND TO EVERY CORNER OF THE GLOBE.

THE SPIRIT AND THE PRIVILEGE OF BEING PART OF THE FIRST, LEGENDARY SHOTOKAN DOJO BUILT BY FUNAKOSHI IN 1944, AND DESTROYED BY THE AMERICAN FORCES ONE YEAR LATER, SPICED EVERY ACTION AND MOVEMENT PERFORMED BY SENSEI KASE. IT WAS A TRADEMARK AND A SIGN THAT HE WAS VERY PROUD OF. WHEN HE DEMONSTRATED ANY OF HIS EXQUISITE SHOTOKAN KATA HE LOOKED LIKE A REINCARNATED KAMI, INVOKING SOME TIMELESS ELEMENTAL SPIRIT. HE WAS A MASTER WHOSE SPIRIT AND TECHNIQUE WERE AS TIMELESS AS MOUNT FUJI AND AS DEEP AS THE SEA OF JAPAN.

Q: When did you begin training in karate-do?

A: When I was 6 I began training in judo since my father was a judo teacher. Judo was much better known during the war, but I started practicing karate in 1944 at the shotokan dojo, where Master Funakoshi was imparting his knowledge of the art of the empty hand. I remember one day I was in a bookstore and I saw a book written by Master Funakoshi. Of course, I knew about judo, aikido and kendo, but karate was something

new to me. I decided then to go to his dojo. This dojo was destroyed by the American Air Force in 1945. This is a very important memory to me because many other great karate instructors never had the chance to train and learn from Master Funakoshi at his original dojo. I'll keep that memory until the last day in my life and beyond.

Q: Who else was there with you?

A: I remember that Master Tsuomu Oshima, who now resides in California, was also training there with me. Oshima was only 13 years old when I was the university captain already. My university was Senshin, and Sensei Oshima went to Komazawa. I used to collect Sensei Funakoshi to go to training. Both the atmosphere and the spirit at the old dojo was very special - very different from the other schools. I firmly believe that there was some kind of magic there. The training we did then with sword was perfectly applicable to the empty-hand methods of karate. You have to remember that we were living in a time of war so the martial spirit was everywhere. We didn't think about tournaments or sport. It was touch and kill, very much like katana training. This was the true age of budo!

Q: Did you only train under Sensei Funakoshi?

A: Well, Sensei Egami and Sensei Hironishi were also my teachers. They helped Funakoshi Yoshitaka in assisting Funakoshi Gichin. I remember that around 1946 Sensei Hironishi was helping Gichen Funakoshi. I also trained under Yoshitaka, his son.

Q: What do you remember about the son of Master Funakoshi?

A: He was really fast and strong. His movements were truly powerful - like a tiger! He was good at everything. Unfortunately, at 38 he was already very sick. Sometimes he had to stop in the middle of the training and go to a corner to rest. Then he would apologize and return to train - even harder. He had been told at 12 years old that his illness had no cure. I guess he wanted to reach a higher spiritual level by training without limits. I truly believe this was the reason for his extraordinary ability and skill in the art.

Q: Some of these names are related to the shotokai branch, right?

A: Yes. For instance Shimoda, Ohtsuka, and Obata, can be considered Funakoshi's first generation students. Hironishi was second generation. I guess this is the reason why I have a very good relationship with shotokai people. We were together, so I never saw a reason to stop our relationship.

Q: What has changed in you and in the art of karate-do since those times?

A: A lot of things! I have changed a lot and the art has also changed. I guess all these changes have been for the good. I have been practicing karate for almost 50 years non-stop, every single day. But there is something that has not changed during all these years and that is the mentality and the training spirit found in Master Funakoshi's dojo. This spirit is still inside of me. From the technical point of view, the art of karate has greatly evolved over the years but I think that part of the old spirit has been lost. And that is not good. I believe that spirit has to be kept within the art because it is the real spirit of karate-do.

Q: You were personally trained by Master Funakoshi. How do you remember him?

A: I met him when he was 70 years old. He had a very structured mentality concerning the art and was concerned about how it should be taught to the new generations. Sensei Funakoshi was continually changing and improving the art. I would say that he liberated karate from the precepts of Okinawan karate. On the other hand, he was a very honest and calm man - very kind and with a deep spirituality.

Q: Do you think Master Funakoshi would approve of the karate-do evolution during the last years?

A: First of all, Sensei Funakoshi was constantly changing and making innovations to the art. I am sure he would agree with the evolution, but it is very important to try to understand his mentality. He was from Okinawa and when he moved to Japan he saw how other martial arts systems like judo had great recognition from the government and the people. He wished the same thing for karate-do. He wanted karate-do to be part of the budo arts. For Master Funakoshi, karate was not a sport but a way of life. He always advised us to practice and keep practicing all the time. In fact, the training we did then with swords was perfectly applicable to karate! Don't forget we were living in a time of war and there was a martial spirit everywhere. The art of karate was practiced and, I think, still has to be practiced that way today - in the same spirit as katana training. I really think Sensei Funakoshi would be very proud of all his students and how the art he brought to Japan from Okinawa is being practiced around world. However, it is important to distinguish three different stages in the development of shotokan karate – the Okinawan, the Japanese and that of Yoshitaka Funakoshi.

Q: You mentioned that Funakoshi did not believe in karate as a sport. What do think about the fact that karate is probably going to be accepted in the Olympics?

A: I agree with the idea of karate becoming an Olympic sport. The sport aspect is a small part of the whole art - a small but important part nowadays. Karate competition is very fashionable these days and it has allowed the art to spread. In itself, that's not particularly bad but it may bring some consequences if we don't keep an eye on it. Competition might impoverish the art because practitioners tend to standardize the way they train, therefore creating a competition style. Fighters end up losing their personality and their training becomes competition-orientated. On the other hand, karate is not only budo, but budo is a big part of karate that has to be kept. It can be used to develop the human relationships. This is why the sportive side of karate is good. But it is only good as long as the techniques are kept in the right context and the karateka understand the tradition that links his spirit to the other parts of the art. I'd say that the sportsman has to respect the budo.

Q: What do you mean?

A: It's important to keep the right attitude and approach to training while you develop the sport, but if you begin to modify the karate techniques in order to be better in sport competition - and you forget about the right zanchin, the right posture, and the right combat spirit - then sport karate will ruin real karate. Sport karate is useful during your youth but the art of karate is for all your life. Karate is karate, boxing is boxing, and tennis is tennis. You shouldn't modify techniques just to score a point. Your technique and spirit have to be strong, never lacking in concentration. I don't see a problem in doing sport competition and preserving the real spirit of karate in every technique you use in combat. This is the right way. Real karate is not just jumping around and grazing your opponent. It's concentration and bang! Game over. You have to think about a life-or-death situation. Karate is a martial art which is practiced bare-handed. You try to render an opponent unable to fight by using a single technique. Period.

Q: You were one of the first JKA instructors sent to spread the art around the world and one of the pioneers in the famous Instructors Course. Is the JKA Instructors Course as hard as it used to be?

A: Not anymore. I still teach some of the classes every time I go back to Japan but these courses are not that taxing when compared to the old ones. In the old days they were very hard, very exhausting and tough. There was an unbelievable spirit in the air with Sensei Kanazawa, Sensei Shirai, Sensei Enoeda, et cetera. Classes today are very hard, but not that hard. After training there we were sent to different countries to teach the art of karate-do. I believe that JKA karate is the most researched and refined karate there is. The instructor training program allowed the students to devote themselves to the art, to completely immerse themselves in study and training. This is what made JKA karate so strong and the true reason why JKA teachers had such a high technical level.

Q: Did this personally affect your evolution and development as a karateka?

A: Well, not only myself but other instructors like Enoeda Sensei, Shirai Sensei, Kanazawa Sensei, et cetera, who have been away from Japan for three decades! Our distancing from Japan meant we had to set our own standards – either to improve or deteriorate as karateka independently. We are always exchanging ideas and I believe our standard has greatly improved. I always look for reality training for myself and my students. I like to analyze the technical and psychological levels of karate and the way it is expanding. I am daily searching for new techniques that are more relevant to the way I see the art these days. When karate was developing there were many gaps to be filled. Master Funakoshi knew that the influence of other methods was essential and that's why I'm trying to incorporate them. I truly believe in a healthy karate. Unfortunately, these days I see too much tension in the practitioners. They become so excited that they forget to relax their muscles. Trying hard is all they do and by the time they develop speed, their muscles are too tense. Therefore they can't relax properly in order to use their natural energy and muscle relaxation

to build up speed in their techniques. Modern practitioners need to develop a sense of balance between the soft and hard side of karate.

Q: What did Sensei Nakayama mean to the art of karate-do?

A: Very much. He was a turning point in the evolution of the art and his dedication and work should be recognized by every practitioner around the world. He opened a lot of new doors for karate, not only for shotokan practitioners but for students of any karate style. Master Funakoshi was a true gentleman and the person taking over should be the same. Nakayama Sensei was a great man and a gentleman as well. Unfortunately, since he passed away the JKA has split and all the great teachers that once were together now are working in different directions. It's sad but there's not much you can do about it. The old top instructors like Sensei Nishiyama, Sensei Okazaki, Sensei Shoji, or myself - we are living out of Japan so a problem was created as far as choosing a leader. The rest is history.

Q: Sensei, you mentioned once that you were "doing your own karate." It is possible to personalize the art of karate?

A: I definitely do my own expression of the art. It depends on my body, my mentality, my spirit, and my attitude. It is based on the way I look at life itself. Everybody is different and after many years of practice and understanding of the principles of karate your own expression of what you have learned will see the light. Sensei Oyama began his training in shotokan but he experienced different arts and decided to add certain things. Later on, he created the kyokushinkai system. Don't misunderstand me, this is not something that can be done overnight. It takes many years of training and above all, a deep understanding of the fundamental princi-

ples of karate and yourself. I don't think the style is that important. For instance, Sensei Tagaki practices shotokai. The technique is different but the spirit is the same. The essence of the art is the same, it has not changed a bit. This is what is really important.

Q: Have you practiced other karate styles?

A: I have a lot of friends that practice and teach other styles, and let me tell you that at a certain level it is not the art but the person that's important. The styles converge, they share the same principles but it's up to the practitioner to make it work. It's like playing piano; you can play Mozart or Chopin but if you are a lousy pianist, forget about it!

Q: What does kata training mean in your perception of karate-do?

A: For the beginners, kata is just a form, an external mold - but when you've trained for many years your understanding expands and kata becomes something else quite distinct. Also, you preferences in kata change with your age and evolution. Some kata may be very difficult for me but easy for you and vice versa. It is the person's ability that causes the difficulty. Unfortunately, in most cases, the kata we see are not real. The judges in competition only look at rhythm. I believe everyone, including myself, should talk to each other about the different aspects related to kata. I think some people are losing the kata internal meaning just for competition purposes. And that's definitely something wrong.

Q: Master Shigeru Egami developed shotokai, which differs from the system practiced and taught by Nakayama Sensei. What is your opinion of Egami Sensei?

A: The shotokai style seems strange to anyone practicing the more orthodox systems of karate-do. The kata are the same as shotokan but are performed in a soft, slow and fluid fashion, reminiscent of tai chi. Egami Sensei was one of the senior students of Master Funakoshi and he was an excellent technician. In fact, he was the model for the kata in the second edition of Funakoshi's book, "Karate Do Kyohan". In the early '60s, Egami

Sensei began his researches on the internal aspects of the martial arts and came upon his unique soft karate. He felt he was continuing his karate development in a way Funakoshi Gichin would have approved. He was an excellent karateka. Sensei Egami found something, but perhaps it was too difficult for him to transmit this to his students. He was very concerned with the "do" of karate-do.

Q: What is your advice for the karate practitioners around the world?

A: I would recommend that they train hard, every single day. Always keep in mind the right spirit and attitude in training. Don't forget about striking a balance in training between kata and kumite because that is the real secret. I am very old but I still train as much as I can accordingly to my age. You never stop learning and this is something that you have to carve in your mind from the first day. From day one to the last day of your life you are always learning. In the end, it is not about the styles of karate - there is just karate. You make progress or you don't - you reach the standard or you don't. That's all. Like I said before it is pretty much like music, it's a question of whether you are a good pianist or not.

Shojiro Koyama

THE PERFECT BALANCE

Born on December 4, 1935 in Tokyo, Japan, Sensei Koyama moved to the United States in 1964 and began teaching at the Arizona Karate Association, where he remains as chief instructor today. He has been promoting karate for more than three decades by teaching as a guest instructor in many other areas of the world, including Pan-America, the Caribbean, the Middle East and Canada.

He is liberal and open-minded about his methods and does not propose his to be the only true path to karate mastery. "All the fighting disciplines have a spiritual quality about them that all practitioners should try to develop," he says. The way he explains the philosophical foundation of karate-do is refreshing and soothing at a time when martial arts in general are leading us to more combative and violent approaches.

Author of several books on karate and health and many articles for leading martial arts publications around the world, Koyama Sensei is the Western Regional Director of the International Shotokan Karate Federation, headquartered in Philadelphia, and is a member of the Japan Karate Association Shihan Kai Instructor's Group. His remarkable contributions to the art of karate brings one to the conclusion that his has been a life well spent, and he has the right to be satisfied with it.

Q: How long have you been practicing the martial arts, and in how many styles of karate have you trained?

A: I began training in Shotokan karate in 1950 at the age of 15. I attended Hosei High School in Tokyo. In my senior year, I became the captain of the school's karate team. In 1954, I entered Hosei University, where I trained under Master Saiki and Master Kimio Itoe. By the time of my graduation, I had become the Co-captain of the university's karate team, and I remained there as a team coach until 1964.

I have only trained in shotokan karate. However, after so many years of karate training, I have had the opportunity to meet masters of other styles and that helped me to better understand other styles and methods of karate.

Q: How do Westerners respond to traditional Japanese training?

A: Western students are very open to absorbing Japanese culture. They tend to be open, accepting and rather obedient. However, although it appears on the surface that Western students absorb the culture, even after 40 years in the U.S., I can't be sure that they absorb the teachings at the subconscious level.

Also, when I first came to the U.S., I taught using the Japanese instructional approach. Pretty soon it became apparent that this style was not a very good fit for the Western mentality. Therefore, I can say that the aim of my teaching remains the same, but my approach to teaching it has changed and evolved throughout the past four decades. To fit the Western psyche, I tend to use more explanations and come at these explanations from many different angles, which is not really the traditional Japanese teaching approach. Japanese students are not used to as much explanation; they are more accepting of basic drilling without verbal clarification.

Q: Were you a natural at karate? Did the movements come easily to you?

A: No, I was very stiff. In the beginning, it was not at all easy for me.

Q: How has your personal karate changed and developed over the years?

A: This is a very interesting question. When I was young, I only studied and practiced my technique, and I thought that my technique would improve through this type of training. My instructors always said that I must also "Seek perfection of character" as part of my training and development or my technique would never really improve. Of course, as a youth I doubted that advice. I believed that "technique is simply technique." Now, however, I think I understand what my teachers were trying to tell me. After a lifetime of experience, I understand that hardship and struggle must be incorporated — in the form of character development — into one's training in order to improve one's performance. I watch videos of my old performances and demonstrations, and I can see a big change in my technique and myself since the earlier days. I attribute that change to the dignity, judgment and composure that I developed through my lifetime of experiences, good and bad, but especially to those that resulted in hardship and struggle. I have always said that karate is a lifetime exercise. If I continued to view karate only as a sport, as I did when I was young, I think that I would never have understood that lifetime exercise and character development actually lead to improvement in technique. This concept has to do with what it is referred to as EQ (emotional quotient or emotional intelligence). In the  Oriental way of thinking, emotional intelligence, born out of a lifetime of experience both good and bad, is very important in every endeavor. This is true for karate as well.

I have come to understand that sometimes American students don't like the Oriental militaristic style of teaching. It is usually the instructor's fault that students fail to understand that the extreme concentration and focus required of a karateka depends on a strict code of obedience and a strict style of teaching. Otherwise, technique will never really improve.

Q: What are the most important points of your teaching philosophy?

A: For me, karate is a mission, a mission that I brought to the U.S. when I arrived in the early 1960s. For example, early on when I arrived in the U.S., I formed the Western States Karate Championship Association. The annual tournament hosted by the WSKCA has always been an excellent vehicle for translating the philosophical pillars of karate into a practical reality.

Also, my karate philosophy reflects my belief that under adverse circumstances and conditions of struggle, a person's true character emerges. This is true in life and in the microcosm of life that karate represents. For example, when a karateka is unsuccessful in a dan exam or tournament competition, his or her true nature is revealed quite clearly. Those people who have begun to understand the importance of character development understand that — when initially unsuccessful — patience and composure are most critical. Failure can be a very good learning experience. Many people do not understand this concept and are always quick to compliment and try to soften the blow when their student is unsuccessful.

However, I believe that this soft approach will most often not bring out strength of character as efficiently as when one simply accepts failure, learns from it and commits to persevering despite of it. This mindset forms the core of educational karate and of karate as a lifetime exercise, and is, I believe, what is really meant by the first tenet of the shotokan dojo-kun: "Seek perfection of character."

Q: With all the technical changes during the last 30 years, do you think there is still pure shotokan?

A: Of course, despite all the changes on the surface, the fundamentals remain the same. These immutable basics (strong hips and body core or seikatandan, solid grounding, et cetera) are very, very important and always will be. That being said, it is undeniable that tournament technique is very different today than it was in earlier times. It used to be that karate opponents faced one another with a "one-punch, one-kill" frontline mindset. Now, karate competition is much more like a game. Nevertheless, basic foundations never change. Good competitors will always need to have techniques grounded in excellent basics, regardless of what current trends are reflected in those techniques.

Life is changing, becoming more complicated economically, geographically, politically... Evolution in karate technique reflects these changes. A strong "one-punch, one-kill" mentality is no longer enough. Nowadays, a successful competitor needs timing, speed and balance, and that comes from developing composure, patience and psychological grounding. Therefore, character development is most important.

Q: Do you think different ryu are important? And what are the main differences between the different shotokan methods that have appeared after the original JKA split?

A: The JKA split resulted in two distinct organizations, but I think that technically the karate in both is very similar. What differs between the two is organizational structure and management, even though basics and style remain the same. I hope that philosophically both organizations follow Master Funakoshi's guiding principles, which form the core and foundation of traditional shotokan, regardless of organization.

Q: What is your opinion of full-contact karate and kickboxing?

A: Although beautiful in its own right, this type of karate is 100 percent different from traditional educational karate. In sports styles such as kickboxing and K-1, victory or defeat is all that matters. Winning is everything and defeat is to be avoided at all costs. In some ways, I think that it is difficult to learn and grow with that type of mindset (one is focused on nothing but winning the next match). A famous professional sports coach once said, "Winning isn't everything; it's the only thing." I don't think this type of mindset is compatible with karate as a lifetime activity. Failure is an opportunity for growth. Sometimes that growth comes many years later, when one has progressed and developed enough to comprehend the lesson in that failure. But it does come when one has the patience to wait for it. Sports karate, wherein "winning is the only thing," is not as conducive to that type of patience or learning.

Q: Sensei, how do you think a practitioner can combine the principle of character development as Funakoshi Gichin described and the art of karate in the 21st Century?

A: Master Gichin Funakoshi wrote, "The ultimate aim of the art of karate lies not in victory or defeat, but in the perfection of character of its participants." He wrote this during the early 20th century, arguably the most aggressive and violent century in history. The generation of that time pioneered modern weapons of mass destruction and engaged in human rights violations of a scale never before seen or even imagined. Certainly, one would have hoped that the 21st century would bring a spiritual awakening and a fundamental change in the nature of human relations as the world began to look back on the tragedies and violence of the previous era. Unfortunately, it seems that human relations remain very complicated. Although the world has had the opportunity to reflect on the possibilities that face the human race in an age in which technology is capable of vastly improving life, or conversely, destroying it. Sadly, aggressive regimes continue to threaten their citizens, nations continue to wage war and terrorists attack innocent civilians. Perhaps human nature is fixed and will never change. If this is the case, it certainly seems that society needs to pursue areas of spiritual growth or peace will continue to be elusive.

Q: Practitioners of Master Funakoshi's karate maintain that the martial arts are different from, and more spiritual than, entertainment sports. How do we differentiate martial arts from sports?

A: To put it briefly, the aim of sports is to win, conquer and dominate the opponent. Losing is "bad" and therefore value is only to be found in victory. But, as Master Funakoshi's quote so eloquently explains, the value in the martial arts, such as karate, is to be found in the lessons learned from losing as well as winning. There are no true losers among practitioners of the martial arts, because both victory and defeat are opportunities for spiritual growth. Throughout life we must all learn to face both victory and defeat with grace and spiritual grounding. Otherwise, the disappointments of day-to-day living, over a lifetime, wear us down, make us bitter and cause us to behave aggressively, discourteously and possibly even destructively toward others. Karate fosters in us the ability to appreciate the learning opportunities inherent in defeat and loss throughout a lifetime of experiences, both good and bad.

One of the most important lessons that karate teaches us is that courtesy and respect are paramount. Without courtesy and respect, the martial arts are exactly the same as street fighting. That is what Master Funakoshi meant when he wrote the 20 basic precepts of karate, in which the very first one states that, "In karate, begin with a bow and finish with a bow." Where one consistently follows this principle, one begins to appreciate that courtesy and respect are more important than "winning." By respecting and valuing our opponents, we become capable of recognizing their courage, guts, mettle and spirit, regardless of who ultimately emerges "victorious." Character development means recognizing that this "spirit" is far more important than the trophy or medal that the winner receives.

For more than four decades, I have tried to operate a tournament that reflects Master Funakoshi's philosophy. At times, it can be very difficult to keep competitors and fans focused on the difference between entertainment sports and martial arts because, naturally, in the excitement of the tournament, many people are more focused on the entertainment value of the event and on carrying home the championship trophy. That, of course, is human nature. But, I will try to continue to promote the importance of the principles that underlie our art and differentiate it from other types of sports, as I have done for 40 years. That is, after all, the basis on which Master Funakoshi founded his art of traditional karate.

Q: How would you describe the life and dedication of the late Nakayama Sensei to the arts of Budo and specifically to karate-do?

A: Master Nakayama was the essence of modern Budo. After WWII, Master Nakayama created a new Budo, which we still follow to this day. It used to be that there were no tournaments, just drilling in the basics with a one-punch, one-kill mindset, albeit confined to a non-tournament setting. This type of training appealed to only a limited number of people. Master Nakayama opened traditional karate to a much broader audience and a wider market of potential students with the advent of tournament karate. However, I think that Master Nakayama might look at the ultimate destination toward which karate seems to be headed and perhaps conclude that the sports mentality has been taken to an extreme. In that regard, as the father of modern karate, he might be a bit taken aback at the direction taken by some of his "children," a direction he probably never envisioned when he pioneered modern Budo.

Q: Do you think that karate in the West is on the same level with Japanese karate?

A: I'm afraid that I can't answer that question yet. My mission was to bring Master Funakoshi's art to the U.S., but that mission is still a work in progress. If one considers only the technical aspects of karate as the basis for comparison, maybe the levels are the same. However, because karate is a form of lifetime exercise and education to me, I cannot judge yet how successful those

who have pioneered shotokan in the West have been. The results can only be judged on the basis of how many people have truly enjoyed life as a result (at least in part) of their training. Because that is the Oriental mindset, it is difficult to compare the Japanese "level" versus the Western "level." The basis of comparison is intangible when one looks beyond technical competence.

Q: In regards to physical capabilities, do you feel that there are any fundamental differences between Japanese karateka and European or American karateka?

A: I'd have to say that, in general, European people are stronger, but Japanese people are more technically "fine-tuned." These differences are analogous to the comparisons between Japanese and European/American technology. Japanese products such as Toyota and Sony are often thought to be more technologically refined, but European and American products are thought of as sturdier and more durable.

Q: Do you feel that you still have further to go in your studies in Budo?

A: I recognize that sports, entertainment and pleasure are very important, but philosophy and education is my field, my life's work. Personally, I believe that learning and studying are essential throughout life.

Q: Japanese coaches and Western coaches have a very different method of dealing with the preparation of a sport competition. Which method do you think is better?

A: There is no better method. Let me give you an example. In the 1964 Tokyo Olympic games, the Japanese women's volleyball team took the gold medal. That year's team coach was a man by the name of Dai Matsu, whose nickname was "The Demon." The Demon was a very strict, very hard man, much like an old-time Japanese military officer or samurai warrior. Many people believed that he was so successful because he was so strict and militaristic. This year the Japanese women's volleyball coach is 180 degrees different from The Demon. However, despite his differences in coaching style, he too led his team to victory in the Asian regional trials. It is very interesting that these two diametrically opposed leadership styles, one very regimented and harsh, one compassionate and gentle, have both been effective at different times and with different teams, although it might be argued that Dai Matsu's style was ultimately more effective because this year's Japanese team did not take home the Olympic gold! I think that the reason that each style has been effective in its own time is that today's players are also very different from those of the 1960s. This difference is characteristic not only of Olympic athletes but also of young people in general. For example, today's young karateka are much more recreation- and sports-oriented and much less focused on discipline. The spiritual and artistic features of karate are frequently neglected in favor of a focus on competition and showmanship. Unfortunately, when we turn completely away from the original cultural ideals or our art, we risk losing its rich and beautiful legacy, which is, of course, very sad. Perhaps even sadder is the likelihood that a focus on the sports-like aspects of karate leaves less room for the philosophical foundations that guide and enrich the life of the true martial artist.

Q: Sensei, you like to talk about some elements of the Chinese philosophy and something described as "the philosophy of kai." Would you elaborate on that?

A: Of course! The Chinese have a very interesting life philosophy. A person's life, they say, is like a bamboo stick. It is organized in discreet sections rather than along one long continuous pathway, as many people seem to believe. Life can be thought of as a learning process composed of five segments or stages. Stage one, sei-kai, is the beginning stage, in which the very young child is focused on being and existing in the physical world. Physical needs are all that the baby knows and is concerned with, and he or she is completely grounded in the present moment. Stage two, shin-kai, is concerned with forming a basic self-identity, which is based in defining a life purpose. In this stage, formal education geared toward an eventual occupation is the all-consuming focus, and the young person begins to develop a future orientation. Stage, three, ka-kei, is the point in life in which one begins to focus on raising a family. Ka means house, and the person at this stage of life is concerned with hearth and home, spouse and children. Ro-kai, stage four, is the beginning of old age. The individual at this stage of his life is starting to focus on defining a meaning for his existence and on finding a purpose in life. A focus on the past becomes important in order to understand and find value in one's lifetime of achievements, accomplishments and experiences. However, living completely in the past is dangerous at this stage because in doing so one risks losing a sense of purpose in one's continued existence. That is the reason that many people die shortly after retirement. They find themselves drifting aimlessly and failing to find meaning in their post-retirement activities. During the  final stage of life, shi-kai, one begins to think about his or her mortality and to prepare for eventual death. This is also a time of contemplating life after death and may bring a new orientation to the future, along with this focus on the afterlife. Depending on culture and religion, one might, for example, begin to imagine what heaven would be like or might wonder in what form he will eventually be reincarnated.

The important point in this philosophy is that a person should not move aimlessly or mindlessly through these stages. Kai means plan or study and inherent in the name of each stage is the implication that successful negotiation of every one depends on developing and following a meaningful personal philosophy during each of these life phases. Remember too that karate follows a similar pattern of development, which elsewhere I have referred to as seasons. The individual who is, for example, exclusively and narrowly focused on competition (the middle stages of his training) will ultimately neglect the latter stages and will fail to find any purpose in the practice of his art as he inevitably retires from the tournament ring. One very productive way of finding value in the post-competition ro-kai stage is by teaching, for example, as a karate instructor. Through teaching and passing on what you have learned, you achieve a sort of immortality. This is what the great psychologist Erik Erikson referred to when he wrote about successful negotiation of old age through the passing on of wisdom and guidance to a new generation. Also, as Erikson said, successful negotiation of any stage depends on successful resolution of previous life stages. In this regard, a lifetime is much like a child's game of dominoes. If an earlier domino is off balance, it will impact each succeeding one in a negative way, ultimately resulting in failure of the entire chain. Remember, in everything that you do, keep in mind the Chinese philosophy of life stages and you will find satisfaction throughout your lifetime.

According to the Chinese philosophy, I am currently in the ro-kai stage of my life. Some people, even those much younger than I, perhaps only in their 50s or 60s, look very old and unhealthy. As they exited what they thought of as the "prime" of their lives, their physical condition declined and their functioning deteriorated. That is, of course, natural and inevitable. However, it is not healthy to merely accept this decline as the beginning of the end, without a plan for the latter stages of life. That is why kai, planning and studying, is so important, especially as we begin to age. That is also precisely why the practice of the lifetime art of karate is so beneficial. Supplemental exercises such as stretching, push-ups, diaphragmatic breathing and so on are excellent methods for reducing stress, increasing mental and physical flexibility, and in general, combating the deleterious effects of aging, especially depression and anxiety. Each stage is an opportunity for study, planning and finding new meaning in all of our activities, such as the practice of karate. However, this opportunity is lost when one passively and fatalistically accepts functional decline as a sign of impending uselessness and deterioration.

Q: How exactly does karate fit into this philosophy?

A: That is for each of you to decide for yourself. Each person's physical condition and capabilities are different. Some people can continue to compete into their 40s while others are no longer physically capable of competing in their 30s. I can provide you with the basic philosophical framework as articulated in the Chinese philosophy of kai, but you must determine for yourself how you will apply it in your own life. One principle, though, is important for everyone, regardless of their personal life stage or circumstances, and that is this: Study and planning are important and are your responsibility. Mindless existence is a waste of your valuable and unique life potential. If you think of karate as only a form of recreation to pass the time, you will not be able to use your art in pursuit of your maximum potential. Instead, use your art as a learning opportunity and a route towards character growth, and you will reap the rewards of following the philosophy of kai toward a successful and fulfilling lifetime of experiences.

Q: How do you see karate in the rest of the world at the present time?

A: One night I was watching CNN and saw something that I think was very sad. The reporter was showing a terrorist training camp in which the trainees were practicing karate. To me, this is a tragic misuse of a beautiful art which celebrates non-violence and prohibits practitioners from using it offensively. On the other hand, I have also seen karate instructors in universities throughout the world teaching young people that karate is not just a form of fighting but also a philosophy and form of mental, emotional, spiritual and physical discipline. That, in a nutshell, is life ... sometimes good, sometimes bad. I believe that karate, even if not always used as envisioned by Master Funakoshi, at the end of the day will continue to reflect first and foremost the principles on which it was founded, in spite of its occasional misappropriation.

Q: Do you think it helps empty-hand karate physically to train with weapons?

A: Of course, in some forms of martial arts, weapons are very important. I am training in an "empty-hand" style, and I consider myself in many ways still a beginner. If I ever finish my course of training, I will pick up weapons training. So, in answer to this question, I am not officially training in a weapons art at this time. That being said, however, I do find that it helps me with my karate basics to train in some basic kendo techniques, such as the shinai. I find that this sort of training is an excellent supplement to my shotokan training.

Q: What's your opinion of makiwara training?

A: Makiwara training is very important. It is very helpful in working the legs and hips. I myself still train frequently with the makiwara. As people age, they become mentally and physically weaker. The makiwara is particularly good for older people because it trains the mind and the body at the same time, requiring sharp mental and physical focus and speed training. Older people often fear becoming slower as they age, and the makiwara helps combat slowing and loss of concentration. Also, the well-constructed makiwara as an opponent is very, very difficult to beat. It helps hone a competitive edge while keeping the user quite humble.

Q: How should a sensei (teacher) prepare his personal training in order to progress in the arts? What elements should be more emphasized once you reach an instructor level?

A: Technique comes from the instructor's personality and personal philosophy. If your aim is to be strong and violent, all you need is technical competence, and philosophy is not important. But shotokan karate emphasizes the first principle of the dojo-kun: "Seek perfection of character." If your personal philosophy or behavior runs counter to the dojo kun, your technique will never really improve or reach its full potential. I already mentioned that when I was younger my instructor warned me that I was concerned with technique at the expense of attitude. I have since learned that if you improve and advance your mind (attitude), your technique will follow. Unfortunately, the reverse does not seem to be true! Personally, I recommend Zen training. Zen training focuses on good, correct posture and breathing. Of course, it is a bit dangerous when an instructor tries to teach Zen to others without first having personal instruction from an experienced leader or teacher. It is relatively easy to read a book and think that you understand the principles behind Zen. However, there can be some dangerous side effects to practicing the art improperly if you have not been correctly schooled in technique.

Breathing is also important. Proper breathing leads to composure and a calm mind, as well as to physiological benefits. Breathing control translates to mental control. The autonomic nervous system (ANS) is not under the conscious mind's control, but with good breathing, a chain reaction of physiological events takes place that ultimately leads to the practitioner's ability to indirectly control the ANS.

Q: Isn't winning what is truly important in a sport competition?

A: Not really. Let me give you an example. Sumo wrestling is a traditional Japanese martial art in which aggressive competition is very important. However, sumo differs from a pure sports activity and illustrates a fundamental characteristic of martial arts in that victory is important but it is not everything. To be a sumo grand champion, one must not only win the tournament but also display a commitment to perfection of character at all times. The deportment of a true sumo grand champion reflects dignity, integrity and honor. Because sumo champions are important celebrities in Japan, they are highly visible and must be willing to recognize and accept their obligation to display integrity and honor in all of their public behavior, in the ring and out. Therefore, non-sportsman-like displays of emotion on the tournament floor, whether one wins or loses, are inappropriate and unacceptable for a competitive Japanese sumo wrestler. It is very interesting to watch a sumo match. Even though it is physiologically unnatural to suppress the intense emotions that accompany aggressive competition, the contestants almost never engage in passionate displays. Consider how different these sumo wrestlers behave than do, for example, many professional

football players after scoring a winning touchdown. This type of moderation is also traditional among practitioners of other true Japanese martial arts such as aikido, judo, kendo, and of course, karate. Students of these activities who do not behave in accordance with principles of modesty, dignity and honor cannot truly be considered martial artists in the traditional Japanese sense. Unfortunately, it seems to increasingly be the case that modern society is so influenced by the entertainment-sports mentality that many students of karate behave more like professional football players than like dignified sumo grand champions.

Q: Do you think that the mental approach of a fighter varies if he is competing in a sport tournament or if he is fighting for his life?

A: Nobel prize winning biologist Julius Axelrod concluded that human mental states (on which all of human behavior is based) are the result of hormones acting on the nervous system. In human beings, as well as in animals, passionate physical and emotional displays are a natural reaction to the secretion of hormones such as adrenaline and testosterone that accompany aggressive physical competition. The body does not know the difference between attack by an enemy and a controlled kumite match in the ring. In both cases, the brain perceives a threat and reacts by engaging the sympathetic (fight-or-flight) nervous system and directing the release of hormones that enable the body to better react to that "threat," whether or not it is actually real. Such physiological reactions are adaptive when one faces a truly dangerous situation, however, they can lead to unhealthy physical and emotional stress when they are too frequent or too intense. The restraint and self-control displayed by practitioners of martial arts such

as sumo helps moderate what would otherwise be unhealthy effects of an overabundance of stress and aggression hormones. Physiologically, this behavior helps counterbalance the arousal caused by the sympathetic nervous system by engaging the calming effects of the parasympathetic system. In contrast to the sympathetic system, the parasympathetic system decreases the heart rate and blood pressure and deactivates hormones like cortisol and adrenaline that can cause unhealthy levels of stress, and eventually illnesses such as heart disease, stroke and even cancer. In this regard, the restraint displayed by martial arts practitioners that may seem to be merely a means to spiritual growth and character development is actually physiologically protective as well.

The two-minute, single point matches of karate are very compatible with moderation of physical and emotional overreaction. The emphasis on control, spatial perception and cool-down between bouts of punching and kicking engage parasympathetic-like elements of the nervous system. This balance of an increase and decrease in physiological arousal is one of the characteristics that helps to differentiate martial arts from competitive sports. Unlike martial arts, many sports can be thought of as promoting only the arousal-supportive functions of the human nervous system, including secretion of testosterone and adrenaline. After the sports competition is over, the athlete goes home still keyed up and physically aroused. In the case of the martial arts, during the match itself, the sympathetic nervous and hormone systems are fully engaged, just like in competitive sports. However, martial artists learn to moderate these reactions as soon as the match is over, thereby engaging the parasympathetic system, cooling down more rapidly and controlling the effects of hormones such as testosterone. We have learned that an inability to control these effects can be disastrous. For example, research shows that many criminals have an overabundance of testosterone and are more likely to react aggressively to its presence.

Q: How should instructors modify their training when getting older?

A: As the instructor gets older, supplemental training (Zen, breathing, stretching, et cetera) become more important. For the older instructor, I have found that the proper ratio is 2/3 supplemental training to 1/3 technique training. This ratio helps promote the practice of karate as a lifetime exercise. Many instructors, in their youth, thought of karate as merely a sport to be won at all costs, much like professional football. And like many football coaches, such a karate instructor may allow himself to get out of shape and out of practice once he is past his physical prime. He still understands logically how to win and he can continue to teach the players to win, but he does nothing to grow in his own practice. Of course, that is OK for a sports coach, but my philosophy is that karate is a lifetime exercise, and therefore, the instructor, as he ages, must continue to train his own mind and body, over time increasing the ratio of supplemental training until he reaches that 2/3 ratio.

Q: When teaching the art of karate, is self-defense, sport or tradition the most important element?

A: I'd have to answer tradition but only when the term is used as a synonym for philosophy. Sports and self-defense, as goals, are limited. When you retire from competition or pass the physical prime of youth, sports as a goal becomes potentially obsolete. And once one has mastered self-defense techniques, one may become bored with training and quit. But for those students who find value in learning and following traditional manners and instructor-student relationships, principles of character development and Oriental philosophy, karate becomes a lifetime exercise for the long-term and shotokan becomes a way of life rather than a temporary hobby or merely a source of entertainment. Of course, everything should be in proper balance. Focusing exclusively on tradition is difficult and must be balanced with a commitment to train in the basics and, for those who so desire, engage in competition and tournament karate.

Q: In training, what's the proper ratio of kata and kumite?

A: Fortunately or unfortunately, students today seem to like sports karate. Therefore, a focus on basics is very important. Seventy percent of training should be in the basics but not only "basic" basics. Kihon with a partner in which application, coordination and practical elements of technique are emphasized is very beneficial.

Q: Some people think it is necessary to go to Japan to train. Do you agree with this point of view?

A: This is a very interesting question. For those who go to Japan for a year or less typically are only able to scratch the surface when it comes to experiencing and understanding Japanese martial arts culture and philosophy. They may come to believe that they understand it better than they actually do, but their understanding will invariably be shallow, and, as they say, a little knowledge can be a dangerous thing! However, the exception would be the person who finds a good guide/mentor, and

immerses himself in Japanese culture with that mentor's instruction and guidance.

Q: What do you consider to be the major changes in the art of karate since you began training?

A: First and foremost, karate has become more sports-oriented. It used to be the case that technical skill, philosophy and attitude were driven by a martial arts-oriented ideology. Now, these same elements are driven by a sports mentality and ideology.

Q: Whom would you like to have trained with that you have not?

A: Master Gichin Funakoshi.

Q: What would you say to someone who is interested in learning karate-do?

A: There is a Japanese saying that states if one wants to train in the martial arts the instructor must insist that one visit the school three times before deciding. Interestingly, the Talmud (the code of Jewish religious law), requires that a Rabbi turn a prospective convert away three times before agreeing to train him for conversion. Perhaps this similarity stems from the fact that, according to Budo tradition, one must commit oneself fully to one's martial art and training, much as a convert is expected to commit body, mind and soul to his new religion.

Q: What keeps you motivated after all these years?

A: Of course, I have a dream, a target destination if you will, but more important is right now, the present moment. Present life satisfaction and mental stimulation are very important. Without intellectual stimulation, a human being becomes like an animal ... the spirit withers and the body soon dies. Training provides that source of stimulation. After every training session, I say, "Thank you God. I did it! Right in this moment I was able to do what I set out to do." That is a bit of a miracle if you think about it, just like the elegant physical mechanisms that underlie all of the body processes that we take for granted, such as simply breathing. Everyone has big dreams. For example, a novice student dreams of obtaining his black belt some day, but what you are doing in the moment is what is really important. Eventually, the little satisfactions and small moments of progress that come day by day will lead you to your goals and dreams, but today is all we ever really have. That is what keeps me motivated.

Q: Do you think it is necessary to engage in free fighting to achieve good self-defense skills for a real situation?

A: When people think bad thoughts, their actions are bad. When they think good thoughts, their actions are good. Very simple! It is dangerous for a person who trains in karate to always imagine himself in a real fight with a real

opponent in the real world. Violent thoughts translate to violent actions. People often make the mistake of envisioning the makiwara or bag as a real enemy. This is incorrect. The purpose of makiwara training is focus and concentration, not imagined combat. Therefore, it ought to represent an abstract rather than a concrete concept in the practitioner's mind. In fact, when practicing with the makiwara, one's body should really operate as a machine, without thinking, and certainly without thinking about real enemies or fights. Relax, empty your mind and your reactions will come very quickly.

Actually, I always say that the dojo kun is itself the practitioner's best defense. I don't really think about real fighting, and I believe that one should keep one's mind clear of thoughts about real-life enemies and fighting when training. Your true opponent is your own mental limitation, not another person.

Q: What is your opinion about mixing karate styles? Does the practice of one nullify the effectiveness of the other? Or, on the contrary, can it be beneficial to the student?

A: All of the different styles are beautiful in their own right. That being said, I think of mixing karate styles much as I would of mixing different cuisines and cooking styles. While prime American steak, well-prepared sushi and gourmet Italian food can be a wonderful culinary treat on their own, mixed together they would lose their unique flavors and even become somewhat unappetizing. While this may seem a ridiculous analogy, it really does illustrate my feeling about mixing styles. As always, there is generally an exception to every rule, and in the case of mixing styles, it is this: As the karateka gets older, and after about 30 or 40 years of practice in one art, he will benefit greatly from supplementing his training with a softer art such as yoga or even tai chi.

Q: Modern karate is moving away from the bunkai in kata practice. How important do you think bunkai is in the understanding of kata?

A: Like most things, bunkai training has both advantages and disadvantages. On the negative side, for any technique, there may be another more reasonable or more efficient application or countermove than what is typically taught in bunkai training. On the other hand, if one is interested in brain stimulation, training and the right hemisphere in particular, bunkai training can be very helpful because it helps develop imagination and spatial perception.

Q: Do you have a particularly memorable karate experience that has remained as an inspiration for your training?

A: I don't really have one particular memory that stands out above all others. But what I can say is that I have been practicing karate for more than 50 years, and everyday training is still satisfying, I sleep well, my appetite is good, and I am still healthy and in good physical condition. That by itself is amazing and wonderful, and I credit my lifetime practice of karate for all of these simple satisfactions.

Q: After all these years of training and experience, could you explain the meaning of the practice of karate-do?

A: When I was young, I used to be preoccupied with big philosophical meanings. But today, as I have gotten older, mostly I just appreciate the benefits inherent in everyday practice, ordinary training and feeling good. That, in a nutshell, is the essence of lifetime exercise.

Q: How do you think practitioners can increase their understanding of the spiritual aspect of karate?

A: Early on I trained to be strong and to get stronger still. But now, through karate, I have come to understand how to be weak, how to recover from weakness, and how to maintain my level of skill and fitness. I have come to understand and accept my weak side because I understand the importance of modesty and humility. Hard, challenging training helps cultivate modesty and humility, which naturally leads to a better understanding of the spiritual aspects of the martial arts. Therefore, keep training, don't give up and don't become discouraged by your moments of weakness. Instead, learn to value and cherish them for the ultimate spiritual growth that they will bring you.

Q: How much training should a "senior" karateka be doing to improve and get better at the art?

A: The how is what it is important and not the how much! Maintenance is the best target for an older senior student. When a senior student always focuses on physical improvement, he or she will inevitably become disappointed or frustrated. He should just try to maintain what he has; it is a more realistic approach. This kind of goal will provide an interesting, simulating and realistic target for the older senior student.

As the instructor gets older, supplemental training (Zen, breathing, stretching, et cetera) becomes more important. For the older instructor, I have found that the proper ratio is 2/3 supplemental training to 1/3 technique training. This ratio helps promote the practice of karate as a lifetime exercise.

Many instructors, in their youths, thought of karate as merely a sport to be won at all costs, much like professional football. And like many football coaches, such a karate instructor may allow himself to get out of shape and out of practice once he is past his physical prime. He still understands logically how to win, and he can continue to teach the players to win, but he himself does nothing to grow in his own practice. Of course, that is OK for a sports coach, but karate is a lifetime exercise, and therefore, the instructor, as he ages, must continue to train his own mind and body, over time increasing the ratio of supplemental training until he reaches that 2/3 ratio.

Q: Is there anything lacking in the way karate is taught today compared with those who were being taught in your early days?

A: Ninety percent of life is composed of the ordinary and the mundane. An appreciation for the mundane is what is missing in today's karate training. For example, when I was a student at Hosei University in Japan, we had no tournaments ... just basic dojo training. Our instructor would say, "Today we are going to do heian shodan 100 times." We would do it and be satisfied. Now, students always seem to be chasing the next big exciting event. Often, as a result, they have little patience for the type of ordinary practice and drilling that we did in the early days.

Shotokan Legends

Q: Speaking of mundane things, you once said, "An individual has to find joy in the mundane." What did you mean?

A: Unfortunately, the vast majority of the human lifespan is spent in mundane, unconscious moments. To ignore and reject them is akin to discounting a large percentage of one's life, which, of course, is unfortunate. Those who are able to rejoice in the mundane are able to make the most of every moment of their lives, and ultimately, to cultivate their abilities to engage the unconsciousness. To engage the unconscious does not mean to bring it into consciousness but rather to use its power to mobilize relaxation and focused concentration, and to open the mind to new experience, growth and progress. This lifelong pursuit of development is the fundamental basis of educational as opposed to sports karate.

While sport karate, which focuses energy exclusively on moments of excitement like competition and tournaments, may seem like the most efficient means of skill development, in fact, the career of the sport karate enthusiast tends to be short-lived, and within the reach of only a very few elite individuals. By contrast, educational karate promotes life-long pursuit of growth and enjoyment and is open to all, regardless of age or innate talent level. Of course, as always, balance is critical. Some degree of excitement, as is found in championship tournaments, builds a healthy competitive spirit and provides short-term motivation. Furthermore, in modern Western society, the dojo that completely rejects the sport-like aspects and entertainment value of karate is unlikely to survive for very long. However, it is our responsibility as practitioners of lifetime educational karate to pass on the importance of the mundane aspects of life and training and to cultivate the patience that allows us to tap into the unconscious power of those mundane moments. Therefore, while tournaments are valuable and exciting, the more mundane events, such as the daily practice of basics and kata, are also important.

Q: How can a parent help the karate teacher in this educational process?

A: Parents play a critical role in cultivating within their children an appreciation for the mundane, in karate as well as in all aspects of life. Children who are taught to value the ordinary learn patience and develop an understanding that real life is not always going to be like a trip to Disneyland! Many modern parents have a tendency to focus on big events such as exams and championship games. They push their children toward greater and greater achievements in high-profile or high-stakes experiences, thereby seeming to devalue the routine aspects of daily study and practice. Unfortunately, these children fail to experience the pleasure inherent in the painstaking pursuit of a goal and the personal pride that comes through perseverance itself. While success in the critical experiences of

life is important, we must also offer our children, as well as ourselves, the opportunity to gain meaning from the lower-profile moments that make up the vast majority of life. These lower-profile moments form the backbone of community karate. I encourage you to take advantage of the ordinary training opportunities that are part of the community karate experience and to recognize that they can be just as meaningful, if not more so, than competitive championship tournaments.

Q: What do you consider to be the most important qualities of a successful karateka?

A: A commitment to everyday training and an appreciation of the mundane. Train hard, finish, bow and say "thank you" for the opportunity to sweat. The most important quality for a practitioner of lifetime karate is the ability to find such satisfaction in ordinary training. Of course, for those students who want to participate in special events and tournaments, I say fine, but don't neglect the basic, ordinary training that makes up more than 90 percent of the practice of the art. Otherwise, you risk boredom and disenchantment in between those special events, which is quite sad. As an aside, the willingness to pass on your skill and knowledge to others as you grow and develop in your own art is also important. It is said that giving nothing to others is akin to harming them. The successful practitioner of lifetime karate is successful because he has had a satisfying life, not because he is a tournament champion or 10th degree black belt. Satisfaction comes from ability to enjoy the ordinary and willingness to pass on one's wisdom as one ages. That's all.

Q: Why do many students start falling away after two or three years of training?

A: They quit because they have no philosophy and therefore no destination or long-term plans and goals. Perhaps, for example, their only goal is to get a black belt. After accomplishing that objective, they may find themselves without motivation. It is the instructor's responsibility to help the student appreciate karate as a lifetime art rather than always seeking a particular rank or a medal or trophy. Students who seek only rank or who view karate solely as a competitive sport are likely to quit when they experience defeat, fail an exam or discover that they are not likely to be the next "Bruce Lee." Those students who understand karate as a lifetime exercise and recognize that karate follows a lifecycle much like the seasons of the year are far less likely to "fall away" after a few months or years of training.

Q: Sensei, you often speak about the four seasons of karate-do. Would you please elaborate on this?

A: I am fond of saying that educational karate differs from sports karate. But, in what way are they different? Educational karate is a lifetime exercise. The original fundamental basis of the art is in Eastern philosophy, in particular, Zen Buddhism. This type of philosophy emphasizes peaceful self-reflection and an appreciation for the natural world. The spirituality of Zen Buddhism is based in self-knowledge and personal growth. By contrast, sports karate has more in common with certain aspects of Western culture that place a much higher value on achievement, accomplishment and external measures of success. Such a value system emphasizes a competitive spirit, which, to some extent is important, but in excess tends to preclude spiritual peacefulness.

Asian cultural symbols are often rooted in images of nature, and metaphors of the natural world are used to describe human material endeavors. So, for example, an analogy might be drawn between a person's practice of the martial arts over his lifetime and the four seasons of the year.

Spring is a time for preparing the soil and sowing the seeds of the future. Although flowers begin budding in the spring, in general, the fruit has not yet fully ripened. In karate, spring represents kihon, the basic foundations of training. At this time, stance training, makiwara practice and fundamental techniques such as five-step sparring are essential. But, like the fruit that is picked before it reaches its peak of ripeness, the karateka in the spring of his training is undeveloped and not yet ready to reach his full potential. The practitioner of karate who rushes his training in order to compete in tournaments is like a green banana that is artificially ripened and rushed to market. On the surface, he may appear smooth, glossy and polished, but at the core he remains immature and underdeveloped. This

type of student may be prone to injury, frustration and eventual burnout, especially when he achieves easy early victories. Then comes the summer phase. Here the basic foundations of springtime training are essential but are not, by themselves, sufficient for the student to fully "ripen." Summertime training involves development of speed, timing and balance. At this time, the foundations that are laid during springtime preparation are further developed and augmented so that flexibility, stamina and strength reach their peak. Summer is when spring's basics are applied in kumite and kata competition. It is also a time of increased risk of injury. Unfortunately, often when a student is injured during competition, he becomes discouraged and quits training. However, the student who continues to train after suffering an injury benefits from the experience of overcoming adversity and surmounting pain. Pain and suffering are inevitable human experiences and carry with them an inherent opportunity for character development. Like an oyster that transforms a painful irritant into a beautiful pearl or the poet who is only able to create his poetry when he is suffering, the true martial artist mobilizes creative energy from his own pain and suffering. Suffering, either because of physical injury or defeat in competition, is an invaluable source of spiritual growth as well. In the world of competitive sports, where victory is everything, the winners are incapable of empathizing with the pain of the losers. By contrast, the martial artist who has experienced loss and injury develops a sense of compassion and sympathy that is typically absent in the highly competitive world of sports karate. During the summertime of karate training, victory and defeat, joy and pain, agony and ecstasy — when properly balanced — contribute to full ripening of the karateka's physical, emotional, mental and spiritual being.

In autumn, the knowledge that is cultivated in youth is harvested, and the practitioner uses that knowledge to form a philosophy and framework for the future. In the natural world, toward the end of summer, the turning of the leaves and the briskness in the air is accompanied by a sense of foreboding. Similarly, for the martial artist, as the physical prowess of summertime little-by-little begins to decline, there is often a feeling of sorrow or regret. The student who was at his peak a top competitor eventually finds himself beaten by a younger, stronger, faster opponent who is just beginning to enter his own "summertime" training. Jealousy, envy and discouragement are natural feelings as age takes its inevitable toll. However, those who understand the value of lifetime exercise can overcome discouragement through the pursuit of beauty and serenity in the practice of their art rather than the single-minded quest for competitive victory.

Finally, in the "winter" season, all the wisdom and skill that has been gathered in youth is ready to be shared with others through teaching and mentoring. The process of aging is accompanied by decreased flexibility and physical strength, and training becomes more difficult for most people. Those who are able to subordinate their own egos can create value by passing on their knowledge to the next generation of students. This is the time when soil must be readied for the next growing season and the seedlings cared for so that they may achieve their own full potential in the coming spring and summer. A discussion of this same basic idea can be found in the works of well-known developmental theorists like Erik Erikson. In Identity and the Lifecycle, Erikson suggested that those who are able to find value in their own histories and in sharing their wisdom and experience are more content as they age, and less prone to despair, depression and loneliness.

Unfortunately, many practitioners of sports karate invest 100 percent of their energy in the spring and summer of their art. They fail to recognize the value of autumn and winter and may become discouraged and lose their purpose once they are past their athletic prime. By contrast, those who recognize the value inherent in each stage of the seasonal cycle can gain much joy from participating in all phases of the natural rhythm represented by that cycle. Thus, in youth, the karateka is taught and coached by his respected sensei. In adulthood, he develops a style and philosophy of his own, based on the earlier teachings of his instructor. As he ages, he in turn becomes the respected teacher and gives back by passing on his own wisdom to a new generation of students. That is the natural order of lifetime karate-do.

The seasons of lifetime karate can also be compared to the pursuit of higher education. Practice of the basics and their application in kumite and kata are mandatory, like the "required courses" in a liberal arts degree. Development of one's style can be thought of as the "masters degree" stage. The "Ph.D.," the highest and most respected level, is achieved by those who pass on their experience as instructors and mentors. Success in competition and physical fitness alone are not sufficient to achieve this last level; spiritual development and the wisdom that can only be achieved with age are also necessary. Those who are fortunate enough to recognize this process will be able to enjoy a lifelong pursuit of happiness through the practice of their art. Those who do not (for example, sports karate enthusiasts who value only the spring and summer of their training careers) are likely to experience frustration and loss of motivation when they are forced to retire from competition.

In karate-do, the greatest value is not to be found in a trophy, or in fame, or the admiration of fans or in higher and higher black belt rankings. The true attainments of value are far less tangible. They come from the personal experience of the performance of the art itself, from practicing, teaching and demonstrating that art. There is a great sense of personal power and energy that comes from performing one's art. As the practitioner polishes and purifies his performance, others have the opportunity to observe, enjoy and benefit from that process as well. In sports karate, the observer may notice and be impressed by the power, strength and athleticism of the competitor. However, those who observe practitioners of lifetime karate are treated to a display of beauty that goes beyond physical power. That kind of beauty is obtainable by the lowest ranking white belt or by the oldest student in the dojo just as much as by the youthful tournament champion.

For many years I have taught college P.E. courses. One night I went to the gym where my class is usually held and found the room occupied. I opened the door to look inside and was surprised to see about 200 people participating in a yoga class! Yoga is also a lifetime exercise, but unlike karate, there is little or no focus on summertime training because there is no competitive component. As a result, yoga appeals to a broad segment of the population that is not interested in or capable of engaging in competitive sports. However, the value of the competitive aspects of training should also not be overlooked. Balance is important, as are all four seasons of the training lifecycle. But, where summer training is emphasized to the exclusion of all other aspects, eventually, the activity ceases to be an art, and becomes instead a pure competitive spectator sport like K-1 or cage fighting.

Right now, dojo enrollment seems to be at an ebb, particularly relative to such activities as yoga. It is not helpful to be an alarmist, but neither is it prudent to ignore a potential problem. Because educational karate retains a core of dedicated students, it is easy to overlook declining enrollment. Eventually, however, we may find that we have passed the "failsafe" point and have lost our students to summer-only activities like sports-karate on the one hand and "summer-less" ones like yoga on the other. If we want to continue to pursue the opportunity to enjoy the four seasons of our beautiful art, we must make sure that we recognize the value of each of those seasons and communicate that value to our younger students. Otherwise, we risk losing those students who fail to understand that the ultimate destination of the karate-ka is not the summertime tournament but is instead a lifelong pursuit of growth, development and fulfillment throughout all four seasons of the karate-do lifecycle.

Q: There is very little written about you in magazines. You obviously do not thrive on publicity like some martial artists. Why?

A: A karate instructor is similar to a golf pro. Some golf professionals, such as Tiger Woods, are focused on competition. Others are teaching pros. The entertainment value and popular interest is in the competitor, not the teacher. I am a teaching professional, not a celebrity. Popularity, notoriety and fame are simply not important to me.

Q: Have there been times when you felt fear in your karate training?

A: When I was young, I always felt fear. But as I have gotten older and entered the later stages of my life cycle, I am no longer really worried about anything. Why are people afraid? I believe it is because they have unhealthy desires such as more and more money and more and more popularity. The possibility of not obtaining these desires makes people nervous. I am approaching the end of my life's journey. I still have aims, plans and dreams, but these are no longer guided by unhealthy desires. In my youth, of course, I had those needs, and therefore, I was afraid. I have discovered in life that the biggest enemy is fear. It is only through abandoning unhealthy desires that one can finally conquer fear. The Talmud, which

I referred to earlier, defines one who is mighty as one who conquers evil impulses. In other words, strength of character is developed through emotional and spiritual control. This same principle is embodied in the dojo kun, which instructs us to seek perfection of character and avoid unhealthy preoccupations.

Q: How important is the principle of balance in karate and life?

A: It is very important, and I'll try to fully explain it. Although I have lived for more than four decades in the United States, I continue to find it very difficult to explain the philosophical principles of karate to American students. While part of this difficulty is due to my own grasp of the English language, in large part it is also because the Japanese way of relating through language is sometimes very different from the Western communication style. As a result, for example, it has been virtually impossible for me to translate Master Funakoshi's teachings directly to my students. I have discovered that — rather than attempt direct translation — it is often more effective to find a similar philosophical concept in Western teachings and to use it to illustrate the ideas that Master Funakoshi expressed so eloquently in his own writings.

For example, Master Funakoshi spoke frequently about the importance of balance in all things. Mental, emotional, physical and spiritual balance are essential to pursue perfection of character, a principle underpinning in the art of karate. Many Western philosophers also discuss the importance of balance in achieving progress and character development. For example, the Talmud's discussion of achievement in the mental, physical, material and spiritual realms relates to the importance of balance. The Talmud poses four important questions that we might all ask ourselves, and they are as follows: Who is wise? Who is mighty? Who is rich? Who is honored? And then find the answers.

Q: What is the answer to the first question?

A: Wise is the one who learns from all teachers. Master Funakoshi taught that humility is essential for the development of mind and body. Of course, we may learn much from our higher ranking, experienced teachers. However, I have discovered during my years as a karate instructor that I also learn from my own students, in particular the beginning white belts.

The technique and skill refinement imparted by my teachers must be in balance with the humility, enthusiasm and acceptance I am taught by my own lower ranking students.

Q: Who is mighty?

A: The one who conquers evil impulse. Here, the Talmud is teaching us that strength of character is developed through emotional and spiritual control. This principle is also embodied in the dojo-kun, which teaches us to seek perfection of character through control and balance in physical manifestations of emotional reactions. A reaction that is too weak leaves one vulnerable and in the position of a victim. A reaction that is too strong is a sign of lack of control and foolhardiness. Again, balance is the key.

Q: Who is rich?

A: The one who is satisfied with his portion. Karate is a lifetime exercise. As we age, our physical abilities change and may not be as impressive as they once were. At the same time, often our spiritual development accelerates, as we grow older. If we are able to accept these changes, we are not disappointed by the loss of physical stamina. When we recognize that the losses are more than balanced by the gains, we remain content with our portion and we are able to continue to gain satisfaction from all areas of our lives. If we fear aging and resent or deny the changes that accompany it, we become discontented, frustrated and ineffective in our practice of karate ... or in any other life task.

Q: And finally, who is honored?

A: The one who honors others. The principle of respect for others is, of course, the underlying tenet of the dojo kun. We are respected only to the extent that we respect others. This balance of respect is illustrated by the formal code of conduct karate students practice in the dojo. Ritualized interactions between students and teachers reinforce the importance of this balance of respect, which, in Eastern society, reaches far beyond the dojo walls.

Q: What are your thoughts on the future of karate-do and what's your opinion about karate entering the Olympic Games?

A: The Olympics provide a wonderful opportunity for the world community to get together in a common endeavor. This is a beautiful thing. The top, most elite athletes perform in front of the entire world and are treated like heroes by millions of people. Kids dream about going to the Olympics some day. Unfortunately, Olympic-level talent and the dedication that it requires are not the norm, of course. Five-year-old kids train 10 hours a day honing their skill, which is amazing and beautiful. Mankind benefits tremendously from that kind of icon. But to focus on the Olympics as an ultimate goal for the vast majority of people in any sport would be ridiculous. As it happens, something like 80 percent of school-aged athletes drop out by the time they graduate high school, largely because they had unrealistic dreams and become disenchanted. So, symbols and icons such as the Olympic athlete are very important, but it is also extremely important not to forget the principle of lifetime exercise. Regardless of whether karate ever becomes an Olympic sport, the majority of practitioners will ultimately focus on the lifetime exercise aspects of the art. Don't quit and keep training. That is the essence of karate-do.

Q: Sensei, what is the value of non-competition practice of karate?

A: Today, unfortunately, many people get caught up in unrealistic Hollywood-influenced expectations of performance and assumptions that — with enough time and practice — they will ultimately become champion martial arts competitors and recipients of higher and higher black belts. It seems obvious that without an extraordinary level of talent and natural ability that it is unrealistic to expect to receive such things. Imagine, for example, that every weekend golfer truly believed that with practice and determination he or she could become the next Tiger Woods. Golf courses would soon empty as avid but ordinary golfers became discouraged and disappointed. Of course, most leisure golfers understand that they will never be Tiger Woods and are satisfied with the enjoyment and pleasure they gain from the activity itself. Karate practitioners must likewise understand that not everyone can become a champion and that happiness can come from enjoyment of the art rather than from certificates, belts, awards and trophies.

There are many benefits that come from participation in sports. For an elite group of athletes who possess a rare combination of talent, single-minded determination and luck — Tiger Woods and Michael Jordan — money, fame and recognition are possible. For most of us, the benefits that we can expect may be somewhat less ambitious, but they need not be any less meaningful. For example, a second group participates in sports activities for purposes of physical fitness and the pleasure that comes from being strong and in good shape. Most of this second group is comprised of healthy young people, a few of whom, with great effort and practice, may some day become elite athletes and champions. A third group participates in sports activities for purposes of physical rehabilitation (to recover from an injury or reduce the risks of chronic illness, high blood pressure, et cetera). A fourth group consists of older people who desire to stay in shape, stave off the aging process and avoid depression and inactivity. In this regard, karate is similar to other sports. Sometimes it seems that everyone thinks they will eventually become Bruce Lee, but of course, it is more realistic and less frustrating to understand what type of exercise is important and which of the four groups is the best fit. Otherwise, where the focus is on tournament performance, many people become quickly discouraged and quit training. Likewise, where the focus is on chasing ever-higher belts and ranks, disappointment, frustration and impatience are common. Internal pleasure and happiness are lost in the quest for external symbols of achievement and glory.

Of course, those individuals who truly have the skill and drive to succeed competitively should not be discouraged from challenging themselves to do so. These individuals may achieve "Tiger Woods" success with lots and lots of practice, sweat and effort, and not a little luck. But, the vast majority of us risk appearing to be ineffective if we focus on glory rather than on development of our art for its own sake. Do not let this dismay you, however. Remember, there are many paths to ultimate happiness. Most of these roads do not end with a tournament trophy. Karate should be thought of as a lifetime exercise. Remember, even champions eventually retire and must seek pleasure in the more ordinary benefits enjoyed by members of the other three groups of sports participants.

The great Greek philosopher Socrates said, "Know thyself." Thus, seek happiness through understanding your real objectives, analyzing your abilities and needs, and deciding in which group of karate practitioners you truly and realistically belong. It is my responsibility to educate the current generation of karateka about the discouraging results of succumbing to the American celluloid image of martial arts and the importance of finding one's true path and true goals of training.

For example, championship fighters may not focus on learning the 26 shotokan kata (and in fact, may not even know most of the kata at all). It is up to the larger majority of us — those who view karate as a lifetime exercise meant to challenge the mind, body and spirit — to study the intricacies of these beautiful traditions and pass our learning on to each new generation of karateka. If we think of the trophy, the tournament title or the fifth dan certificate as the ultimate "work product" of karate society, most of us will feel that, our karate seems to be purposeless. We should not fall into the trap of believing this to be the case, however. According to Master Funakoshi, perfection of character and improvement in body and soul, not a tournament trophy, should be the ultimate goal of the practice of karate. Many benefits may be discovered along the journey toward self-improvement but it is only when one ceases to focus on external symbols of success and instead looks toward more meaningful goals of internal happiness that physical strength and spiritual fulfillment can be attained. We must avoid fixating on championships and glamorous tournament performances; otherwise, we risk spinning our wheels, forever chasing an unobtainable goal.

Q: What do you think are the main reasons why people come to your school, and how do these motives affect their progress in the later years of their practice?

A: Just recently, I distributed a questionnaire at the dojo to collect student opinions about our training program and the quality of instruction. Preliminary results indicate that, in general, students are very satisfied with training in kihon (basics) and in karate's philosophical principles. Furthermore, many students rated kihon, kata and mental/spiritual development as the aspects of training most important to them at this time. These results greatly encourage me because they suggest that the areas rated most highly and deemed most important by my students are, in fact, the very ones upon which I focus my teachings, and those that are most essential to Master Funakoshi's basic principles of shotokan. I do not believe that the survey results are mere coincidence, rather that they are a reflection of my students' understanding of the critical role of basics in shotokan karate. This being the case, it seems that I have succeeded in passing on to my students some of the most important teachings of Master Funakoshi.

Q: Why have you chosen to refocus your teaching on the basic skills rather than on more flashy or intricate techniques and applications, even though some people may consider the basics less interesting?

A: Unlike in most other sports or activities, kime and ki (spirit) must also accompany the practice of these techniques; otherwise, improvement will be elusive. Therefore, you must understand the importance of this type of basic training and believe in the benefits you will receive from it. In karate, the focus of basic training is development of the body's core, known in Japanese as the seikatanden, and its connection with the hips and legs. The triad of the seikatanden, hips and legs forms the fundamental body structure on which all stances and techniques depend. If I were to focus in class on more fancy and elaborate techniques, students may find class more exciting; however, the benefits to the fundamental body struc-

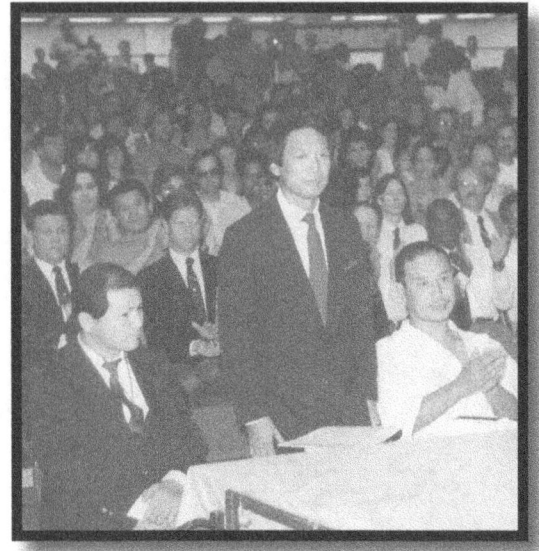

ture would be more limited. By focusing on the basics, over the long term, one begins to appreciate the improvement in one's form and will notice the positive effect that a stronger, better developed fundamental body structure has on one's ability to perform the more elaborate aspects of karate. In time, I guarantee that the development of fundamental body structure will, in turn, be reflected in a stronger, healthier mind, body and spirit, as well as in better karate!

In addition to a renewed focus on basics, I also provide more training in kata, both because my students have expressed an interest, and because I believe in the maxim that "knowledge is power." The more you know, the more you will desire to learn, the more interested in your art you will become, and, paradoxically it may appear, the greater will be your commitment to the basics. In shotokan karate, we have 26 kata. Of course, I do not expect to learn all 26 kata to perfection; that would be impossible. But kata, performed with grace and ki, can ignite the imagination, inspire the spirit and provide meaning to one's practice of karate, as well as foster an appreciation for solid fundamental techniques.

Q: How does the concept of knowing yourself affect a karateka's training and his personal development as a human being?

A: There are four different kinds of people. Members of the first group never even ask for advice or instruction. Everything they do has to be done "my way or no way." Often, they act without thinking at all, and certainly without considering other more qualified opinions. Members of the second group may ask for advice, and when they receive it, they hear it but do not listen to what they hear. While they may solicit expert opinion, they continue to do things their own way, never changing in response to the suggestions they receive. The third type of person solicits advice and then incorporates it in its entirety, but without critically evaluating it or tailoring it the specifics of his situation. The fourth and final group is the one I think of as superior. Members of this group seek qualified advice, listen to that advice, evaluate it and then incorporate it selectively and thoughtfully into their unique situations.

Many students exclude themselves from membership in the third or fourth group of people, not because they are unwilling to heed advice, but simply because they fail to ask for it! Of course, many students are reluctant to ask for instruction because they are intimidated, shy or overly reserved, or they do not want to interrupt their busy instructor. However, with the proper modest and respectful approach, an interested student can and should request assistance, feedback or advice. A smart student looks for an opportunity when the instructor is free and approaches the instructor with a well thought-out question. Once the student receives a response, it is his responsibility to make use of it. By pondering the response and incorporating it thoughtfully along with other qualified advice and instruction, the student gains membership into the most superior of the four groups.

People live their lives according to many different styles. As the philosopher Victor Frankl observed, "Suffering gives meaning to life." Without pain, one cannot fully appreciate pleasure. And without personal suffering, one is less capable of feeling true compassion or empathy. Suffering makes philosophers out of all of us, even those who have gone through life mostly thoughtlessly.

After more than 50 years of karate training, I believe that I understand how suffering can lead to philosophical growth and character development. Socrates said "Know thyself." Examine yourself, and critically evaluate what kind of person you are. Do you have a philosophy? Do you appreciate the ordinary as well as the extraordinary? Use the pleasure and pain your karate training brings you to help you increase your self-knowledge and enjoyment of life. Do not wait for bad news or tragedy to make you into a philosopher. Live each moment as if it is the most important one of your existence, for "right now" is all we really have. The past makes us what we are, but we cannot change it, nor can we predict the future. The present is what is important because it is where we learn from the mistakes of the past and plan for whatever the future may bring.

Q: Sensei, is there anything else you would like to add?

A: I came to the United States more than four decades ago with a mission to spread Master Funakoshi's philosophy and teachings. That mission remains a work in progress, and I will never give up, no matter what circumstances may bring. It is my life's work, my passion and the raison d'etre for my dojo. I hope that you will make it your mission as well, so that we may pass the baton on to the next generation of karateka, and ensure that we and generations of the future may continue to benefit from the beauty that is Master Funakoshi's karate. And, if the results of the survey may be considered any indication, it seems that I have, at least in part, done my job in transmitting to my students an appreciation for the beauty of basics and simplicity that is inherent in Master Funakoshi's philosophy.

Takayuki Mikami

THE ESSENCE OF PERSEVERANCE

Born on December 10, 1933, Takayuki Mikami had no interest in the martial arts beyond the required physical education programs of judo and kendo. When Mikami finished high school in 1952, he went to Tokyo to attend Hosei University and it was there where he started karate training.

In 1958, at the second All-Japan Championships held by the JKA, the community of karate got the ultimate lesson in spirit, power, and combat psychology. Takayuki Mikami and Hirokazu Kanazawa had what it was described as the most stirring and important moment in the history of the Japan Karate Association. That match went down as legend.

In 1963 he traveled to the United States, planning to stay only a year, but destiny had different plans for him. A firm believer of karate being a bridge between cultures, and an effective tool for self-improvement and understanding, Mikami Sensei is one of the few senior instructors who held technical positions with both the JKA and the WUKO.

With the 21st century beginning, Takayuki Mikami is still considered one of the top karateka and instructors the JKA ever produced. Although he never trained directly under Funakoshi, Mikami represents everything the Shotokan founder originally conceived when he created the art.

Shotokan Legends

Q: Can you tell us about your beginnings in the art of karate?

A: I joined the karate club as soon as I entered Hosei University. I was a little boy from a farm and Tokyo was a very tough city. I guess since I felt the need to build my confidence and improve my physical strength I decided to join the karate club. The first instructor I had was Mr. Saiki and then Mr. Kimio Ito. The training was very hard and there was a high level of dropouts, particularly during the first year. Once I started karate training I lost interest in everything else, so unfortunately my thesis for my major in Japanese Literature was four years late.

Q: So you didn't start your training in the JKA?

A: No. When I was in my fourth year at the university, Ito Sensei told me about entering the JKA to become an instructor. At the time they didn't have their own dojo or instructor program - everything was under construction. This special training began in the Spring of 1956. There were a lot of good karateka. Students from other universities joined the course, which helped to raise the training level. It is true that many dropped out, mainly due to political problems, and in the end very few of us remained training at the new JKA dojo where Masatoshi Nakayama Sensei was the Chief Instructor. We used to do a lot of kihon - thousands of repetitions of each technique. Master Nakayama was a very tough instructor. The old training was very samurai-like. We used to drill, and drill, and drill without the instructors explaining anything. If you didn't understand the technique, you did it 100 more times. You had to find it out by yourself. In Japan this way of teaching is called "teaching through the body."

Q: What are your memories about early days in the Instructor Training Program?

A: As everybody knows it was very hard, but let me explain this carefully. When I say "hard," I mean really hard and not just concerning physical training. It was comprised of two different parts; we, the students had to do all the work - I mean from cleaning the dojo to preparing the food, et cetera. We were doing practically everything to keep the whole thing going. Of course, we were being watched all the time, 24 hours a day, by

our sempai. Nakayama Sensei kept an eye on us and when he couldn't, then Mr. Ito and Mr. Tagaki would watch over us. We couldn't be found chatting or things like that. In the training aspect, don't forget that karateka from all over were anxious to check us out since we were receiving special training. I remember that teachers from Kansai area, which was very strong at that time, used to send up to ten students to test the three of us. The Takushoku University coach used to do the same - send a bunch of people to train with the three JKA instructors - and we three had to fight the whole line! Also some other groups and styles came to the JKA to challenge us. The sparring classes were very tough. It was free-sparring with no referee whatsoever.

Q: Who were the other two?

A: Sensei Kanazawa and Sensei Takaura. Everybody knows Kanazawa Sensei but Mr. Takaura is not so well-known because he stopped training karate.

Q: Did you ever train under Master Funakoshi

A: No, never. He was very old at that time but I saw him many times at the JKA headquarters. He was always present at the belt test watching what you were doing. He was so old that he looked like a god to me.

Q: Why was that particular generation of practitioners so special?

A: I guess we were happy to have the chance to leave the country to spread karate around the world. It was like a mission to us. We were ready to give everything we had in training. We worked extremely hard in a very

difficult time for Japan, just after the war. We never looked for the easy life; our motivation for training was very, very different from the practitioners today. Also, it was a very important that we were allowed to constantly train - and this intensified our practice sessions. The JKA was well-regarded for its high technical level. For instance, after the instructor's program I kept training full time for another seven years! That's the reason why the JKA had such a great technical level compared to other schools and styles.

Q: Do you think it is not the same in the present?

A: Of course not. To begin with, the people training in Japan have to no plan to leave the country whatsoever. They don't need to go through the hard times and difficulties. This will definitely affect the future of the art. Technique-wise I believe it will be the same but as far as concerning the spirit, attitude, and philosophy it will not be.

Q: Is it true that you designed the Instructor Program for the JKA?

A: Yes, it is. The course was composed of two parts; one was strictly physical technique and the other consisted of a series of reports that the students had to submit. These essays touched different subjects. A good instructor is not only a good technician. He must know how to teach a class, how to instill karate values, and how to deal with his student's psychology. Not all the people taking this course were interested in getting an instructor's certificate. Some of them just wanted to improve their technique and knowledge.

Q: Why did you decide to come to America?

A: Well, the JKA sent me to teach. I was sent to Philippines in 1957 to teach an introductory course in Manila. This three-month period was extended to one year. After returning to Japan I remained as a JKA instructor until moving to America in 1963. I began teaching in Kansas City but after having some problems with my sponsor I talked to Mr. Hidetaka Nishiyama and he said it was OK to leave Missouri and move to New Orleans where somebody had requested a Japanese instructor. But not everything was as easy as it sounds. When I arrived there I thought I was going to live in an apartment, not sleep on the dojo floor; and that my food was going to be provided - but none of that happened. Everything was very different from what I had expected. Let alone the legal problems.

You see, I was in America on invitation, with a flight ticket paid by my hosts. The Immigration Department wanted me to go back to Japan and apply for a permanent residence visa. Once I had to travel back to Kansas City to teach for another karate group. But the person who initially sponsored me got mad and reported me to the authorities. Fortunately enough, I had already applied for a resident visa, but my passport was with my lawyer. They came to check me out during the weekend and of course my lawyer's office was closed. Since they didn't believe me, I had to spend a couple of days in jail.

Q: What was your first impression of American karate?

A: To be honest, I had a very bad impression. I attended what it was supposed to be a karate tournament, but saw no karate that I recognized. That day I realized how great of a misunderstanding the Americans had about real karate. I felt I had to stay and teach the art properly.

Q: What's your opinion of karate as sport?

A: People come to martial arts for several reasons and sport training is only around 10 percent. What we are seeing is a new karate born of a blend of Japanese tradition and Western customs and culture. Even in Japan many karateka call their teacher "coach" not "sensei." They conceive it more as sport. These days, karate has an sportive aspect, even the so-called traditional exponents go to tournaments and enjoy the sport. Let me tell you that I don't think this is bad as long as we keep it in the proper perspective. Today, even the most traditional Japanese arts engage in contests. Unfortunately, in order to win, many competitors do wrong things such as cheating, acting, et cetera. And, of course, this is completely opposed to the spirit of martial arts. I don't think competition has to interfere with the traditional principles of the art. Winning or losing is not the most important thing in competition. The sport competition teaches us a lot of thing that can't be learned in the dojo such as pressure in front of people, mental control in an strange environment, et cetera. But like I said

you have to keep the right perspective.

Q: Don't you think that mixing two cultures is kind of confusing?

A: It might be, and honestly I think it is. The Japanese philosophy and the Western philosophy are different. Maybe the goal is the same but the approach definitely is not. The Western practitioner in a final match will jump and celebrate after scoring a point. In the true spirit of budo, you must concentrate and stay calm and focused, keeping all your emotions under control. This allows you to develop energy while exerting control over the ego. In the West, the karateka build their energy using their ego. Doing it this way is a very easy method to get a big head. And once you lose your spirit it is very difficult to get it under control again.

Q: What does karate means to you?

A: This is a very difficult question to answer. I can tell you, though, that I'm proud I never changed my direction in karate. I don't care about all the difficulties and hard times I went through, I always got self-satisfaction and spiritual development by keeping the same path throughout my life. Sometimes when I got bored I kept doing the same basic things over and over again until I reached a new level. I always tried to communicate with everybody, although the old JKA policy was not to. I believe that communication can help you to find your own way. I also believe the one must be honest and sincere, putting 100 percent into everything you do because without effort nothing is gained. Karate is about effort and sacrifices. It is true that sometimes we make mistakes but we must always make a real effort.

Q: How do you perceive the correlation between kata and kumite?

A: They are two parts of the same whole. I know some people think they don't need kata in their quest to be great fighters but they are wrong. This is an incorrect approach to karate. The student has to dedicate the same amount of time to both aspects but keep in mind that kata needs a very in-depth study. The analysis of one single kata may take years; by this I mean

the different uses of the same technique, and its application in kumite and self-defense. I recommend to study deeply one or two kata, although you can get a lot of knowledge and inspiration by learning others as well. Kata teaches the correct body positioning, the proper execution of the techniques, focus, balance, et cetera. One gains powerful techniques from correctly using the body. Why do you think the best kata people are the best fighters? Unfortunately, practitioners today rely too much on their own physical power instead of learning proper form and technique.

Q: Why do some change the kata?

A: Well, Funakoshi Sensei changed all the Okinawa kata to better fit into his conception of shotokan karate. Originally, the stances were narrower and higher, but JKA changed to deeper and lower positions in order to increase the difficulty and improve the training methods to achieve better physical development. The original stances were made for fighting but since the purpose no longer holds they adapted karate to the present day, looking for a better overall physical development.

Q: Your fight against Kanazawa Sensei is considered a classic in karate circles. How difficult was it?

A: That was the hardest match I ever fought in my life! Kanazawa Sensei and I knew each other very well since we sparred in the dojo all the time. I was aware of his longer reach so I had to be very careful while trying to break through his guard. He was cautious about my speed so he didn't want to close the distance improperly. After a while we were very tired, both physical and mentally. Concentration was a key factor. A lot of peo-

ple from my hometown of Nigata where watching, including my family. Kanazawa Sensei had support from his family as well. Neither one of us wanted to disgrace or disappoint our families. I realized that Kanazawa was thinking the same way. So I said, "Why should I give up?" I knew that I had to use all my speed to score on Kanazawa since he is a strong fighter. We faced each other for four overtime periods, stalking each other and seeking that decisive psychological moment to launch the final attack. But that attack never came. There was nothing left in our bodies. Only our spirits kept us fighting. Finally, we were both were declared champions. It is the only time this has ever occurred. The next year I won both the kumite and the kata titles. But I have to tell you that without all that support coming from the people there I would have quit or even lost the match!

Q: What's your definition of traditional karate?

A: Let me tell you that all dojo do some kind of sport competition, at least a little. In real traditional karate if you had to fight, you would kill and you can't do that today. So what do people mean by traditional? Traditional karate is not about technique like the people like to describe, it is about attitude. It's about life or death and not about doing hikite when you punch gyaku-tsuki. I guess karate has lost some of its essence. It was originally for self-defense but the demands changed with the times. We were trained based on the fact one was a warrior.

Q: Do you think karate must change with the practitioner's age?

A: Of course! Your body changes so the way you do things has to change. Not the inner principles behind the motion, but certain aspects of it. I started to modify some things according to my body when I was 50. Shotokan is a great style but it is very difficult for older people. It is important to find ways of adapting the methods without losing the principles. Unfortunately, power and speed in techniques is over-emphasized and a lot of karate techniques do not need that much power or speed. As your joints start to hurt, you need more effective, practical techniques. It is very important for the practitioner to be aware of the sho-ha-ri principle which is the normal way of the martial arts in Japan. First you strictly train under your teacher and you imitate without questioning - sho. Then comes ha, where you master the physical techniques and gain your own insight into the nature of the art, spirit, and techniques and incorporate these insights into your daily practice. Finally, after many years comes ri, where you separate from your instructor and go out on your own.

Q: Have you ever studied other arts?

A: Yes. I studied iaido. I'm also very attracted to some circular motions of tai chi, aikido, and jiu-jitsu. Weaponry training is very good as a supplementary aspect. It must be extra, not the central part of your training.

Q: Would you give any advice to karate practitioners in general?

A: Sometimes karate is boring and I understand. Everything is boring if you do it everyday for 30 years! The secret lies in not giving up, but in training the simple things until you feel better. That's the real test of budo. The hardest thing to teach in martial arts is spirit, but it is the most important aspect the art of karate can offer to its practitioners. The mental and spiritual aspects of the martial arts can help one to overcome any kind of difficulties. That's the key - learning how to keep going day-by-day.

Masaru Miura

SLICES OF BUDO

SENSEI MIURA IS ONE OF THE DIRECT STUDENTS OF MASTER MASATOSHI NAKAYAMA. DURING HIS COLLEGE YEARS HE STUDIED KARATE AT THE TAKUSHOKU UNIVERSITY, WHICH IS THE JAPAN'S LEADING KARATE TRAINING CENTER. AFTER GRADUATING SENSEI MIURA CAME FIRST IN ENGLAND AND THEN IN ITALY. MIURA'S REPUTATION AND TECHNICAL SKILL LED TO MASTER NAKAYAMA SUGGESTING TO TRAVEL TO INSTRUCT IN EUROPE. THE PART HE PLAYED IN THE POPULARIZATION OF KARATE IN ITALY CANNOT BE DENIED, AND HE IS NOT ONLY A LIVING LEGEND, BUT A CREDIT TO HIS TEACHERS AND WILL ALWAYS BE RESPECTED AS ONE OF THE GREATEST KARATEKA TO HAVE EVER LIVED. ALL WHO TRAIN WITH SENSEI MIURA ARE MESMERIZED FOR HIS STYLE AND PERSONALITY. HE IS ONE OF THE MOST DYNAMIC SHOTOKAN TEACHERS TO HAVE EXISTED, AND HIS MOVEMENTS ARE BEAUTIFUL, PRECISE WITH FULL OF ENERGY AND ECONOMY OF MOTION. HE IS ONE OF THE MOST FAMOUS KARATE INSTRUCTORS TEACHING TODAY AND HIS DEEP SKILL AND EXTENSIVE KNOWLEDGE MAKE HIM A MARTIAL ARTS TREASURE.

Q: Sensei, would you tell us where you were born?

A: I was born on April 22nd 1939 in Shizuoka prefecture, Japan, which is 150 miles west of Tokyo.

Q: How were your beginnings in the Martial Arts?

A: When I was eight years old, I started practicing Judo. It was during World War II that my family had to move from the city to a country village

to avoid the city bombing. Since I was very little and came from outside of the village, I was bullied by other kids every day. The reason I decided to take Judo lessons was very simple. I wanted to become strong and to avoid being bullied. I started taking Judo lessons at the local police station. Once I started learning Judo, the other kids stopped picking on me. After I knew some Judo techniques and gained confidence, I began challenging other kids, who were bigger than me.

Q: When you started Karate training?

A: When I turned the age of thirteen, I started taking karate lessons. I thought that the karate techniques were fancier and stronger than the Judo techniques to defeat an opponent. I wanted to master some karate technique so that I could knock down the opponent with only a soft touch. I read about it in a martial arts magazine. I recalled that it must have been some acupressure techniques. The name of my first Karate Dojo was called "Shunpu-Kan".

Q: Would you tell us some anecdote during your early days?

A: One day, when I went to the dojo, two guest instructors were visiting from Tokyo. They were Masters Nakayama and Kanazawa and they were in the middle of a karate demonstration tour. When the kumite practice began, I ended up facing Master Kanazawa. During the sparing drill, I swept Mr. Kanazawa by accident. My timing was perfect. At that moment, I thought that I had defeated the JKA instructor and I was very proud of myself. But at the same time, I had great fear and regretted that the other dojo senior students were going to punish me later. I felt very bad and tried to help Mr. Kanazawa get up. I apologized deeply and said, "I'm very sorry, sir!" I expected that Mr. Kanazawa would get revenge on me later in practice. However, Mr. Kanazawa was very gentle and whispered to me, "It was a good technique!" and tapped my shoulder with a nice smile. I was very impressed with Mr. Kanazawa's reaction and wanted to become like Mr. Kanazawa, who is a strong and gentle karate-ka. This was when I was a high school student.

Q: How influential was Sensei Kanazawa in your life?

A: Soon after, I decided to go to Takushoku University, where Mr. Kanazawa had graduated. I would not be a Karate instructor today without this little incident with Master Kanazawa. When I was a member of the karate club in Takushoku University, during my junior year, Mr. Ochi was in my senior year and was the team captain of the karate club.

Q: We have heard you did get in trouble there....is that true?

A: A little! One day, one of the club members caused a lot of trouble and the school suspended their club activities for a year. At that time, all the club members were living in the school dormitory, but they had to leave there during this suspension period. They needed to make some money to rent a new place to practice and to live in and all the members got a part time job. Me and other students worked at a department store. Our job was to deliver packages from the store to a store in another location. I was the only one who had a driver's license so I became the truck driver. The other members rode in the back of the truck and would carry the packages from the truck to the door. One day during the summer, it was very hot. I was driving the truck, the other members opened one of the gift packages and started drinking the cold drinks and eating the food. I thought that this was unfair. I was the only one who was not able to taste anything. One day, when I was by myself, he stopped the truck, sat down on the grass by a river, and was eating the sausage from one of the gift packages.

Shotokan Legends

All of a sudden, someone hit my head so hard from behind and pushed me into the river water. I got so angry, turned around, and yelled at him, "Who are you? What are you doing?" After I wiped off my face and looked at that person, I realized that it was Mr. Ochi. Mr. Ochi punished me because I was skipping the job, and I was stealing the food from a business package. Mr. Ochi was monitoring everyone to check whether they were working hard or not. Since he was the captain of the club, he had a huge responsibility to raise the club money to get back their dojo space and dormitory. This is my best memory with Mr. Ochi.

Q: What did you do after graduation?

A: After I graduated from Takushoku University, I worked at the local city government office for 6 months but I did not like the job. One day, I met Master Nakayama at the karate dojo again and he told me that I should go to Europe to teach karate. When I was in college, I had experienced many different types of jobs and had saved up enough money to travel to Europe so I was able to accept Master Nakayama's suggestion.

Q: What it was your first impression in Europe?

A: In 1964, I arrived in London, United Kingdom. Before I arrived to England, I used to imagine that all the people in England were very gentle and polite, just like how the Royal family behave in public. However, when I rode a taxi in downtown London, I saw that the driver spat from the window. After I saw this, I wanted to travel around Europe to explore how the world acts. He had traveled for approximately 6 months in European countries until I spent all of his money. When my money was all gone, I was in Torino, Italy.

Q: What happened then?

A: Since I spent all my money, I was sleeping under a bridge or shelter in the town. One morning, I was practicing karate by the river, and a man came up to me and asked me for karate instructions.

He was my first student in Italy. Of course, he did not have enough money to rent or buy a dojo, so I used a butcher shop and practiced in their kitchen. They had to move the machines to make enough room to train and move around. This is how I started teaching karate in Italy. Forty years later, the number of my students has increased to a very high number. My organization has become one of the largest in Europe today.

Q: Tell us about Sensei Okazaki…

A: I have a fond memory with Okazaki Shihan. I went to see him off at the Tokyo airport when Okazaki Shihan was departing to the United States in 1961. Okazaki Shihan was my senior from the same college and he used to come to teach at my school but I was not able to have any chance to talk to him while Okazaki Shihan was in Japan.

Q: How do you see the future of Karate?

A: My ideal vision for the future is for students to be able to visit each other more freely and frequently from different countries. I think that we should develop this kind of close relationship between any organizations. In this way all students would be able to exchange goodwill and develop friendship.

Q: How do we have to change the combat approach as we get older?

A: When we age we can't bounce back and forth and move like lighting anymore, we simply can't. We need to conserve energy and don't waste our energy in feints and fancy movements. We need to change the approach to combat and be decisive. We need to learn to move when we are sure that we are going to hit the opponent, remaining almost static the rest of the time. Speed is not the answer, timing is. The approach should be very simple: to hit the opponent, to win. There is no need to be flashy, just get the job done. We need to reach the point of not having to have a guard. Master Funakoshi mentioned that guard is for the beginners. But to start fighting without a guard we need to change radically the way we fight and focus on real Budo fighting concepts.

Q: What advise can you give to all practitioners regardless of style?

A: Karate belongs to everyone, not only young strong people, but also older and smaller people. My techniques show that you do not use muscle strength to defeat an opponent. I am always using physics or architectural knowledge and uses the entire body to execute the technique. To reach

Shotokan Legends

this level, would take a long time but there is no fast path in Budo. You must keep training every day. This is the only way that you can become a good technician. Of course, nobody can keep hardcore training forever. When you get older, your muscle strength decreases. You need to change your training method. And this is the most important point to study Budo. You need to keep having a clear mind and good attitude. You should be a humble person. For example, you must run when an instructor calls you. You must put your shoes together if you take them off. Those small things will develop your clear mind. That will help you develop good technique. Karate is lifetime training. You must keep training with the right mind.

I want students to learn the techniques so that a smaller and older person can defeat a bigger and stronger person. I have studied these for many years and want to share them with my students.

Q: How much the concept of "change" should be part of the evolution of Karate?

A: I think flexibility to change is one of the most important qualities a good instructor should have. Please note that I am now referring to simply change things for the sake of change. Change should come after any years of study and a process of trial-and-error with experimentation. It is important to study the principles that the techniques are based on and then "adapt" things to the circumstances. The old way is good but we should not afraid of using "new" ways of doing things if these methods are proven to be correct. Karate is based on interaction and it should be no locked on one single way of doing things. Karate should be fun.

Q: Finally, what advise can you give to teachers and instructors in general?

A: I really think that school and dojo instructors should reflect dedication in all areas. For instance, some teachers are 30 or 40lbs over his standard bodyweight. This doesn't show a lot of physical dedication to keep training. In order to teach one should keep training and be an example for the students. Yes, a complete example by training and being in shape. Obviously at 55 years old we can't be the same than when we were 25 but you get my point. How many hours do you train "teacher"? How is your diet? Do you keep yourself in good physical condition that shows an example for the students or you are overweight?

Look at sensei like Okazaki, Kanazawa, the late Nakayama, Nishiyama, Asai, etc. they were in very good physical condition for their age. That shows respect for your teacher, for the art and for your students. Wearing that black belt, having a high rank and being called a sensei is not enough.

Masatoshi Nakayama

A LEGACY OF EXCELLENCE

ONE OF GICHIN FUNAKOSHI'S TOP STUDENTS, NAKAYAMA WAS BORN IN 1913 INTO A FAMILY OF KENJUTSU INSTRUCTORS OF THE SAMURAI TRADITION. HE STUDIED KENDO UNTIL HE ENTERED TAKUSHOKU UNIVERSITY WHERE, BY MISTAKENLY READING THE CLASS SCHEDULE, HE BEGAN KARATE-DO TRAINING UNDER THE LEGENDARY FUNAKOSHI. UPON THE DEATH OF MASTER FUNAKOSHI IN 1957, NAKAYAMA WAS APPOINTED CHIEF INSTRUCTOR OF THE JAPAN KARATE ASSOCIATION, AND WAS PUT IN CHARGE OF DEVELOPING THE STANDARDS FOR THE NEW ORGANIZATION.

IN 1971, NAKAYAMA, WHO WAS ALSO AN ACCOMPLISHED SKIING INSTRUCTOR, HAD A TERRIBLE ACCIDENT WHEN HE WAS STRUCK BY AN AVALANCHE. THE DOCTORS GAVE HIM ONLY FEW DAYS TO LIVE AND HIS FAMILY WAS CALLED TO HIS BEDSIDE FOR HIS FINAL MOMENTS. BUT SENSEI NAKAYAMA NEVER GAVE UP AND, AGAINST ALL ODDS, PROVED THE DOCTORS WRONG AND LEFT THE HOSPITAL FOUR MONTHS LATER AND RESUMED HIS TRAINING.

WHEN HE PASSED AWAY IN APRIL OF 1987, DUE TO A STROKE, HE HAD SET NEW STANDARDS FOR THE ART OF KARATE-DO AND INFLUENCED THOUSAND OF PRACTITIONERS WORLDWIDE. MASTER NAKAYAMA WAS A GREAT TEACHER IN THE TRUE BUDO TRADITION, AND IS CONSIDERED TO BE AMONG THE MOST INFLUENTIAL KARATE MASTERS OF ALL TIME. HIS LEGACY OF EXCELLENCE, DEDICATION, AND TRUE BUDO MAKES HIM AN EXAMPLE TO ALL KARATEKA REGARDLESS OF STYLE, AND ENSURES THAT THE WILL LIVE ON FOREVER IN THE HEARTS AND MINDS OF THOSE HE SO DEEPLY AND PROFOUNDLY TOUCHED.

Q: How did you begin in martial arts?

A: Budo was part of my family. My grandfather belonged to the Sanada clan of Samurai. Budo was always present in my education. My father was a disciplinarian since he was a military man. As far as my training, I did kendo before entering Takushoku University.

Q: Is it true you entered Takushoku without your father's permission?

A: Yes! I always wanted to visit China and Takushoku was the best university for getting training and education to work and teach overseas. So I secretly took and passed the entrance examination.

Q: How did you start practicing karate-do?

A: I already had kendo training so I looked for a kendo class at Takushoku. I checked the training schedule and I misread the timetable and showed up at a class where everybody was wearing white uniforms! I had read a little bit about karate and all those movements were kind of amusing so I decided to sit there and watch. Suddenly, one of the men approached me and challenged me to try it and I did. Very soon I realized that it was not as simple as I thought. That day I had my first challenge of trying to perfect the karate movements - and I still have that feeling of wanting to perfect karate inside of me. Up to this day, I still wonder what the schedule for the kendo classes was!

Q: What was Sensei Funakoshi like in and out of the dojo?

A: Sensei Funakoshi always kept a very strict discipline inside and outside the dojo. Karate-do was a way of life for him, not something to be left behind when you left the dojo. The training under him was very hard and demanding; the classes consisted of long hours of performing each technique hundred of times. Kata was repeated 50 or 60 times and makiwara training was done until our hands bled. Master Funakoshi used to join us for makiwara training and hit the post with his elbow thousands of times. He seemed to enjoy that particular aspect of training.

Training and traveling with him allowed me to see the man he was from many perspectives. For instance, he always seemed to be in a constant state of vigilance, no matter where he was. This made a big impression on me. Many times he did things to teach me that I was still young and immature and that I needed more self-discipline and self-restraint because those aspects are where true courage lies. He showed me that it takes more courage to walk away from a fight than to get into one. He was a visionary who was able to see that the students – who mainly came from kendo and judo, where sparring was a usual aspect of training – needed sparring in karate-do training. He devised sets of five-step sparring sequences the students could practice in a more combative environment than the techniques of kata. Don't forget at that time we only had kata and kihon as methods of training. Of course some of the students were hot blooded, and if you failed to counter-attack at the right time they would hit you right away without waiting for you! As I said, the training was very hard and from the original group of 50 or 60 students, only five of six were left after a couple of months of practice.

Q: Few people know you trained in Chinese martial arts.

A: I trained in 1937 when I was sent as an exchange student to study Chinese language and history. To be totally honest, I was not impressed by the Chinese methods of fighting because they emphasized circular movements and at first sight they seemed to lack focus. But after training with several teachers my opinion started to change. I studied mainly under an old teacher called Sifu Pai, of a northern style. He was really good with his legs and his defensive actions were marvelous . Since the northern styles emphasize the use of the legs, I developed two new kicks. One was the pressing block with the sole of the foot taisoku uke, or with the lower shin, haisoku uke, and the other was the reverse roundhouse kick, ura mawashi geri. These techniques were added to shotokan later in 1946 when I returned to Japan and, of course, with the permission of Sensei Funakoshi.

Q: What else did you do in China?

A: During my stay at Takushoku University I majored in Mandarin Language and Chinese History so it was natural for me to go there. I planned a trip and in 1935 traveled on foot across the Greater Khingan Mountains of Outer Mongolia. In 1937 I returned as a exchanged student,

as I mentioned before, and that was when I studied the Chinese martial arts.

Q: Did you have time to practice karate-do in China?

A: Of course! I practiced every day. When you find yourself in a strange country you feel lonely, afraid, and insecure. But because of those struggles I became aware of important things such as self-reliance and self-confidence which helped me to overcome my loneliness and fear. Those situations are when the values of budo have to be used in real life.

Q: What happened upon your return from China?

A: I had the intention of teaching the Chinese language, but I soon realized that was impossible. There was no way I could get a teaching post after the war ended. The economic and social chaos were huge. So I end up making a living selling underwear!

Q: Did you get in touch with your karate colleagues?

A: Yes I did, but it was hard. Many of them had died and even Gichin Funakoshi's son, Yoshitaka – who was going to be the heir and leader of the shotokan - had died of tuberculosis in 1945. On the top of that, martial arts were banned after the occupation authorities issued an edict. The situation was really bad in all aspects.

Q: You were one of the top instructors for the Strategic Air Command when the US incorporated unarmed training, right?

A: Correct. It was very interesting because all of the students were young men in their early 20s who were in Japan for only six months. I was traveling round Japan teaching the soldiers who were stationed there. It was rewarding to meet some people today who come up to me and tell me that I trained them at that time! It's a great and enjoyable feeling. Teaching these American students allowed me to realize that we needed more detailed explanations of "why" we were doing the techniques in the way we practiced them. The American students required explanations of the movements, so we started to analyze the movements and come up with theoretical explanations based on the laws of physics. Our Japanese students never asked these kind of questions. I guess it has to do with the culture and education of the people.

Q: How did the Japan Karate Association start?

A: A friend of mine had a great relationship with the head of the Japanese Ministry of Education. The ban of karate was not lifted until 1948, and in 1949 Sensei Funakoshi had a meeting to discuss the martial arts and the future of karate after the war. It was in that meeting that the nucleus of the JKA was formed and I was put in charge of the technical standards for the new organization. In 1955 the JKA was incorporated as an educational body under the Ministry of Education. We had to come up with the technical and grading standards to be registered

with the Ministry of Education. Under the total supervision of Sensei Funakoshi I began to formulate the instructor program. I received great help from other karateka such as Teruyuki Okazaki, Hidetaka Nishiyama and Motokuni Sugiura. In 1957, after the death of Sensei Funakoshi, I was elected the Chief Instructor of the Japan Karate Association. In 1958 the JKA was declared an official body by the Japanese government and we made a great effort to unify many of the other shotokan karate schools in Japan.

Q: You were one of the students Sensei Funakoshi took to visit Kenwa Mabuni of shito ryu. What can you tell us about that meeting?

A: Sensei Mabuni was a very respected karate-do master and Gichin Funakoshi had high respect for him. He was a living encyclopedia of kata from many different sources. Sensei Funakoshi took me with him to visit Sensei Mabuni and he told me to learn two kata from him - ninjushijo and gojushijo - so we could study them later on in detail and more carefully. Eventually, we changed the format to specifically suit the structure of the shotokan method, conforming the movements that are not practiced by our members. Gichin Funakoshi wanted to grasp the essence of the different karate-do styles and incorporate them into his method. It's important to remember that these kata were added to the basic 15 kata that Funakoshi taught. For instance, his son Yoshikata, went to Okinawa and returned with sochin. All these additions definitely improved the art and never in any way changed the basic concept of the karate taught by Sensei Funakoshi.

Q: Everybody speaks about the confrontations and the brutal sparring between schools in the old karate days. Was that true?

A: In the early days of karate-do, for some years after 1935, college

karate clubs all over Japan held inter-school matches. They were called kokangeiko, which translate as "exchange of courteous practice." The participants freely attacked each other with all the karate techniques at their disposal, and the original purpose was to promote friendship between clubs, not to beat anybody up. For instance, one person attacked only once. Then his opponent counterattacked, again just once. They continued in strictly controlled alternation. But sometimes, the young blood of the students ran too hot to be satisfied with such tameness. They could not resist the temptation to use to the fullest the techniques they had learned and the powers they had gained through daily training at the dojo. There would be five or six contestants from each university in these free-style matches. If something happened or went out of control, it was the responsibility of the judges to step in and part them. The truth is, the judges rarely had time to exercise their responsibility. Some of the contestants had broken teeth or twisted noses. Others had earlobes nearly ripped off or were paralyzed from a kick to the belly - the injured crouching here and there around the dojo - it was a bloody scene. It was tough.

Q: There weren't any kind of rules at that time, right?

A: Not at all! Karate in its early days had no match rules, although there was a gentlemen's agreement to avoid attacking vital organs. Despite the wounded, the custom of holding such matches remained popular for some time. I was a student in a karate club in those days. If the custom were to continue, I feared, karate would degenerate into a barbarous and dangerous art. Yet, defeating an opponent is the common aim of all the martial arts in budo. Don't forget that karate was developed in Okinawa, where the people were strictly forbidden to own weapons. Practitioners used

train themselves through practice centering on kata. They held no matches. Although we can maintain our technique through practice without an opponent, we cannot improve our mental and physical conditioning in preparation for actual battle if we adhere to the kata method all the time.

Q: How do you think a practitioner can develop that particular aspect without crossing the line?

A: Well, the practitioner needs to learn how to overcome anxiety and how far he should stand from an opponent. Without practice against an opponent, we cannot have the chance to work at our greatest capacity. Fighting is dangerous, but fighting is indispensable. Only through it can we maintain the essential skills of karate. Even after graduating from college, I still kept hoping to see the development of a true match that would make karate a modern martial art. Once I organized a match with the contestants wearing protective gear, but the special clothing was an obstacle and turned out to be itself the cause of unexpected injuries. I had to keep looking for a solution. That was just before the beginning of World War II.

Q: What happened then?

A: After the war, even Japan abandoned the militarism of the past and made a fresh start as a nation based on pacifism. The college karate clubs kept holding their wild fighting contests, and the number of injured kept mounting. In the new climate of peace, violence in any form was a hateful thing and not accepted in the society. If karate remains as it was, I thought, it will be regarded as the embodiment of violence and will eventually fade away. Yet judo and kendo were developing as sports. The glori-

Shotokan Legends

ous contests of swimmers and baseball players were brightening the postwar gloom. Young karate practitioners began to hope that karate would become a sport, and in order to do that it would have to have rules for matches.

Q: Was that the reason why you developed match rules?

A: I thought it was the right time for us to make a sport of karate. I studied the rules of many sports and observed matches. Finally, I developed rules that allowed contestants to use karate techniques to the fullest without injuring each other. However, if we put too much emphasis on fighting, we become loose in our technique. To prevent that I made a kata competition, too. The kumite matches I had worked out were first performed in Tokyo at the All-Japan Grand Karate Tournament in October 1957, under the auspices of the Japan Karate Association. They were most impressive - attacks and counterattacks with rapid, powerful, well-controlled techniques. Not one contestant was injured in the free-style fighting and they were a great success. That was the beginning of the free-style fighting matches performed today in karate tournaments around the world. Finally a match form close to actual fighting had come to the public.

Q: So you finally succeeded

A: I think I did, but I'm still afraid of one thing, however. As karate matches become popular, and they are these days, the karate practitioners become too absorbed in winning. It is easy to think that gaining a point matters most, and matches are likely to lose the very essence of karate. Karate matches are degenerating into mere exchanges of blows. Moreover, I cannot say whether the idea of free-fighting styles matches the soul of karate as taught by Master Funakoshi, the founder of karate-do. The soul of his karate requires quite a high standard of ethics. And we can't ever forget that.

Q: Do you think Master Funakoshi would be against these type of matches?

A: Let me tell you this, Master Funakoshi often recited an old Okinawan saying: "Karate is the art of virtuous men." Needless to say, for students of karate to thoughtlessly boast of their power or to display their technique in scuffles goes against the soul of karate-do. The meaning of karate-do goes beyond victory in a contest of mastery or self-defense techniques. Unlike common sports, karate-do has a soul of its own. To be a true master is to understand the soul of karate-do as a martial Way. Karate-do has grown popular these days, and its soul is apt to pass from our minds. We must strive to strike a balance and I believe that if the practitioner trains with the right spirit, then the balance can be reached. Don't forget that in karate there is no initial movement.

Q: What exactly does that mean?

A: It is said that karate has no initial move or sente. That is an admonition to practitioners not to launch the initial attack and concurrently a strict prohibition against thoughtlessly using the techniques of karate. The masters of karate, especially Master Funakoshi, strictly admonished their pupils with those words again and again. In fact, it is not going too far to say that they represent the soul of karate-do. The idea of no initial attack in karate is embodied in the kata. As far as I know, there are 40 or 50 kinds of kata and each begins with defense or uke. You may argue that since karate was born as an art of self-defense, it is natural that it has no initial move. That is certainly true, but if you immediately conclude from the words, "There is no initial move in karate," that you can freely counterattack, you have not yet fully grasped the soul of karate-do. The underlying meaning of those words is much deeper. In addition to refraining from attacking first, practitioners of karate are required not to create an atmosphere that will lead to trouble. They also must not visit places where trouble is likely to happen. To observe those prohibitions, the practitioner must cultivate a gentle attitude toward others and a modest heart. That is the spirit underlying the words, "There is no initial move in karate" and that "Spirit is the soul of karate-do." One master says, "Karate is based on attempts to avoid any trouble, so as not to be hit by others and not to hit others."

Q: Is that when karate-do becomes more than a fighting art?

A: The soul of karate-do is the wish for harmony among people. Such harmony is based on courtesy, and it is said that the Japanese martial ways begin with courtesy and end with courtesy. Such is the case with karate-do. Master Funakoshi collected the kata of his forerunners and then systematized them into 15 kinds of kata for practice. One, called kanku, symbolizes the wish for harmony, the soul of karate-do. Unlike any other pattern, it begins with an action unrelated to defense and attack. The

hands are put together, palms outward, and the practitioner looks at the sky through the triangular hole formed by his thumbs and fingers. It expresses self-identification with nature, tranquility, and the wish for harmony. The practitioner of karate must always have a modest heart, a gentle attitude, and a wish for harmony. Karate is truly the art of virtuous men.

Q: What about the saying, "There is no posture in karate?"

A: This concept summarizes the proper attitude in training or actual fighting. And together with the previous one is an integral element of the soul of karate-do. When we say, "There is no posture in karate," we basically mean that you should not stiffen your body - you should always relax yourself to be ready for any attack from any direction. When the gale blows, the stiff oak resists and breaks, the flexible willow bends and survives.

But even if there is no physical posture, you may think a certain mental posture is necessary. You cannot relax your attention. That is why in karate-do, there is posture but no posture. Practitioners assume a mental posture but not a physical posture. Actually, that is not the highest stage of the art. At the highest stage, practitioners of karate should in actual fighting have posture of neither body nor mind. Herein lies the deep meaning of "There is no posture in karate." It is this highest stage, the essence common to the art of budo.

Q: Has this something to do with the idea of "no mind?"

A: Definitely! In the 17th century, the Zen priest Takuan gave Yagyu Munenori a treatise which had a great influence on the ideological side of the martial ways of Japan. It is popularly called Fudochi Shinmyo Floku and in it, Takuan wrote, "If you place your mind on the movements of your opponent, your mind is absorbed by the movements of your opponent. If your mind is on the sword of your opponent, your mind is absorbed by the sword of your opponent. If your mind is on cutting your opponent, your mind is absorbed by cutting your opponent. If your mind is on your sword, your mind is absorbed by your sword. If your mind is on not being cut, your mind is absorbed by not being cut."

Where, then, should the mind be! You should put your mind nowhere. Then your mind is diffused throughout your body, stretched out, totally unfettered. If your arms are important, it serves your arms. If your legs are important, it serves your legs. If your eyes are important, it serves your eyes. It works freely in the body wherever necessary.

Takuan further said, "If you concentrate on one place, your mind, absorbed by that place, is useless. If you are worried about where to place your mind, your mind is absorbed by that worry. You should throw off worry and reason. Let your mind go over your entire body, and never fix your mind on a certain place. Then your mind must accurately serve in response to the needs of each part of your body." In short, the Zen priest says that the mind, if placed nowhere, is everywhere.

Q: Does this mental state affect the physical performance of the practitioner?

A: It sure does! I'll give you an example; when we first learn how to drive a car, we find it very difficult and take every precaution. But once we have thoroughly mastered driving, we can be quite at ease while we drive and still not break the rules. We aren't very conscious of our driving technique.

This is the highest stage of actual fighting in karate-do, where we do not have posture of mind. In the martial arts, when we have attained the highest stage after long years of training, we return to the first stage. In the first stage, where we do not know any posture or technique, we do not fix our minds anywhere. When attacked, we simply respond unconsciously, without strategy. But as we come to understand posture, the use of technique, and fighting tactics through our study of technique, we occupy our minds with all sorts of things. The mind is divided into attack or counterattack and loses its freedom. After a long period of further practice, we can move unconsciously, freely, and properly.

That is the highest stage of karate-do, the true meaning of, "There is no posture of mind." That stage can be reached only after hard and painstaking training, but it has nothing to do with physical strength. In the West, physical strength counts for much in the martial arts. Men of a certain age must quit. Karate-do, however, emphasizes technique based on the prac-

tice of kata. We can continue to practice this martial art for a lifetime, no matter how much our physical strength declines. The more we practice, the more gracefully we can move.

Q: Do you think there is a danger if karate-do becomes a simple sport?

A: That danger exits, but everything is in the instructor's hands. Karate, if practiced properly, can be used as self-defense and a sport without losing its essence. If the principles are taught properly it won't matter what the practitioner is doing - he will be doing "karate-do." The art has to be used to develop the person and it's when the student trains only for competition when the direction is wrong. The secret is to train "in the art," not "in the sport." We must train with a balance in our minds. Competition karate has to maintain the idea of ikken hisatsu, which will keep the seriousness of true budo and not simply allow the sportive scoring of points. If we do this, karate-do will keep its essence as an art and will be practiced by people of all ages, because is not simply a sport but a complete art used to develop the whole individual. The art of karate-do is about daily practice and if you follow this, the real truth will come to you because life is the same as karate training - a daily and constant practice.

Q: What do you think of those who train in different systems at the same time?

A: Everybody can do what they please, and I respect any position. For me, as a budoka, the idea of budo is to train, study, and develop one art so using this as a vehicle we'll improve as human beings. The important aspect is not to learn more and more systems but to go deep into one art so you can develop the correct spirit of budo, which goes deeply into life. If you use logic, in a lifetime it is impossible to develop true mastery in many styles and methods; maybe you'll reach a level of simple physical skill but not true mastery. The correct idea of budo is to concentrate on something and master it. I always compare this to a doctor. There are many branches of medicine but doctors become specialist in their fields. They know more than any other average doctor in that specific field. In short, the idea is to go deep into one art since after many years of training you'll be able to understand any other system and grasp the essence of it. Once again, I want to emphasize that this is the budo attitude and approach.

Q: You had a terrible accident when skiing. What happened?

A: I was a ski instructor in 1971 and I took some students to the Japanese Alps. The conditions were so bad that I ordered the students to take off the skis and walk. The snow mass suddenly started to break and after I put the last of the students in a safe place the avalanche struck me. I was sent to the hospital where the doctors said that I had only just a few days to live. My family was at my bedside ready for me to die. Fortunately, I didn't! That accident happened when I was 58 and I truly believe my karate training saved my life. I was in a very good physical condition for a man of my age, and my body could take the stress of everything it had to go through. The doctors said that it was a miracle that I recovered the way I did. I think it was simpler than that - the art of karate-do saved my life.

Q: Any fear or regrets after all these years?

A: No, not really - no regrets. Maybe a few things could have been done in a different way but I always tried my best to promote and expand the art of karate-do all over the world. And fears? I hope when I die and meet Sensei Funakoshi that he's not angry with me for introducing the sportive aspect into the art. After all, he wanted to see his art practiced and recognized all around the world and the sportive aspects did just that.

Hidetaka Nishiyama

KARATE'S DRIVING FORCE

He was one of the truly great masters and pioneers of Japanese karate, his classic work, "Karate: The Art of Empty-Hand Fighting," was published in 1960 and is still considered the definitive textbook on the subject. A direct student of Gichin Funakoshi, Sensei Nishiyama began his study of karate at the age of 15. In 1961, Sensei Nishiyama moved to United State and founded the American Amateur Karate Federation. Before leaving Japan, he was one of the founders and leading exponents of the Japan Karate Association, in charge of the famous Instructors School where masters like Kanazawa, Enoeda, Mikami and Shirai came from.

Few people know that the legendary Bruce Lee was highly impressed with Sensei Nishiyama's kicking techniques and leg control, and that after witnessing a demonstration given by Hidetaka Nishiyama, decided to change his training methods for kicking. Although Master Nishiyama lived in Los Angeles, he was one of the foremost ambassadors for karate in the entire world. Without a doubt, his zanchin still expressed decades of grueling training forged under the samurai spirit.

Q: Sensei Nakayama was a father figure for many JKA instructors. How did you feel when he passed away?

A: Really sad. I felt tremendously sorry that we lost him. I always felt that karate needs people like him to reach higher stages of development. He worked very hard until the last day of his life giving seminars, lectures, coaching at the university, giving demonstrations, et cetera. During the war he went to China to research karate's roots. What is more, he took his wife and two children along! He was a big influence in my life, along with my kendo teacher, Morio Mochida. I can only say that Sensei Nakayama devoted his life to the promotion of karate-do.

Q: You wrote a great book about karate many years ago. Any plans for a new one?

A: Several different publishers have been asking me to write a new one. I guess that when I get time I want to produce a new book specifically for instructors – not for students – a pure textbook for instructors that would require a program on how to use the book. To me it's sad to see how many good karate-do practitioners ignore how to coach or instruct in a professional way. It is not enough for the teacher to demonstrate the technique and for the students to repeat it in the old way. We must advance more in order to progress.

Q: Why did you found the International Traditional Karate Federation?

A: There were just too many kicking and punching courses being called "karate." Basketball, soccer, and handball are "ball games," but yet are not the same. The ITKF is based on the original idea of karate-do, not "new" or "sport" karate. To avoid confusion, and therefore to clarify what real and traditional karate is, I founded the ITKF.

Q: Are you against sport karate?

A: Not at all, but I'm against a conception of karate as simply a sport. Competition is good but only while keeping the real values of traditional karate. Don't forget that karate-do is based on the art of self-defense. In karate there is something called "todome" or "finishing blow." It is very similar to the idea in the old fencing schools of killing the opponent with only one action. Of course, the final idea of any martial art is to win without fighting.

Q: When did you start training in martial arts?

A: It was a very long time ago. I think it was about 1943. Karate was not popular at that time, but judo and kendo were. I did them because martial arts training was incorporated into the school system. But I liked them very much, so it was not a problem for me. I heard about karate and I got interested. Unfortunately, I had to look all over Tokyo but finally found Mr. Toyama's dojo. I began my training there and a lot of people began telling me that I should go to Mr. Funakoshi's dojo. I stayed with Mr. Toyama for over a year-and-a-half and then I went to Master Funakoshi's school.

Q: Was Gichin Funakoshi your actual instructor?

A: Yes, he was. Sensei Funakoshi instructed me at that time. Remember that it was wartime – all the senior instructors were away at the war. So mostly at the university we saw only Master Funakoshi and Master Kuriyama. I did train sometimes with Master Funakoshi's son, Yoshitaka. He was young and very strong. I remember that all the young students were trying to copy him. Master Funakoshi's techniques were in principle the same as Yoshitaka's, but the external form was different. I guess some of the youngest students didn't understand that, since they were only looking at the external form.

Q: Why did you drop judo and kendo for karate?

A: It is not that I didn't like kendo or judo, but having a small body I was not well-suited for judo practice. In karate, small size is not a drawback.

Q: So when you started to train, karate wasn't popular?

A: That's right. The number of karate practitioners was very small because the war created a big blank in the instructor's ranks. Karate was an almost unknown martial art. That's why it was so difficult to find a dojo – only in three or four universities could you find one.

Q: You mean that the best instructors were serving in the war?

A: Yes. All the top instructors were at war, so the senior people were those from the university. It wasn't until 1949 or 1950 when these instructors returned to Japan, that things started getting back into order.

Q: I guess the post-war period was not the best time for karate reconstructions.

A: It was not, but they had to do it. I was the captain of the university team and we started a rotation training in different university dojo because almost everybody had forgotten their kata. People who had studied for a long time couldn't remember, so we all had to get together, pool our information, old reading materials, and our personal experiences. We also used to gather to train under Master Funakoshi.

Q: I've heard that there was a difference of opinion between the seniors and the people at the universities.

A: I think it was more a matter of loyalties and not so much a difference of opinion. The older ones felt they were more traditional, and in the university there was a little bit of class distinction, so some egos came out. Then we decided to start the Japan Karate Association. I recall that we had no dojo so we still rotated around the universities. Without a central dojo, things were no as smooth as they should have been. Master Hironishi was very good in bringing people together but later on he decided, along with some other shotokan schools, to form the shotokai.

Q: How was the training at this time?

A: Well, we didn't practice many techniques or combinations. No variety at all. One hour kiba dachi (horse stance), 1,000 punches, 1,000 kicks, and pretty much that was it! Sometimes we would repeat the same kata a hundred times in a row. We had this kind of training all the time. The first day I went to class, my teacher showed me the kiba dachi stance and left me there for an hour! I was so mad, I don't know why I went back the next day. The instructors did not teach with a lot of explanations. This was not the way during those days. The student had to pick up things for themselves and to do so they had to study their master's daily life – how he worked, how he lived, how he expressed himself in different circumstances. After three or four years, the master would decide to start teaching techniques, but without much detail – maybe just a few special points. They never liked coaching or teaching scientifically. You had to find out for yourself the right way, just by feeling the technique. And of course, you were never supposed to ask questions.

Fortunately, for many, these days there is more teaching, more explanations, and more help on the instructor's part. Curiously, the principles are the same, they haven't changed. We have new ideas and training methods but the fundamental principles are the same. Sometimes I wonder how the old masters knew about the right physics and dynamics of the human body.

Q: Do you think the same principles apply to all different karate styles?

A: Yes, of course! The principles are the same. Goju ryu, shito ryu, shotokan, wado ryu, et cetera, all share the same basic principles. It just happens that the explanations are a little bit different and the form looks different. For instance, goju ryu uses short movements since it was devised for short distance fighting. They look for developing strong muscle power for close range techniques. Shotokan put more emphasis on wider movements and dynamic body actions – getting the power more from rotation and body shifting.

What it is true in any style is the fact that regardless of the style, every karateka needs to know how to develop power in short range and long range using strong muscle actions and contractions. We must think how to make power in different ways. All the actions must start from the floor for external force. This is the very basic principle of momentum and as Newton mentioned in his 1st, 2nd and 3rd laws, without an external force you never increase energy and momentum. It has to be remembered that all the actions in karate are from the floor. I practice shotokan, but shotokan is not the only karate. We must never think shotokan is complete or that shotokan is the best.

Q: Who do you remember from the old days who is still active in karate?

A: Sensei Kase, Sensei Kanazawa, and Sensei Mikami – I can't remem-

Shotokan Legends

ber anymore! Taiji Kase was a student of Sensei Hironishi and Hirokazu Kanazawa and Sensei Mikami were among the first people to graduate from the Instructor's School. That was around 1957 or 1958. 1 remember that I met Sensei Kase and Sensei Sugiura just after I graduated from Takushoku University. Mr. Sugiura is a very nice person and very serious about everything he does. I recall that Mr. Kase was working for a company at that time but that we always found time to get together for training.

Q: You mentioned very important names in karate history. How do you think they reached such a high level?

A: They continued training and studying – they never stopped. They always looked for their own personal development. That's the reason they are so good. Look at instructors such as Enoeda, Shirai, and Kanazawa. They were very young men when I first met them as the chief of the JKA instruction department. I have to tell you that there were many instructors who were at the same level as them, even better than them, and with more and better understanding of the principles. At that time they were not so special. But these other instructors did not continue their development and quit. Conversely Enoeda, Kanazawa, and Shirai dedicated their life to the art of karate. You have to keep studying and training for self-development in the art if you really want to reach a very high level.

Q: Why was the art of karate being taught at the universities?

A: Sensei Funakoshi was responsible for this. In the beginning he brought karate to the universities. But after the war, General MacArthur passed a law that no martial arts could be practiced at the universities. So we kept training by going to Mr. Yoshida's backyard after finishing classes at school. After a while we returned to the university because the law was relaxed

Q: It is true that you used to put on a white belt and go into the Instructors School classes?

A: Yes! It was during the beginnings of the Instructors Course at the honbu dojo. I did it to see if I could learn gyaku tsuki or kiba dachi. I tried to think just like a beginner and I took notes about the instructor's perfor-

mance and teaching ability – then I brought it up in the course. I know it was very difficult for the new instructors but it was also for me. I knew that I had to do it so I could find out by personal experience if the beginners were receiving their instruction properly. After all, that's what karate-do is all about – personal experience.

Q: It is said that at this time there were a lot of challenge fights.

A: No, that's not correct. There was great rivalry and the kumite matches had no rules and no control, so it was very hard. This used to happen during kokan geiko or exchange training. But no challenge fights happened. In fact, we developed a great friendship through these special training sessions.

Q: Was kokan geiko only for shotokan members?

A: No, other styles were invited also. It was not restricted to shotokan schools only.

Q: Do you think karate competition with rules is better than the way you used to fight – with no rules, no control, et cetera?

A: I'm not against sport, but the problem with modern competition is that you don't need to feel budo. In real karate, if you miss your block you are going to get hurt. There's no second chance. This state of mind changes your whole conception of what you're doing in kumite. You must pay much more attention to your training. If there's no contact in sport karate, why train the kihon? You don't need power! The punch might make contact and the fighter score the point, but in a real situation, there is no damage! For me, this is not karate and I believe that the sport side is growing a lot and the spiritual and budo side is going down. Of course, it is better to

have a set of good competition rules, but I guess it's very hard to please everybody. I support the traditional conception of karate-do.

Q: What's your personal opinion of kata?

A: Kata is karate. All karate techniques are taken from kata. Let me put it this way: if you look at the history of karate, all the old masters developed certain katas based on their perception of combat. Original kata is very valuable. What some people don't understand is that while they were going through this research, they found out the very essence of movement in the body. What they did was to understand the principle behind the physical motion, and its relationship with the body, and use it in the application of the technique. In the old days, we never referred to kata as form, as we understand it today. Kata used to mean "symbol," although it was written in the same way. The physical movement was just a vehicle to understand and identify the internal principle. Only after that did they began to apply the technique. It is very important to teach these aspects in the right way, with the complete spiritual dimension that is called in Japanese "fudoshin."

Q: How do you think a student should approach their kata training?

A: The practitioner must first study the kata at the outside form, but seek the principles. Kata is like saying "for example." Later on the student must connect the principle to the application. The old masters experienced these applications. Therefore, the practitioner has to study the outside form first, then understand the principle, and later on connect the principle to the actual application. Unfortunately, many teachers and students have decided to change the outside form right away. You must study and understand – not just look at the outside form which is just an example. The old masters would first study the outside actions of the kata then digest it. They would make the kata their own, but not by changing the techniques and movements, but making it match their own body. For instance, I visited Master Kenwa Mabuni's shito ryu dojo for several days to learn kata from him. His kata was very beautiful. He had a very skillful body. Some people have very strong kata but are not beautiful. This is because they have not made the kata match their body. This is something very important to remember for every karate-do practitioner. Unfortunately, once you have trained the wrong way it is very difficult to change, because your body structure is set and bad habits are almost impossible to change.

Q: What it is karate-do for you?

A: As a physical art I could say that provides an excellent all-around exercise to develop coordination and agility by using all body muscles in a very balanced way. As a self-defense method, and through the training and use of the principles and knowledge of the art, the student is prepared to both physically and mentally defend himself against any attack. Of course, the sport is important but only if we follow the precepts of the art and we don't forget the very essence of it. On other hand, karate is art not science. It is an art that uses scientific principles. Science doesn't make karate. Personally – and because I learned my karate from the feel of the techniques – I think no science can explain this feeling. It can only explain the way the movements are done and the physical science behind the movements.

Q: What is your idea of perfect training?

A: It depends very much on the instructor. The first thing a good teacher has to do is to make the student understand how to develop internal energy. It is very important to assimilate and develop the energy coming from the ground. You only have to look at golf players and the kind of shoes they use; their shoes have cleats in order to better adhere to the

ground. If you apply the same concept to karate training, it is easy to understand why rooting to the ground is so important. The energy goes from the ground to your feet, all the way up to your legs and hips, to be exerted from the limb doing the punch or the kick. In karate, this kind of energy is explosive if you focus it right at the moment of impact.

Q: Is there a way to get a student to actually use this power?

A: In a way. I have gone through this kind of training myself. The idea is to give the junior student the right spirit. If a junior can fight different seniors after five or six hours of hard training, and still have the spirit to face them, then he has overcome great psychological barriers. The junior is always afraid of his senior, this is the first barrier. It is not physical, it is mental. So the senior hits him and pushes him by yelling Kick! Punch! Get up !" He doesn't beat him badly but pushes and forces him to fight back.

Q: Did you ever met the founder of aikido, O'Sensei Ueshiba?

A: Yes, I had the opportunity of talking with him on a private basis. I was very close to Sensei Gozo Shioda since we were at the same university. I remember the three of us talking about the tai-sabaki principle. Of course, you can find this principle in other arts but I always tried to use valuable knowledge and apply it to the art of karate.

Q: Is it true that you have been studying Chinese chi gong?

A: The real masters of chi gong have great mental power. As a young practitioner, I remember trying to find a gap in my kendo master's defense, but I could never perceive any flaw. After all these years of training, I came to realize it is the mental part that is decisive in real combat.

Q: In every karate style there are different interpretations for each kata. Do you think this is correct?

A: Like I said before, kata is the symbol of karate so it never changes. Unfortunately, 95 percent of the people don't understand kata meaning –

only the outside movements which are irrelevant without understanding. Each kata evolved out of the experience of the masters. Through it, they embody the principles of karate. The good student has to learn through careful imitation and endless practice. This is the traditional way, not only for karate but even for other things like flower arranging, for instance. The student must copy the designs for a long time and, in the end, once he has picked up the principles, develop his own way.

I always say that you have to develop you own way, but this is where scientific explanations of each movement come in. If you copy Picasso or Van Gough or Monet, this might be OK just as a means for learning. When you look at the work of these masters you see art at its highest level. They didn't change the art, they were art. That's the difference.

Every karate practitioner has a different body. Through training and understanding kata in the right way, they seek their final form – they become their own masters for expressing karate. The principles are there and they come out naturally. The good karate master teaches his students to find their own way, not to follow his. Students that venture out on their own too soon, or without the right amount of knowledge and understanding, will never know what they're doing. In martial arts there is not a "set logic," everything is a matter of experience.

Q: What is your final advice for all karateka around the world?

A: All traditional karate is one – karate-do. Traditional karate is budo. We must keep this philosophy. We must continue developing new teaching methods to give the next generation the best possible karate. This is our responsibility as leaders.

Hideo Ochi

WISDOM OF AGE

BORN IN 1940, HIDEO OCHI STARTED KARATE DURING HIS DAYS AT THE FAMOUS "TAKUSHOKU UNIVERSITY" IN TOKYO. A FORMER GRADUATE OF THE JKA'S INSTRUCTOR PROGRAM IN 1964, HE BEGAN TEACHING AT THE JKA HONBU DOJO ON A REGULAR BASIS AFTER PASSING HIS FINAL EXAMINATION.

AN ACTIVE COMPETITOR IN HIS YOUTH, SENSEI HIDEO OCHI WAS ALSO A FORMER ALL JAPAN GRAND CHAMPION PLACING FIRST ON NUMEROUS OCCASIONS. IN 1970, SENSEI OCHI WAS SENT OVERSEAS TO GERMANY AND IN 1993, HE FORMED HIS OWN ORGANIZATION "DEUTSCHE JAPAN KARATE BUND" (DJKB) TO HELP RETURN GERMAN KARATE TO MORE TRADITIONAL ROOTS AND AWAY FROM SPORT KARATE WHICH WAS BECOMING EVER MORE PREVALENT IN THAT COUNTRY. IN 1997, HE WAS AWARDED THE GERMAN MEDAL OF HONOR FOR HIS CONTRIBUTIONS TO THE DEVELOPMENT OF GERMAN KARATE.

Q: Sensei Ochi, how were your early days in Germany?

A: It was hard because I had no idea of how to speak German so the communication was pretty much the same than other JKA instructors at that time...show the technique and use some basic Japanese words. I learnt few basic words in German to give directions during classes but I was far from being able of maintain a conversation of any kind! I had to teach by example and showing with my body. The students couldn't rely on their brains to try to "learn" my body movements since the "logical explanation" of the technique was impossible. They had to "copy" me. The body usually learns faster than the mind so I believe it was good that I

Shotokan Legends

couldn't speak German in the beginning!

Q: Did you keep your connection with the JKA Headquarters in Japan?

A: I always maintained connection with the JKA Headquarters and with Nakayama Sensei in Japan and Okazaki Sensei in the U.S., although we were separated by thousands of miles. I remember the old days with a great feeling of happiness because I think it is fair to say that JKA had at that time the best group of karatekas in the world. I am not saying that Shotokan was [or is] the best style but the way Nakayama Sensei structured the training, the instructors program and the vision of expansion of the style around the world was years ahead of any other and tat is the reason why Shotokan is spread all over the world the way it is.

Q: How do you remember Sensei Nakayama?

A: He had a vision and knew how to make it happen. He knew what kind of blocks we were going to meet ahead because he used to travel to China and actually lived there for a while. Everybody respected him because he was a unique combination of seniority, knowledge, experience and practical wisdom.

Q: How it was the training with Sensei Nakayama and Sensei Okazaki?

A: The training was very spirit oriented. Karate should be approached spirit first and technique second. This is the traditional way. You use basic techniques like oi-tsuki, gyaku-tsuki, mae-geri, etc...to build the spirit. Every technique was repeated thousands and thousands of times with no rest. Obviously you develop a very good basics but the main goal is to 'break' the students' spirit and then build it up from the scratch. Today the training in based on technique first and eventually the spirit will developed. The times are different and the society is different. I know that you can't push students as hard as we were pushed. It is that simple. Nowadays, you can't have people hitting the makiwara 1,000 times with blood in their hands. I feel that in general the technical aspect of karate has evolved a lot. People's technique are much better than ours when we were young, better conditioning, better training methods, etc...but the new generations are lacking of the 'spirit' that we had. I think you win some...you lose some.

Q: Do you think that with the modern way of teaching – less hardcore - part of the traditional spirit is being lost?

A: Many karate-do instructors still have a traditional attitude. They like to teach and preserve the art in the old ways, like a treasure and the training is reserved to a few chosen students. On the other hand, other instructors are more progressive and think that the art has to be taught widely in our society to prevent it from dying. Both approaches are good and it depends on the teacher how he decides to share the art. There are good and bad aspects for both ways and that is normal. To be honest, karate is a very personalized art. It was developed by the masters based on their own perception of the old Okinawan methods. Masters like Funakoshi, Mabuni, Miyagi, etc…gave a personal expression of the material they learnt from their instructors and their styles are an example of that. Shotokan, Shito and Goju are different in concept and application because they are the personal expression of these masters. I believe they did a great job by studying and formatting their principles. I really don't think we have to "reinvent" the wheel and create more styles or combine any of the ones that already exist. Why? We have all the right set of tools in each style of karate, we simply need to understand which method or style fits better to our body type. And even then, I don't think that is a relevant point since you may like a style that may not be the best to match your body type. For instance, Goju Ryu seems to fit better for short people. I am not that tall and I have been doing Shotokan all my life! I think this is an example of how the style will mold the beginner's body to fit the demands of the particular style.

But I would like to say that Funakoshi Sensei never talked about styles or "ryu" when he talked about karate-do. Just karate-do. We should think about this.

Q: What advise would you give to the instructors?

A: One of the things that leading instructors need to remember is that is their responsibility to teach the complete art. I will explain. We all, including instructors, develop our own preferences in kata, kihon and kumite. Things and techniques that fit better to us and we like and enjoy to train and therefore to teach more often. This is alright but we can't empha-

size these kata and techniques more than the rest when we teach our students. Our preferences are "our" preferences and should not be imposed on our pupils. If we do that, eventually we are helping to develop an "style within an style" instead of teaching Shotokan, Shito, Goju, etc.

Once you truly understand the art of karate-do, you realize that it is a very flexible art but certain principles should be followed and maintained because forcing the student to follow a rigid shape and fixed format is not truly the way of allowing the students to eventually express themselves. The art of karate-do provides a way to accommodate the need and abilities of every student. The existence of many styles is a fact but unfortunately not all the styles have a complete training system and progression. Some people are advocates of developing one single style or method of karate but I don't think this is the right direction to go. The principles of Shotokan not necessarily are compatible with the principles of Shito Ryu or Goju Ryu and vice versa. Instead of trying to unify karate we should be more preoccupied with unify the instructors who teach it!

Q: How do you separate the students in your classes?

A: In my classes I have always separated the training into different levels. This gives to the students an idea where they are what they need to do to progress to the more advanced levels. Some students are too clever and they try to copy and practice the advanced movements and kata even before they are ready for them but their foundation od not good enough and eventually they will make big mistakes in the future, like trying to compensate the lack of technique with other physical elements. For instance, in kata you have different levels that you have to 'master' before learning kata from a more advanced level. Just because your body is capable of doing "Unsu" or "Gojushiho" and your brain can remember the sequence of movements it doesn't mean that those kata are meant to be practiced but someone of your level. Maturity is the key.

Q: What do you mean when you say "karate techniques are not simple"?

A: It is important to remember that at an advanced level, karate techniques are not "simple" in application. What we can see as an attacking movement at a beginner's level it will become a defensive action at an advanced level. And vice versa. An attacking punch can be also a blocking move. The focus of the physical action must be changed as the situation demands and that is the reason why it takes a certain level of understanding and skill to make it happen.

Q: Sensei Okazaki is a very important figure in your karate-do development. What can you tell us about him?

A: Training under Okazaki Sensei was very hard. He always wanted for us to give the most and the best we had within and never allowed us to give up. Giving up was simply not an option. He emphasized basics and spirit training. He knew how to build up our spirits and give us the necessary confidence to face many of the challenges that he knew were waiting for us abroad. Every class and training session was a serious feeling of strain without relaxing. But I was happily aware that I became stronger and stronger whenever I participated in a class.

Q: You often mention of the "stillness" in training as a beneficial tool for the progress. What do you mean by that?

A: We tend to think that exercising is only based on moving the body but old masters discover that stationary activity brings a lot of benefits. The idea of no movement equals no exercises it is not true. For instance, get your "kiba-dachi" stance and hold it for fifteen minutes. Don't move. After few minutes your legs are getting a very serious workout...either you believe it or not. Maintaining the stance for thirty minutes not everybody can do, not even professional soccer or football players can hold it that long. Unfortunately we only understand physical training when is measured in sweat. It is important to appreciate other ways of developing the human body and how to better learn to use it for karate purposes. Nakayama Sensei traveled to China and discovered many other training methods used by Chinese martial artist that he knew were very interesting and effective for all practitioners. Also if you look at Funakoshi Sensei's stance and movement they were the same as that as Shito Ryu; short stance and higher. But young men must have wider, deeper stances.

Q: Are those two training method complementary to each other or not?

A: They totally are. When doing physical exercise based on motion the individual focuses more on the external aspect of the activity. When we train with a static method like the "kiba-dachi" exercise I mentioned before, we need to calm down and focus on the internal aspect of the stance, the breathing, the tension, etc. It is a different aspect that is emphasized. These two methods do not conflict at all. They are complementary to each other and both are beneficial for the development of the karate practitioner.

Shotokan Legends

Q: You seem to emphasize very much stance training in you classes. Why?

A: The stances in karate are extremely important because they are responsible of the karateka's ability to move. The hips determine most of the body movement. Therefore, it is important that we develop new ways of stance training that can be used for the students' development so they can reach their true potential. The transition between stances is a very important aspect to train since they teach the student how to coordinate the body in a single, unified motion. All instructors should examine their training methods and develop creative ways of stance and body turning training.

Q: What should be our goal in karate-do training?

A: Karate technique and kata should not be practiced with the intention of hurting another human being or destroying an opponent. The training should focus on perfection of character and betterment of the human beings. That's the true goal of karate-do training and its real value for the modern society. With the perspective of many year of training I can tell you that any practitioner that spend years of training trying to make of his body a killing machine or lethal weapon is missing the point of karate-do training. Your training should enhance and educate the body, the mind and the spirit.

Q: What advise would you give to those looking for a karate school?

A: I would recommend seriously check the "DNA" of the teacher. Don't simply start training with someone because he or she is a champion or well-known. Make sure that that teacher has a solid base in all karate-do aspects including the moral aspects of the art.

Q: How important do you think competition is in the development of the practitioner?

A: I think it is important to test yourself. We train everyday but it is hard to really know where we are and how much we are realistically improving when it comes to the actual use of karate techniques against others. "Shia" means "testing" and that is why it is a positive part of the development of the karateka, if used correctly. You test yourself and you test the opponent.

Q: Do you think the Olympics would be a positive step in the evolution and development of karate for the future generations?

A: I do not think that karate is a sport although competition is important. I am seriously afraid that a big distortion will happen if karate-do enters in the Olympics — Judo is an example of it.

I don't like the attitude of players in the Olympic Games, which is to win, no matter what, by any means. I do not think winning is everything, definitely not in Budo training. The desire to win, when it becomes a hindrance of practice, is contrary to my philosophy. It should not be our goal the mere victory in a sportive competition.

Q: What is you opinion of how the art of karate is being taught around the world?

A: I have to admit that many schools, not only in Japan but also around the world offer 'family friendly' karate. I am not against this "family-friendly classes, because they may attract many people and lift up the 'grassroots' of karate in the world. But I also worry about how much of this approach can actually damage the true are and specially the spirit of karate-do. We also need "hard-spirited training" for karate to prosper. Real karate-do trainingusing the Budo spirit is not a "joke", it is not "fun". Karate is martial arts on which the concepts of life and death should be present at all times. I demand that my black belts students train karate seriously and earnestly.

You moved to another country, to another culture...do you think karate-do is better understood by Japanese and therefore only Japanese should lead the art in the future?

Karate should be open to anyone, and the person who trains the most eagerly and have the right Budo attitude, should be qualified to take a leading position. Nationality or gender should not matter.

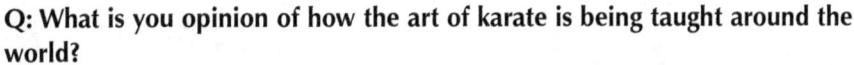

Teruyuki Okazaki

HEART OF FIRE

MASTER OKAZAKI WAS BORN ON JUNE OF 1931 IN FUKUOKA, JAPAN. IN 1947 HE STARTED HIS KARATE TRAINING WITH MASTER FUNAKOSHI AT TAKUSHOKU UNIVERSITY. IN 1961 HE WAS SENT TO THE UNITED STATES TO TEACH THE ART OF THE EMPTY HAND WITHOUT KNOWING A SINGLE WORD OF THE ENGLISH LANGUAGE.

HIS PHILOSOPHY, CHARISMA, AND VITALITY IS SECOND ONLY TO HIS HUMILITY. HE IS A MAN DEVOTED TO THE PRINCIPLES OF GICHIN FUNAKOSHI AND A FIRM BELIEVER THAT THE OLD VALUES TRANSCEND TIME AND CHANGE. HIS MOTIVATION LED HIM TO MEET DR. MILORAD STRICEVIC, A RESEARCHER IN THE FIELD OF SPORT MEDICINE. TOGETHER THEY WROTE A BOOK, KARATE DO: A MODERN TEXTBOOK THAT IS PROBABLY THE BEST BOOK EVER WRITTEN ON KARATE. HE IS THE CHIEF INSTRUCTOR OF THE INTERNATIONAL SHOTOKAN KARATE FEDERATION.

HIS GOAL IS TO EDUCATE STUDENTS ON THE MEANING AND VALUE OF KARATE AS A WAY OF LIFE, NOT AS A SPORT. SENSEI OKAZAKI SPENDS ALMOST THE WHOLE YEAR TRAVELING TO INSTRUCT HIS STUDENTS ALL OVER THE WORLD. HIS GOAL IS VERY SIMPLE - PRESERVE HIS TEACHER'S ART AND PRECEPTS AND "KEEP TRAINING."

Q: You studied directly under Gichin Funakoshi. How was the training?

A: Usually, Master Nakayama led the classes. Master Funakoshi would sit down and tell Nakayama Sensei what to do. He was always there

observing. Master Funakoshi always stressed five important points in his teachings: the mental aspects, the physical aspects, staying calm, being exact, and being natural. He liked to explain how the human body works and how important it was to use the corrent techniques to attack the right body parts.

Q: Was it the way you expected?

A: No way! The training was very hard, very difficult. I recall that for the first three or four months all we did was punching techniques - straight punches. The training sessions were up to six hours each day, six days a week. Master Funakoshi never said that we should copy his form because he understood that his body weight and his body-type made the stances and the form of the techniques that way. He was a very scientifically-minded person - don't forget that he was a school teacher. He developed the physical techniques in a certain way but he used to say, "Don't copy. Judge it by your body type." It is very difficult to explain his movements. They looked almost without power, and more like a beautiful ballet.

He was very open-minded. For instance, he never taught us kobudo but he introduced it to us, like history. For him karate was empty-hand, but I remember him saying, "If you ever have to use a weapon, use the best one to fight with!"

Q: How many people left?

A: Many of them. A lot of people left. We would stand in kiba dachi and punch for two hours in the morning. Then the same for another two hours in the afternoon and for another two hours in the evening. Most people just gave up. The next three months were dedicated to kicking - just kicking techniques. After six or seven months of this kind of training, they started to combine both aspects and kata training was incorporated into the classes and became the focal point.

Q: What was the purpose of this training?

A: We were like machines. This kind of training built up our muscles to an extraordinary degree. Our arms and legs were really powerful. But I didn't understand that back then. It took me over a year to see that the more hard work I put into my training the more benefits I got from it. If I

missed one training session I didn't feel good at all - not my body, not my mind. But it wasn't like this in the very beginning.

Q: What do you mean?

A: Well, in the very beginning I was training in kendo because kendo and judo were the common arts. I didn't enjoy judo very much, mainly because it had been thrust upon me from my early days in grammar school, so I was kind of rebellious against it. Anyway, at Takushoku University the captains from each martial art came and gave demonstrations to introduce the arts.

Q: So you were impressed with karate?

A: Yes, but also with aikido. I really liked them both. So I signed up for both classes.

Q: Who was the aikido teacher?

A: Morihei Ueshiba himself! I was very fortunate. My karate teacher was Gichin Funakoshi and my aikido teacher was Morihei Ueshiba!

Q: Was the term "shotokan" used to describe Funakoshi's style of karate?

A: No, not at all. There was no style. Master Funakoshi just called it karate-do because he wanted it to be called karate-do. But out of respect his students started calling it "shoto" which it was Master Funakoshi's pen name. At that time, we did not have any style. We were practicing karate-do. Of course, Master Nakayama wanted us to train under other karate masters, that's why he used to invite Gogen Yamaguchi from goju-kai and Hinori Otshuka from wado-ryu to teach us a different approach to the art.

All these instructors gave lectures on their methods of karate and taught us various kata. I really think this was an excellent approach to help us better understand the complete art of karate-do.

Q: Did Master Funakoshi get together with other top teachers like Master Kano or O'Sensei Ueshiba?

A: Yes, of course! Master Funakoshi enjoyed very much being with Master Mifune of judo, Master Morihei Ueshiba of aikido, and Master Nakayama of kendo. They used to give demonstrations together. He always said to us that he respected very much Master Jigoro Kano's thinking of the martial arts. I know Master Kano helped Master Funakoshi when he started to teach the art of karate in Japan. He always felt that judo had to study some karate techniques. They were very close friends and they had a lot of respect for each other. I remember that every time we passed in front of the Kodokan, Master Funakoshi always took off his hat and bowed. "He's my teacher," he used to say. "Of course," we all answered, "but he's judo." And Master Funakoshi replied, "It doesn't matter, a martial art is martial art and I must respect it!"

Q: How did you decide to concentrate on karate-do?

A: It's a funny story. The training in karate classes for the first three weeks was only usaki tobi or rabbit hops. Thousands of them everyday, for hours and hours. Non-stop. We would get so tired we would literally fall over on our faces, but there was Nakayama Sensei and other senpai to push us until we got up and kept going. I wasn't happy with that and I decided to quit. I told my roommates, their names were Irie and Onoue, that I was going to quit and concentrate on aikido training. They were my very good friends, we had been together for a long time. Pretty soon, they started to make fun of me, calling me "sissy," and saying that they would never give up. This made me so mad that I promised myself that if they could do it, I could too. So when I was going to be accepted by O Sensei as a regular student, I stopped aikido and concentrated on karate, only to keep face with my two roommates!

Q: So what happened to them?

Well, we were going to test for black belt under Master Funakoshi, so I was very serious about it. My roommates decided they wanted to quit. But I had made a promise and was pushing them to their limits in the training sessions in the early morning and in the afternoon. I insisted that they train for their test. Well, they passed the test but I flunked! Master Funakoshi said I was not good enough. My attitude was bad, very bad. I flunked many times because of it. I was a young guy thinking in the wrong direction. Master Funakoshi picked up on this right away. It was not my techniques which made me fail the test, since it was equal to the other students who passed, but my attitude. Finally I got

really depressed so I went to ask Master Funakoshi why I failed the test. Of course, everybody was shocked that I actually went to speak to him. That never happens in Japanese traditional culture.

Q: What did Master Funakoshi say?

A: He said that he really understood my problem and that he was going to tell me the essence of karate-do - but that I should be very prudent with it use. Then he sat down, and I did the same with great ceremony. I was so excited, and Master Funakoshi seemed to be really concentrating. I was nervous, and after a while he leaned over and said, "You know Okazaki, the true essence of karate-do is keep training - keep training everyday."

Q: Was that what you expected?

A: I don't think so, but I haven't stopped training since. After that, my attitude changed and finally I got my black belt. There is an interesting story about myself right after I passed the test. I was really proud of it and Nakayama Sensei was the person in charge of teaching the beginners. One day he said, "I want you to assist me today!" Of course, I was more than pleased. All of a sudden, Master Funakoshi came in and started to look around. He remembered my name because I'd been there for a long time and he asked me: "When did you pass the black belt test?" Right there I thought, "Master Funakoshi is getting old; he's getting forgetful." "Sensei, you took me for the test" I answered. Then he said, "If you are a real black belt you have to prove it. I'm sure you will be able to knock me down. Punch me or kick me. Go ahead!" I was really scared and thought, 'No way. If I touch him, my seniors will kill me right here!' The problem was

that I was a very short-tempered guy and I said to myself, "OK. I might die but I have pride and I'm a black belt!" So, I attacked him in front of the whole class, with all the students and Nakayama Sensei looking on. I charged and punched at him. I thought that he was on the floor when I felt somebody tapping me on the shoulder. "You need more practice Okazaki!" I don't know how he did it. My classmates said that I did a good job, but it looked as though I went through Master Funakoshi's body. Definitely, he was something special. Nakayama Sensei told me that Master Funakoshi knew how to absorb and use the attacker's energy against him.

Q: Do you ever feel a great responsibility at being one of Master Funakoshi's students?

A: Yes, all the time. My generation was very fortunate to have trained under Funakoshi Sensei and to have been led by Nakayama Sensei, but I guess that no one considers themselves good enough to do the job we have to do. We were educated to believe in high quality karate-do, both technically and spiritually. This is the only way karate can be passed down to future generations.

Q: Sensei, you have a wonderful sense of humor; was there an incident with Sensei Funakoshi's Cat?

A: I had some years of experience, but after ten years of practice under Master Funakoshi, I was assigned a special job. I was scheduled to visit his house once a month to meet with him, exchange papers or information, and bring back his written responses. Because he was a very famous calligrapher, the senior instructors would ask me to take him papers to write something for them. Master Funakoshi would always agree and a month later I would pick up the papers, with beautiful calligraphy and his signature.

Then, one day, he invited me to have lunch at his home. I told the senior instructors about this invitation but they didn't believe me. They thought it was a joke. However, Master Funakoshi was used to my visits and knew me as one of his faithful students. As wise as he was, he could read my character and ambitions. As a member of the younger generation, he knew I was most interested in developing more speed, more focus, and getting a black belt. He was right; that was my mindset. He had been teaching us that the dojo kun was the real goal. But no, I wanted more speed and more focus. Master Funakoshi knew these thoughts were in my mind. He told me to spend more time "thinking" about the training. And I said, "yes sir, yes sir," but on the inside, I thought, more speed, more focus. Upon my next visit, I had this experience...

Master Funakoshi's cat attacked me! Yes, he bit and scratched me, and I was unable to protect myself. That cat was a very smart animal. Whenever Master Funakoshi would come into the room, the cat would curl around behind him. I don't like cats, so when Master Funakoshi left the room, he'd try to come over to me but I would just smack it and the cat would jump and escape. On this occasion, as soon as Master Funakoshi left the room, the cat jumped into my lap. As I reached out to smack it, the cat bit and scratched me in one motion. I was trying to hide the blood and scratches from Master Funakoshi when he reentered the room by saying, "Oh, you have such a nice cat." He knew right away what I really thought, and that I was trying to hide the truth. He said, "What is the problem? You cannot defend yourself against my pussycat? Your mind is wrong!" You know, I still have the scar from that incident. It is a constant reminder of my impetuous youth and Master Funakoshi's wisdom and guiding principles.

Q: Sensei let's talk a little about your days in College, what was the name of the university you attended and the years you were there?

A: I went to Takushoku University. I was there from 1947 – 1953 when I graduated. In my generation the educational system was based on the same as England which was high school for 5 years then college for 3 years but after the war the educational system was changed to the same as the United States. But since they were changing the rules when I was there they said I could go to the college after 4 years of high school so I was the youngest in my class in college because I went there 1 year earlier than my classmates.

Q; May I ask what your degree was in?

A: Political Economics.

Q: When did you begin training in Shotokan, college or high school?

A: College in 1947. Master Gichin Funakoshi used to come to all of the

colleges and universities to teach once a week. At that time Master Masatoshi Nakayama was Master Funakoshi's assistant so when Master Funakoshi was not there, Master Nakayama taught. You know, at that time no one could go to Master Funakoshi to ask him any questions. If I had any questions I had to go to his assistant – Master Nakayama. Those were old fashioned times, and that is one of the things I changed which is to be more accessible to my students.

Before the war there were no other sports such as baseball, basketball, etc., only martial arts. It was militaristic. And the war was ending when I went to school so things were changing. During my school years I was in the new system but when I graduated it was the new system.

Q: It must have been a confusing time for you as well as everyone else.

A: Yes it was. However, even though many things were changing, martial arts never changed. Karate as a martial art never changed. At the present time it is the same as at that time. It is Budo and as you know Budo means to stop the fight, stop the conflict.

Q: Sensei, because it was the transition from the war, did it change the attitudes and way of thinking of the students then? Was the mentality different?

A: Organizationwise it changed. It changed to a democratic organization because before that everything was like a military. After the war we could not train in the dojo for 2 years. Martial arts training was not allowed because the authorities thought it was just for fighting. They did not know anything about martial arts. The Second World War was over but they thought we would want to fight but as you know the main purpose of martial arts is not to fight. General MacArthur was in Japan at that time. It is on record that all of the masters from the different martial arts – Master Funakoshi – karate, Master Kano – Judo, Master Ueshiba – Aikido and Master Nakayama (same name but not our Master Masatoshi Nakayama) – Kendo went to General MacArthur and had a meeting with him to try to explain to him what the martial arts were really about and that martial arts are a culture of Japan, and that the main philosophy for martial arts is Budo which is to stop the fight, and for self-defense if someone attacks you but it is never to start a fight or conflict. Technically it looks like just kicking and punching but all the real martial arts are for peace and self-preservation. For 2 years General MacArthur checked what we were doing and would send the MP's (Military Police) to come to check all the dojo's to see what we were doing. Of course at that time we were young kids and we liked to kick and punch and spar. We would have someone outside watching and if they shouted "hey, the MP's are coming" we would stop and do kata movements. They did not know and if they asked we would tell them we were doing a type of Japanese dance. After 2 years we were able to practice martial arts again in the open.

Q: Sensei, did you try other martial arts besides Shotokan karate at that time?

A: Yes, at that time martial arts were mandatory. In grammar school before the war, it was mandatory to practice Kendo. Kendo is the oldest Japanese martial art. The instructor always explained to us what a real martial art is; however, we were young and didn't listen. We just wanted to hit each other (Master Okazaki laughs and displays a glimmer of youthful mischievousness). But in martial arts you never fight anybody. I practiced Kendo for 5 years then when we went to middle high school we could choose which martial art we wanted to study. As I said, Kendo is the oldest martial art in Japan and that is why they taught it in grammar school. And not just technique, they also taught how to bow correctly and those kind of things. If you did not do those things correctly the teacher would yell at you. Then in high school I tried Judo. I didn't like it very much so I went back to Kendo again. I studied Kendo for 10 years. Then, when I went to the university I studied Aikido. A friend of mine was doing it and so I tried it and studied with Master Ueshiba. I went every day and tried the best I could. Then one day Master Ueshiba called me over. He knew why I was training and said get out. I was trying the best I could so I got very mad inside. Then I saw a karate demonstration and I thought it was the best fighting technique and I'm going to study karate and challenge Master Ueshiba. I was just a kid.

After that I started karate. We started at the beginning, how to bow, mokuso, step by step, everything just like we do now, how to make speed and focus, etc. In high school there was no ranking test. Master Funakoshi started ranking tests because he knew it would get people to train harder to get to the next step. When I first went to the university there were no ranking tests, then after 2 years we began to take tests. This

challenged the students to be better. It is a mental attitude. When I was a brown belt we practiced morning, afternoon and evening. Then it was time for me to take my black belt test. After the test I said to my friend, I think I did really well and I asked him, what do you think to you think I made black belt? He said, yes, I think so. Then after the test, right away they gave the results of the exam and Master Funakoshi called the names. But he did not call my name. I told my friend, maybe he forgot my name. He said maybe so. As I said at that time you could not go to Master Funakoshi to ask any questions. So I went to Master Nakayama and I asked if I could speak to Master Funakoshi because I wanted to know if maybe I needed some kind of special training to pass my black belt test. He said ok, you can go to him and ask him. I went to Master Funakoshi and I told him I needed help and asked him if I needed some kind of special training he said – just train. I expected some kind of technical advice and he just said – just train. Then my mind changed and I thought I did not care about the black belt anymore and just trained. Then I passed black belt and my mind changed again and I got a big head. After that, Master Nakayama did not have any assistant so he asked me to help him with the new members and I tried the best I could. Master Funakoshi's house was about 15 minutes walking distance from the university and as I said he would teach once a week but sometimes he would just walk around to check to make sure everything was alright. On the day that Master Funakoshi would come to visit, Master Nakayama would stop and say Shihan is going to teach. Master Nakayama would make everyone stop and bow to Master Funakoshi and then we would start training. And Master Funakoshi looked at me and said "what are you doing?" I said "I am now teaching". He said, "I don't think so, I don't think you know enough to teach, really you are a black belt?" I said "yes sir, I got it, you gave me the test". Before when I was teaching I was very proud and had a big head, but after Master Funakoshi spoke like this to me in front of the students I felt like I was a lower level. Master Nakayama stopped the class; he knew what was going on. Master Funakoshi said you cannot even punch, let me see how you punch, hit me. At that time Master Funakoshi was in his 80's, 86 or 87, an old man, and I thought because I was Master Nakayama's assistant he would kill me

if I did that. So I looked at Master Nakayama, and he said go ahead, he knew what would happen. So I went in slow motion and punched but did not touch him because I thought I cannot hit him, he is an old man. Master Funakoshi started laughing like hahaha! He said "that is not a black belt". Then I said to myself, ok, I am going to show him, I am going to knock him down. So I went in really hard to punch and Bam! (I was a stupid college kid). But somehow I did not hit him and ended up behind him. I didn't know how that happened, the students who were in the class said it looked like I went through his body without ever touching him. It looked like I went through him, and I thought oh he is an old man, but his reaction was quicker and he turned around and went in front of me.

At that time I needed a job and Master Funakoshi was a very famous calligrapher so Master Nakayama gave me the job of delivering requests to Master Funakoshi to do calligraphies and I would go and pick them up when they were finished to deliver them. One day I was at Master Funakoshi's house and he had a cat. I did not like cats, and I was sitting in a chair and the cat came around and jumped on my lap and I wanted to hit it but I would say "oh you have a nice cat". On another occasion the cat came around again when Master Funakoshi was not in the room so I pushed it away and the cat scratched me. Master Funakoshi saw the blood on my hand and said "you cannot defend yourself against my pussycat and you have to continue training until the scar goes away". I still have some of the scar today so I have to keep training.

Q: Sensei, when you were in the university were there any rivalries with other colleges or universities?

A: Yes, we did not have tournaments at that time but we would have a shiai or special type of goodwill training. We had that kind of special training sparring with the other universities. And of course we wanted to beat the other teams. At that time Master Funakoshi was against tournaments because he said it is not a sport, it is a martial art. So we would have a shiai with all of the universities and we would travel all around Japan.

Q: Was karate an accredited course in the university?

A: Yes it was.

Q: How many people did they have in the class usually?

A: It depended on the university but I would say a minimum of 50 – 100. When it became one of the subjects for physical education many young people became interested. They already knew Judo, Kendo, Aikido so this was fairly new because as you know Master Funakoshi brought it to Japan from Okinawa.

Q: Were there women in class at that time?

A: At that time they did not accept women in the karate class. Women and men trained separately in martial arts. Women mostly practiced Naginata (stick fighting).

Q: You were always recognized for your amazing kicking ability. Were you a natural kicker?

A: I always try to follow Master Funakoshi's principle. He said in daily life, you do not use the legs much, just for walking. The hands, yes, they are already coordinated. He said that is why you have to practice leg techniques 50 percent more than hand techniques. If you do punching 10 times, then you should do 15–20 kicking techniques. That is what I followed and it makes a good balance. Yes, kicking techniques can have more power than hand techniques and we studied how much different they are. Kicking techniques are stronger and that is why I followed Master Funakoshi's advice and practiced kicking techniques more – to help them to develop. As he said, have a good balance. Of course it depends on the distance when you are defending yourself. Maybe kicking would be more effective, or punching would be more effective. He said it doesn't make any difference, but you have to practice kicking techniques more to develop coordination. That is what he said and that is why I did it. Of course, each individual has something he or she is better at; maybe someone is better at kata or another person may have stronger punching techniques. But I practiced kicking more than anyone else and that is why. Everything must be balanced.

Q: In 1955, alongside Master Nakayama, you helped develop the Instructor Program. Do you remember what the primary goals were in developing this program?

A: Master Nakayama followed Master Funakoshi's principles, technically and philosophically, and everything. He taught us that when we taught we should think about our members, which is the most important philosophy. Of course, when Master Nakayama was developing the Instructor Trainee Program, he changed a couple of things to make them better.

Q: What were the most important skills that you wanted to give the graduating instructors?

A: Shotokan karate is a Martial Art and a real Martial Art means never to fight – Master Funakoshi said karate is never to attack first. That is the most important principle. Of course, if someone is trying to kill you, you must defend yourself. That is what karate's techniques are for – to defend yourself, but never attack first. Or maybe some crazy person tries to attack someone else, you have to help them. It is not only karate, but all Martial Arts. It is not to fight; Martial Arts are to stop the fight or stop the conflict. It is a way of life that is the real Martial Art. When you analyze the kata, they give us very important principles technically and philosophically. When you analyze all of the kata movements, all of those masters studied these kata and told us it is a lifetime of training, and they gave us this message that this is karate's techniques and philosophies. So I always say, when you analyze the kata and even techniques, 60 percent of techniques are blocking techniques. Why blocking? If someone attacks you have to hit, but why block? They say it is to stop the fight. Those are the things they are teaching us. That is why everyone has to understand that blocking techniques must be strong because they are also striking techniques. You must stop the fight and you do not have to knock them down. That is why kata is a very important principle to karate's techniques.

Q: Could you please share some memories or stories from the time in your life where you were developing the program?

A: I am a really lucky guy to have studied under Master Funakoshi and Master Nakayama, to observe their ideas and their philosophies. My experience was that when you are young, after we started tournaments, every-

Shotokan Legends

one would like to be a champion. Nothing is wrong with that; it makes everyone train harder to develop their technique physically, but mentally they have to think why they are training. After the tournament, the instructor's minds also change. They think they would like to make their student a champion. The teaching method changes, how to get a point especially for sparring. Then Master Nakayama got upset. He came every year to our Master Camp until he passed away. We would have a meeting and he would say, "we have to change some rules and how to teach because look at how their attitudes are changing. It is not a real Martial Art anymore." So those are some of things we would discuss: how to change some rules, etc., even how to bow; if their attitude is bad, they should lose right away. Tournaments can help by motivating people to train harder; they will get a lot of benefit. But it is the instructor's responsibility to remind their students why they are training. After tournaments, they stop training. The same thing happens with ranking. When they are working toward the black belt, they train harder; when they pass, they stop training. That is why we have a rule here at honbu dojo; we wait one year before they get their certificate. If they do not train, they do not get a certificate. They must practice continuously. Then they understand why they are training. I always say, tournaments are the same as dojo training. It is a special type of dojo training. That is Master Funakoshi and Master Nakayama's important principle – everything is dojo training.

Q: How Master Jigoro Kano influenced the ranking system in Karate?

A: Master Kano was a very famous Judo master and he was very close with Master Funakoshi and he suggested that times were changing and if you have ranking system students would train harder. So Master Funakoshi agreed and he stared the ranking system. From the nineteenth to the twentieth century many things changed, but the principle is exactly the same and we still keep it. But the training method is different. In our time, for one month we may have done only punching, one month only kicking, those kind of things. Then medical science analyzed things: the best way to develop the body; if you train this way or that way, you can make more speed and focus. But a long time ago, it was more mental development when practicing the techniques. Now, we have to have a balance of both mental and physical. That is why we have a tournament, to develop both of those things. But sometimes some people only think one way, to develop for a tournament or ranking system. This is wrong; Master Funakoshi would say that is not training.

Q: You taught the very first batch of instructors on the Instructor Program, including Hirokazu Kanazawa, Takayuki Mikami, etc. What do you remember of the success and weaknesses of the course in its first year, and were there any revisions to the program for the second batch of students on the Kenshusei?

A: The first batch was sort of a test case. As I said, I stayed in the dormitory with them and every morning we had running and training and I would push them harder to teach them, and I would report to Master Nakayama how they were doing. After the training, they had to study and write a report every week. And Master Nakayama would ask them why they wrote this or said that. After that, when they had the knowledge and ability, we would give them a written and physical test and they would become official instructors. After that, we planned to send them overseas. Mr. Mikami was being sent to the Philippines and Mr. Kanazawa went to Hawaii to teach. So those two got some experience outside of Japan and when they came back they gave a report. After that, the second group was Mr. Yaguchi, Mr. Asai, Mr. Yamaguchi, and Mr. Shirai, and they did it exactly the same.

Q: When you first developed tournaments with Master Nakayama, did you see a difference in the way the students trained?

A: When we first developed the tournament it was just for demonstration purposes. We traveled all over to do this but then after 2 years Master Nakayama explained to Master Funakoshi if we have an event here and invite all of the public everyone can come to see it. It is a small island and easily accessible. That was one of the reasons. We got Master Funakoshi's permission to do it, sparring and kata but he said to make sure there are rules. After the 2 years Master Nakayama tested out many different rules but most important rule was never to make contact. Martial arts are never to start the fight. It is good to test your skills in sparring and kata

but never make contact. At that time Mr. Mikami, Mr. Kanazawa, and others were all instructor trainees and were going to be in the first tournament. It was 1957. I wanted to participate to test my skills but Master Nakayama said no, I need your help to judge. I was disappointed but had to judge. In the tournament there was a lot of kicking and punching and not enough rules. Then Master Nakayama said we better change the rules to make them stricter. Master Funakoshi agreed to have the tournaments as a way to show the public what karate was about and also just like ranking tests it would motivate the students to train harder. Anything that made students train harder would give them a benefit. Unfortunately, some instructors began to teach how to make a champion and Master Nakayama began to notice that and every year when he came to Master Camp he would tell me to change the tournament again. But one rule we will never change is that tournaments are good to test your skills but they are just like dojo training. That is why we line up, do seiza, bow and again at the end of the tournament and always say the Dojo Kun.

Q; How would you describe your relationship with Master Nakayama?

A: He would come to the college three or four times a week and I had the same experience with him as with Master Funakoshi. They could read my mind that I was thinking only about how to improve speed and focus. Master Nakayama always followed Master Funakoshi's direction. After I graduated, Master Nakayama picked me to coach the team, and every time he went somewhere I would ask him if I could go with him. One time, he went to Thailand and I went with him. He invited the Thai government to come and watch because Thai boxing was a little different from Karate and he wanted them to see it. We put on a demonstration and they said, "Oh, that is a little different." Thai boxing did not have techniques like Karate's kicking and punching techniques. They wanted to have a competition with a Thai boxer and me. So I went every day to watch how they boxed. After observing them, I knew which kind of techniques they did not have, so I thought, "I can knock them down!" Then I spoke to Master Nakayama and I told them, yes, I can accept and I can fight. He said you cannot do that; that would not be fair. There have to be some kind of rules. Then they came and said you can't do this or you can't do that. Master Nakayama said we have to be able to use all of Karate's techniques. The said, okay, we could make a rule that you can use this technique or that technique. Then Master Nakayama said okay. Master Nakayama and I put on a Karate demonstration and they sent the champion of Thai boxing, who put on a demonstration of their techniques. The newspaper came and took pictures and then they wrote a story about it. I could not read it but I found out that they wrote that a Karate master came over from Japan to challenge the Thai boxer. Then  one day, Master Nakayama and I were walking down the street and a young kid came up and said, oh, you are the Karate master and he kicked at Master Nakayama's head. The next thing I knew, the kid was lying in the street. Master Nakayama said: "do not say anything; let's go right away." This was just like Master Funakoshi, no one could touch them. I didn't say anything but now he is upstairs, so I can say it. Almost any place he went, I went with him – practice, demonstrations, etc. He was like an older brother or father to me. I used to stay at his house and Mrs. Nakayama would take care of me.

Q: Do you think Sensei Nakayama vision of future is the reason Shotokan Karate is so internationally popular today?

A: Master Nakayama travelled around the world and he understood different cultures. He knew we had to keep our principles while at the same time respecting other people's cultures and differences. I think that is one of the main reasons he was so well accepted around the world and was able to spread Karate-do to these other countries. Even now, I know from travelling around the world myself that other countries appreciate that we accept their differences and at the same time they do their best to maintain the Japanese tradition within Shotokan Karate.

Q: Why did you decide to move to the United States?

A: Master Funakoshi's last years were taken up with instruction and preparation to send instructors all over the world. In 1953 we did a nationwide US tour for judo and karate. After that tour, Master Funakoshi received a lot of letters asking for instructors, so they sent me over in

1961. But there was a big problem. I couldn't speak a word of English. It was terrible for me. They sent me to Philadelphia because they thought it was a more convenient location. Anyway, the major problem with that plan was my English! You know, in the beginning I couldn't read the menus at the restaurants so I used to point at something. It could be soup or chicken, or steak. I had a very hard time. Like karate training! But my English improved thanks to my wife. The most important thing is do your best. Not only in karate but in everything you do in your life. We are all human beings, there no way we can be perfect. But the idea of getting better and better everyday is what's important. Just do your best.

Q: Have you found that your teaching has changed over the last forty years?

A: Before I came to the USA Mr. Kosaka, who was the president of the Japan Karate Association and the Japan Foreign Minister, hosted a farewell party for all the senior instructors. He came to me and said, "Okazaki, the first thing you have to do is to have some friends who are lawyers and doctors." At that moment, I didn't understand what he meant. Now I do. When I came to this country I tried my best to make people understand karate-do, I had to be strict – but have control at the same time. You cannot be physically abusive. I always used a shinai stick but it depends how you use it. If you hit hard it is not good, but sometimes it is good to make a loud sound so the students wake up. Think about it as an instructional method. Times and society have changed both here and in Japan. The basics are the same because we are human beings but the mental attitude has changed. Students think that if they pay this much, they must get that much. That's what they believe and we can't blame them because they are like part of a machine. The youth don't practice how to think. Karate-do or other physical discipline teaches them that if you don't sweat and work really hard for something, you'll never get anything. But if I used the same teaching methods that I did forty years ago, I wouldn't have any students!

Q: Did you finish your studies in the Takushoku University?

A: Yes, I did.

Q: When did you become an official JKA instructor?

A: I guess the Japan Karate Association was officially organized around 1955. So I was hired as an assistant instructor and quit the job I had. I became the first coach at the instructor's course. Master Nakayama had plans to make official instructors and I became a kind of guinea pig, because he used to give me several projects to study, practice and report on. He analyzed everything I gave him and later on he started the official instructors program. Like I said, I became a coach to the instructor trainees. The first graduate was Mr. Mikami, and then Mr. Kanazawa, and Mr. Takakura. The idea was that becoming a karate instructor was to be the equal of studying the curriculum in a university to become a teacher. We had courses on how to teach the techniques, how to practice by yourself, and on subjects like physics, scientific aspects, et cetera. One of the prerequisites was a degree from a 4-year college. So this course became sort of a Master's degree.

Q: You consider karate to be a sport?

A: No. Karate-do is budo and budo is not a sport. The real meaning of budo is to go into life more deeply and improve physical and spiritual qualities through hard training. The essence or concept of sport is to get away with the toils of life and have some fun. Master Funakoshi was against tournaments but I remember Nakayama Sensei telling him that it was a good way to promote the art and introduce it to the public. Nakayama Sensei stressed that it is not about trophies and medals but to bring the art into the public eye. Master Jigoro Kano also recommended that Master Funakoshi have a ranking system as a motivational tool. These old masters were training for personal development and didn't need these kind of external rewards. But the times changed and people think and train for different reasons. The environment and the economic situations are all very different. But these masters reached a very high level with the old methods. That's why I keep training - to reach their level of excellence. That's the real challenge for the modern martial artists.

Q: So you are against karate being accepted in the Olympics?

A: I would like to see what Nakayama Sensei suggested before passing away - the Budo Olympics. All budo arts together, exchanging techniques and training methods where there are no winners or losers. This would return us to the original concept of budo and we could educate people about the art and the true meaning of the Way of the Warrior. Nakayama Sensei said to me, "We must make people understand the true martial arts way." And this is what I'm trying to do, and the very reason why even after a tournament we still do the dojo kun.

Shotokan Legends

Q: Did Funakoshi ever get involved in grappling or throwing techniques at all?

A: Yes, he did. In fact he explained that many of the kata applications, the bunkai were throwing techniques. But he always stressed that before you throw your opponent to the floor you must punch or kick in order to finish them first. He liked to throw the opponent in front of the next attacker, using him as a kind of protective shield.

Q: Do you try to preserve Master Funakoshi's and Sensei Nakayama's teachings and philosophy?

A: Of course. That's my goal and purpose. Nakayama Sensei was like a father to me - sometimes like an older brother who was always there helping me and guiding me. Master Funakoshi was like a grandfather. I must fulfill my obligation to my original teachers. Karate-do was taught by Master Funakoshi and Master Nakayama as a way of life. He gave us, his proteges, the "Shoto Ni Ju Kun" or "20 Precepts To Live By". The idea of those is that karate-do is budo and its goal is to develop character in human beings and to avoid conflicts.

Q: Is getting a black belt the ultimate goal of karate-do?

A: Not at all. A black belt is just the beginning of a journey. It is a degree of skill but not of ability or understanding of the teaching methods. These are two very different things. I strongly emphasize to my instructors to be patient. To understand. It's important that the instructor knows how to communicate and "give" something to the student so we create a better society.

Q: Do you have any plans to go back to Japan?

A: My teacher came over here in 1961, so here I am. I was ready to go back anytime they decided, but it didn't happen. Unfortunately, both of them have passed away. Compared to them, I am nothing. I hope they feel proud of me wherever they are now.

Q: Do you think karate-do keeps you young?

A: Daily training gives you vitality, energy, and health. Keep training! keep training! We can never reach perfection, but we must keep training.

That's my challenge and responsibility as Master Funakoshi's student and a teacher of his philosophy.

Q: Now that you have 50 years of experience teaching and with all of the countries you have been to, if you could go back in time with all the knowledge you now have would you have done anything differently?

A: I respect each countries culture such as in some countries instead of shaking hands you bow. That kind of thing. But I always tell everyone, no matter what country you are in, in the dojo you have to follow the Japanese culture 100% at the same time respecting each other's culture. Outside the dojo you learn about the other cultures and respect it. It's funny but even at Temple University, some of the students want to continue after the semester and they come here to headquarters to continue their training, and the funny thing is that some of their other professors tell me that the students forget where they are and instead of saying hello to their teachers they bow. But it is still showing respect no matter where they are and they appreciate that. I would not change anything.

Q: What would you like your last will to be?

A: I would tell my students the same thing I always have and encourage them to follow Master Funakoshi's philosophy and seek perfection of character, respect others, always endeavor to avoid violent behavior, and be sincere. Those are the final goals we are all aiming for.

Tsutomu Ohshima

STRICT EYES

Publicity he does not seek. This legendary martial artist, born on August 3, 1930, seems to prefer the solitude of his Santa Barbara home and the view of the vast Pacific Ocean.

Since 1955, when he arrived in the United States of America, Mr. Ohshima has tried to keep his version of Shotokan karate the way it was originally taught by his teacher Funakoshi Sensei. Ohshima never accepted a higher rank than a 5th-dan because that was the highest rank his teacher ever gave. Mr. Ohshima acknowledges that the bombs in Hiroshima and Nagasaki — the birthplaces of his mother and father respectively — are a very important element to understanding who he is today. He studied under Funakoshi Sensei while attending Waseda University in Tokyo and was selected by Funakoshi himself to be the captain of the university karate club.

In 1955, Ohshima left Japan to live in Los Angeles. He formed Shotokan Karate of America and has maintained it as the most traditional branch of Japanese karate in the world. In 1962, he went to France to teach, invited by Mr. Henry Plée, and developed the foundation for the art of karate in Europe.

He cannot understand why journalists seem unable to converse with him at a certain level of direct knowledge and disregard the actual words he speaks. This is Tsutomu Ohshima, an accessible human being and a gem of Budo.

Q: How would you describe Funakoshi Sensei when you started training?

A: I remember he was teaching at Waseda University. At that time, he was already an old man and we had to carry him up the stairs to the dojo and then back down again after class. I believe he was in his 80s.

Q: Is there any special anecdote you remember?

A: There are many, but these would be only anecdotes and probably wouldn't have a long-term benefit for anybody but for those whom were there. But there are some stories that helped me to understand Funakoshi Sensei better. For instance, at a certain point in time, the students were confused about the proper way to perform a sidekick. Master Funakoshi, when showing the techniques, would only make a small, low motion with his foot. This movement was very similar to a front snapkick except that his was body facing to the side. Many of us thought that the reason why he was doing the kick that way was because he was an old man and couldn't perform it otherwise. So we kind of changed it a little bit and executed the sidekick with a more powerful movement, as well as fancier and higher. I did the technique this way for many years. One day I started to feel pain in my back. Then Obata Sensei, the first captain of the Keio University Karate Club, came to the United States.

Q: What happened then?

A: I explained the back pain and mentioned that it really hurt when I was doing this kick. He looked at me and said, "I think there is something wrong with the side up motion that you are using you to perform the kick. If you do it this way, it is very bad for your lower back. That's not the proper way to do it. Didn't you see how Funakoshi Sensei did it?" I was shocked. Master Funakoshi was showing us the proper way to do it all along, but I didn't understand that until many years after.

Q: How did Japan change after the World War and how did these changes affect Budo and Japanese society?

A: Before the war, the Japanese were very proud of our traditions and cultural beliefs. Not only in the martial arts but also society in general. As for fighting, we believed that our samurai were the best fighting men in the world, but the atomic bomb changed many things. Japanese society was shocked, and we were to believe that foreign technologies were stronger. So after the war, we lost respect for what we had and the new generations accepted a more materialistic attitude. They began to copy Western ways of behaving and thinking. I saw that after the war. My countrymen no longer respected their own culture, and immediately I felt that there was something that had to be saved. My grandfather was a samurai, and you can say what you want about the old samurai. Maybe they were cruel; maybe they were missing something that we consider important today ... I

don't know. But I can tell you this: They were honest, truthful and courageous. They were willing to face themselves, they could overcome their fears and they did not have to ride from anyone. This is a mental development from which modern society needs to learn.

Q: How do you remember those dramatic days?

A: We knew the day was coming. My friends and I were training very hard every single day. We thought many times that we all were going to die. That was the mentality. So courageously, we prepared ourselves for the moment. We were all ready to die.

Q: When you came to the United States of America, how did people react to your training?

A: During the 1950s, right after WW II, the Japanese thought that going to America was best. I came to the U.S. and soon questioned why people who had the opportunity of playing all these games — football, baseball, basketball — wanted to learn the martial arts from me. They knew they weren't going to learn another sport from me. At that time, some of my friends told me that we should try to change karate into a sport to make it more appealing to the masses! But I never wanted to do that because tradition and the ethics of Budo would be lost and practice would have no other meaning than trying to beat someone else. My idea was to show the American people through karate-do that our culture was not stupid or a second-class thing and that it was a serious and intellectual activity. In 1955, people didn't really know what to expect from karate classes. They viewed them as a hobby, something to give them a sense of what Japanese culture was all about. I don't think they realized that karate is a serious business and not something to be taken lightly. The United States of America and the Western world have tremendous potential power. All

human societies have. Our enemy is not some other place. Our enemy is in our own minds. We always have to project improvement for ourselves. This is what all these great people throughout history have taught. This is what the martial arts teach. This is what the Bible teaches.

Q: How would you summarize the philosophy of karate-do?

A: Well, I can summarize my own opinion, but I cannot speak for my masters or my seniors because they may have a different opinion. To me, it's important to try to face yourself directly, strictly and honestly. That [philosophy] has had a very strong impact on my life. At one point, I thought that I was OK. When I started to look at myself through different eyes, I realized that I'm full of weakness and cowardice. That gave me more reasons to push myself. So, what is the karate philosophy? As I previously said, I think it is when you face yourself and are honest. For example, during one of our seven-day special training sessions, there were some movements that I could not do. The best way to handle that is try harder next time. That is when and how I learned how to bring up the best in myself.

When you are young, you are full of energy. Of course, I wanted to be strong, and I did not want to cheat. Anyway, I jumped into special training. The first practice was OK. The second practice was OK. The third practice was OK. After five or six days, however, I was exhausted and had lost my concentration. I thought to myself, "What is this?" For a few seconds, I did not like that. If I look back on my life, I did the special training about 100 times. During those times, I think I did a good job during the special training two or three times. I think. Maybe I forgot. But most of the time, probably 99 percent, I could not push from the bottom to top.

Q: Tell us about your special training.

A: We have had about 100 of these special sessions and some of those have occurred here in the United States. During this training, all we do is practice, eat and sleep. These are the most important events for any karate student because they push themselves to their limit. Some of them have described this training as 'the most demanding and strenuous mental and physical experience of their lives." Right now we do this for a minimum of eight times [per year], and they last 3 1/2 days. The training includes things like practicing at midnight, executing 1,000 techniques and/or holding a horse stance for 90 minutes. It is not easy, and that is why we call it special training. It's not ordinary, easy practice.

People think that someone is a loser because nobody follows him or because nobody recognizes him. For example, I have always tried real hard and done everything straight, but that [type of lifestyle] is not always interesting to other people. That can be disappointing and frustrating. The general public does not always care about quality or depth. They want to take the easy way out and go with the flashy things. And that's OK. For me, however, I want someone to remember me in 200 years. Of course, I will not be here. But when people talk about me, I want them to say that this guy was OK. He did a good job. He tried somehow. I realize, of course, that 99 percent of the people are not going to care about the human mind or show any interest. Again, that is alright. That does not hurt me. I am not looking to be popular. I just want to try my best.

Q: Were you expecting that Westerners would accept these extremely hard and demanding training sessions?

A: In the beginning, many Japanese instructors thought that American students would quit if they were forced to do the special training. They thought the Americans students wouldn't be able to handle such training because they're too materialistic. When I started the special training in 1959, it was very experimental. People did have trouble adapting to the physical discipline. But all the tough guys wanted to take on this crazy Japanese guy and prove that they weren't chicken. I challenged them to show me how strong they were, and they ended up adjusting very well to the demands of the training.

Special training is beautiful because the intense mental attitude of the students makes for a good atmosphere. Everybody tries so hard and works so hard. No one is perfect, and we all make mistakes. But no one who gets through the training has failed on any level. I always say at the end of special training that the students can quit karate the following day, and it wouldn't take away anything from what they have accomplished.

Q: Do people try to leave once they see what they got themselves into?

A: The answer is yes. Some of them do, usually after one day or two. They see the possibility of getting hurt, and they feel the exhaustion in the bodies due to the strenuous physical training. Bruises heal, but mental scars don't. You have to give 100 percent because the idea of all this is to forge a new power in yourself, a new mental level. The ability to fight is really the lowest achievement of karate.

Q: How important is confidence to a karate practitioner?

A: Let me give you my definition of confidence. First, a humble person often comes across the same as a person who has an inferiority complex, [but that doesn't mean he has the complex]. Second, a person with confidence has no need to hurt anyone. Why? Because he has confidence. Next, if a person without any confidence gets a position of power, money or strength, he will become cruel, mean and bad. On the other hand, if a person with confidence and humility gets the same position, he will not be this way. These philosophies do not apply just to the martial arts. There is actually no connection. I am not a moralist or even a crazy person. OK. Now, let's think about a period of time from the ancient days until today. If a selfish, mean, nasty guy survived [some ordeal], everyone would look up to him. He would be [considered] a winner. The martial arts show, however, that that type of mentality is a weakness. What kind of human being is a real winner? A genuine human being. It's very clear. If a genuine human being cannot be a winner, I would have quit a long time ago.

Q: What do you mean when you say that you must face yourself with strict eyes?

A: When someone else does something wrong, we don't forgive him. However, when we do something wrong, it's OK and we expect others to forgive us. That is ugly, stupid, immature or a sign of a weakness of the human mind. So, when I talk about facing yourself with strict eyes, I'm talking about making yourself stronger every day. Can you do this without being selfish and without forgiving someone every day? You can't. Of course, we try, and so do I. But I am not successful every day. It's important, however, that we try really hard.

Q: What is the purpose of meditation before and after class?

A: Zen meditation was important to the samurai about 800 years ago. They called it the martial arts of moving Zen. When we get excited, we move around, but we hope that our mentality is clean and calm like the Pacific Ocean is today. We want to feel the same thing before and after. After WW II, about 1945, I went to Japan. The people were struggling, and many were trying to cut off the traditional mentality, such as Zen. Many said that was junk.

Q: What does it mean to achieve a black belt?

A: To my students, reaching a black belt is something priceless. It is not a trivial thing. It is not a badge only of physical accomplishment, but a sign that a person has achieved a certain mental level. These people have learned to face themselves, and that carries over to the rest of their lives. I wouldn't be teaching this art if I thought that it was only about punching and kicking. After I left Waseda University, I could have gotten any kind of good job. I didn't have to teach karate, but karate is much more than fighting.

Q: Do you think practitioners should only focus their attention on karate practice?

A: And become a failure like me? I hope not! I don't encourage this approach at all. They should have other things in their lives to have a balanced existence.

Q: During your training sessions, you refer repeatedly to the importance of penetrating an opponent and you emphasize the importance of breathing properly. Why?

A: Actually, you should first penetrate your opponent with your mind and technique will follow. Of course, deep breathing and the subconscious mind also play a role in this. These all go together simultaneously so you can penetrate an opponent. If your mind doesn't want to go and your body does, it will never work. If you do not have confidence, you will not have luck against any opponent, even if he is weak, sick or dying. It's important to face stronger, tougher opponents comfortably or they will destroy you.

If you stop [breathing] for a couple of minutes, you will die. Seriously, breathing is important in any field, not just in the martial arts. It's important for musicians, athletes, carpenters, etc. It's funny that breathing is the same character in Japanese as secret points. That makes me really proud of my country as a culture. They understood that.

Q: How do you develop confidence?

A: If I could express in a few words and you could understand right away, I would be a multimillionaire. Seriously, you have to train yourself continuously. It doesn't work with just words, and it doesn't happen overnight. You cannot change that easily.

Q: Mr. Ohshima, you mentioned once that those who have a higher position should sacrifice themselves for the benefit of others. Would you please elaborate on that concept?

A: There are many kinds of individuals on the earth and they all have the right to live equally, but the truth is that not all are equal. Some are mature, and some are immature. Education plays an important part on how an individual will be when grows up. Usually, when we get older, we become more selfish and greedy, with no time or energy for others. It is important to have a good educational system that doesn't spoil the young generation. Everybody wants to lead, but a leader has to be a first-class human being. He can stand by himself and work hard, but he cannot do everything for himself. He has to do things for others. In the martial arts, we are racing toward [a situation in which we will see] who can be the strictest with himself. The martial arts contribute to human society in this way. We are racing toward who can be the strictest with himself and honest with himself. This was the original idea in the martial arts. Unfortunately, many people don't get this message. In the old times, this was the most important idea in Budo ... reach a higher level and become a strong human being. But strong doesn't mean big arms; it means who can be a more strict human being with himself. That is the idea of the martial arts, and that is the essence of Budo.

Q: Do you need a lot of techniques to be successful?

A: It depends on your definition of successful. Do you want to move your hands 100 times in one minute? Do you want to face your opponent and just look at him so he cannot attack you? If one of those is the goal you want to reach, I do not know. I am not a poor technician, so I do not know. I do not depend on one technique.

My black belts know that what they are learning is not for appearance or just for the use of competition or self-defense, but for their own spirit and soul ... for their lives. They have learned to recognize their own imperfections and ugliness. They can be proud of it, because it is not an easy task. In the world, there are good people and dishonest people. What is important is that good people don't give up to the crooked people. One little stone in a big lake makes a ripple that spreads out very far, and that's what we try to do in the martial arts. What is the essence of this? To end the ugliness and selfishness in the world, we have to cut out our own ugliness and selfishness first.

A successful individual in our modern society is someone who has a lot of money and properties. "He is a successful person," they say when the see a millionaire. But what they don't realize is that there is no connection between the material things that person has and his mental maturity. There are many immature and lucky "successful" people in the world. In terms of success in the Western world, I am not successful at all. But I am successful in my terms because I have good members and good friends who trust me very much. So I am quite happy. I never have any troubles of my own, nor do my members who have been practicing seriously for many years. Everything I have belongs to my students. It is not mine, regardless of how expensive the things surrounding me may be. My students gave them to me.

Q: How important is it to have an open mind when practicing the arts of Budo?

A: Look at me. I'm an old man who is 70 years old. An opponent could destroy me within a few minutes. I know in my mind, however, that I've got to face this guy, and it could be a fight for my life. What I feel is strong, and I will go into it [the encounter] with an open mind. I feel that way. I will forget my age; I will forget that my body has a herniated disc and I will forget that my legs will not move like they once did. I do not

know how to resolve this, but I'm ready to make the best of it right now. I will make my fists right now and maybe the technique will follow. For me, it is like that.

Q: What does penetrating with fullness mean?

A: When you are sick, you experience emptiness. Emptiness occurs when you are old, especially compared to the fullness of younger people. There is also emptiness in your body and mind when you exhale. This movement is formed on emptiness. Everybody, every day, breathes when they are at their strongest. When you cannot move or do anything, that is emptiness. When you cannot think or move or do anything, that is emptiness. So, I was talking earlier about a small lady who has to defend herself against a big guy. That is why the fullness penetrates emptiness. She has a chance to survive.

Q: What targets do karateka look for on an opponent?

A: You are asking me to answer that question as a karate-ka, but we never think of that. On the other hand, everyone has a target for his life, and I am certainly trying to provide the way that will enable him or her to accomplish a beautiful life. When we die, we hope that we have had a wonderful life with few tears or sadness. We should appreciate everything we have until the last minute. To me, that is my call and my target, and I am sure I will be there.

Q: Many styles have dozens of kata and some practitioners even create their own. What is you opinion of this?

A: Let's say that one teacher creates a kata. Years later, 20 of his students create another 20 new forms; by the next generation, there are more than 1,000 kata! This makes no sense. How can I change what I was taught by Funakoshi Sensei? I don't think he ever considered what he taught as some kind of style or school. The fundamental element of shotokan is that we try to be strict with ourselves because there is no limit to what we can accomplish. We must be straight and honest with ourselves. This is the tradition of Funakoshi Gichin.

Ohshima

Q: Master Funakoshi only taught a limited number of forms, correct?

A: Yes. Before he went to Tokyo from Okinawa, Funakoshi Sensei visited and trained with many masters to learn their forms. I assume that maybe he learned 60 or 80 kata, but I believe that he probably didn't spent many hours on each of them. The idea, as Funakoshi Sensei showed in the later years of his life, is that it is nonsense to memorize dozens of kata. It is ridiculous. He never told me this, but his teachings were in that direction. In the Western world, the people think that if you know 60 kata, you are better than the practitioner who knows only 30. And that is wrong. This exemplifies a process of accumulation in which the truth is that true Budo and true karate are just the opposite. It is about simplification. We have to simplify, simplify and simplify what we do. Quality in our acts, not quantity. Quality in our kata, not quantity of forms. If you know 20 kata, then make 10 better. If you only know 10, make five extremely good. Even five is too many for a true Budo-ka. Put yourself into the kata. Make the form 10,000 times. Then, when you think you have grasped the essence, go back and repeat it another 50,000 times. Only when you reach the threshold of repeating a kata 150,000 times can you start to think that the kata is yours.

Q: How does repetition bring maturity to kata?

A: Kata is not simply the memorization of a series of movements. I'm a very creative person. I could have created 100 new kata, but what and why? Kata training is the opposite of that. Kata is for the spirit, for your own maturity. If you digest kata, you become one.

Q: What does it means "to become one"?

A: Both your unconscious and conscious are directly connected to your physical movement. If those two move with your body, they idealistically will take a long time. The idea is to become one with what you do, with the kata, with the physical movement. You express your best with all of your energy. That is the direction of the true karate. And kata training is for that. To invent a new kata to impress a bunch of people is not karate ... it is being a Hollywood star.

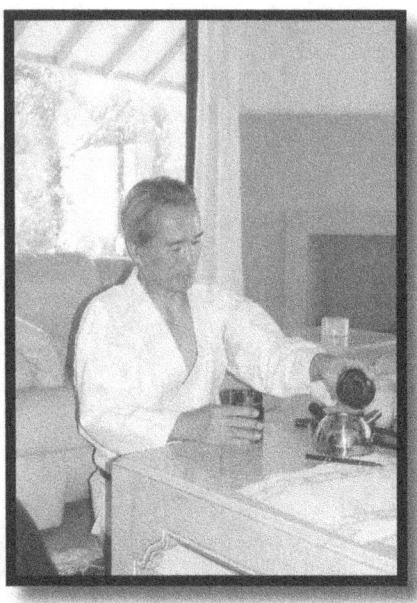

Q: During your early days, is it true that you cleaned the dojo yourself?

A: Yes, I did and it is something of which I am proud. Many people don't understand this. Cleaning is not a low-class act. All my students used to watch me doing it, and I never asked them to do it. In fact, some students used to joke and say things like, "Mr. Ohshima, you like cleaning, uh?" I used to say, "Yes, I do!"

When you clean the place where you train, you are showing appreciation and respect to the place that gives you a chance to practice. Don't forget that polishing the floor is in fact the art of polishing your own mind. I thought some day my students would understand. Some did, some didn't, but that's life. Interestingly enough, after over two years, most of the students were cleaning with me! First, the black belts did, and then the rest of the students realized that if the black belts were doing it, they better do it, too. Nobody asked them to do it; we don't have slaves in this country. The top guy has to work harder so other people will follow him. Somebody who can't demonstrate shouldn't be respected in his position just because of the size of his arms. Younger generations have to learn. But these young people should see that the person at the top is pushing them for them and not for him. Karate is a crystal of the human spirit and its heritage is a gem I intend to preserve. We are all trying to get out from underneath our stupidity, blindness, weakness and cowardice. We must open our heart to the right way to act.

Q: Do you think karate philosophy is some kind of religious belief as some have described?

A: I am a modern man about religion, and I have doubts. I don't believe that I need some messenger, a preacher. Maybe I'm a little bit critical. Karate is a way of life, maybe a little lower than what we understand as "religion," but it can used to achieve a higher level of mentality. Even if they are not intellectually motivated for pursuing religious or philosophical ways, they can find spiritual attainment through training hard in traditional karate. Karate tradition and practice are cultural gems. Many aspects of the art are aesthetically pleasing ... the cleanliness, the purity of form, the power of the body performing a technique, the respect between students and teacher, et cetera. The movements found in karate are more than one man's idea of how to fight. They are the product of a long cross-cultural evolution. They [movements] are more than the most efficient control of the human body. They are part of a spiritual path that is based on physical reality.

Q: What are the differences between Budo and religion?

A: With religion, you always deal with abstraction. It is easy to lose your way, to become proud or confused. In the arts of Budo, there is the experience of the total moment. When you are waiting on an opponent or waiting for an attack, your mind is empty, your body is awake and totally relaxed, and you experience something that can't be put in words, simply because it has nothing to do with words. It is experience. During meditation, you come into contact with a feeling that is much more than just a cultural treasure and more than just an ability to fight. Of course, the martial arts are very related to Shintoism, so I'm very fond of that study. I have been strongly influenced by Zen, and every night, no matter where I go, no matter how late I stay out, I never miss my sitting in meditation.

Q: How do you see yourself in the future?

A: I'm not sure, [but I do know that] I want to live comfortably without money. That's enough for me. I make my best and my members make their best. And though I won't have a chance to see it, it makes me happy to think that maybe after 200 years somebody will still be practicing karate here where I have taught.

Yoshiharu Osaka

KARATE'S PERFECT FORM

OSAKA SENSEI WAS BORN IN FUKUOKA, KYUSHU IN 1947. HE WON THE JKA KATA WORLD TITLE NINE TIMES AND BECAME THE WORLD CHAMPION IN BOTH KATA AND KUMITE. WITH A GENTLE DISPOSITION, HIS CALMNESS HIDES HIS GREAT PASSION, ENERGY AND DEDICATION TO THE PROMOTION OF THE ART. CONSIDERED BY MANY AS HAVING "PERFECT FORM" IN THE STYLE OF JKA SHOTOKAN, YOSHIHARU OSAKA TRAVELED EXTENSIVELY UNDER THE TUTELAGE OF THE LATE NAYAKAMA SENSEI. OSAKA NOT ONLY PROVIDED ASSISTANCE FOR HIM DURING SEMINARS, HE ALSO HELPED WITH THE DEMONSTRATIONS.

WHAT LOOKS SIMPLE AND GRACEFUL WHEN HE PERFORMS IS EXTREMELY DIFFICULT FOR WE MERE MORTALS. HE IS A VERY RESERVED MAN WHEN TALKING ABOUT OTHER INSTRUCTORS OR STYLES. HIS QUALITIES AS AN INSTRUCTOR ARE SECOND TO NONE AND FOR MANY HE IS ONE OF THE BEST TEACHERS IN THE WORLD. HE HAS A GREAT ABILITY TO MAKE STUDENTS FEEL CONFIDENT ABOUT THEIR POTENTIAL, MAKING THEM UNDERSTAND WITHOUT HARSHNESS OR EMBARRASSMENT.

I HAVE KNOWN OSAKA SENSEI SINCE I WAS A TEENAGER PROVIDING ASSISTANCE FOR HIS SEMINARS IN EUROPE. CURRENTLY THE TECHNICAL DIRECTOR OF THE JKA HONBU DOJO, OSAKA REPRESENTS MORE THAN WHAT MANY PEOPLE UNDERSTAND TODAY IN KARATE CIRCLES. HIS DEPTH OF TECHNICAL KNOWLEDGE IS AS BIG AS HIS STRONG SPIRIT AND DELICATE KINDNESS. A TRUE WARRIOR, A TRUE SAMURAI. A TREASURE THAT THE WORLD OF KARATE SHOULD BE MOST PROUD.

Q: When did you start training in karate-do?

A: It was in 1963. In 1966, I entered Takushoku University and trained there for more than four years. Eventually, I was asked to join the JKA instructor's course.

Q: How was the training at the University?

A: Very hard. The atmosphere was very competitive and that made everything more difficult and tougher than any other place. I really enjoyed my time there because there was a sense of honor in winning trophies and tournaments for your university.

Q: Sensei, are there differences between Japanese and Western practitioners? If so, how do they affect physical techniques?

A: Once you have been taught the correct body mechanics and physical elements of a technique, you'll see that those are relevant to how the human body moves and they have nothing to do with the color of your skin or your genetics. But to answer your question, yes, there are some differences. Some are physical and others are cultural, and those are obvious for everybody to understand. Westerners usually try to think about how and why and then [they] do. The Japanese are taught to do [things] first and get used to the physical movements. The thinking about how and why comes later. For some reason, the Japanese approach makes things stay longer with the practitioner because his [the practitioner's] first experience is physical and not intellectual. There are some other differences that can't be seen at first and require a deeper look to detect. For instance, Western karate-ka are very good at performing kata, but you can see weaknesses in the way they use their ankles and hips when going from one stance to another. Another aspect is that the Japanese focus on the transitional phases of the movements in kata. Western practitioners tend to think in terms of completed movements, but they have to pay more attention to what is happening between the end of one movement and the end of the next. Let me explain this a little better, please. Let's take a shuto-uke in kokutsu-dachi as movement one and oi-tsuki as movement two in any given sequence. Western students normally tend to forget how the hip, the muscles in the legs, the tension in the back, the relaxation in the shoulders, and the spring action of the ankles should act during the transition between action one and two. The final point of the movement is not as important as the transitional phases between them. The only way to correct this is focusing is in strong kihon practice. This is the only way to truly develop these transitional phases ... not the repetitive action of the kata without paying attention to the details.

Q: You always mention that the details are the key. What do you mean?

A: For instance, everybody knows how to do a gyaku-tsuki, but what is truly important to know is how to use the body parts in a sequence in

which the previous segment of the body pushes the next and the next does the same thing with the following. The ankle moves, then the knee, then the thigh, then the hip, then the trunk, the shoulder, the elbow, et cetera. If we pull the hip before we bring it into play with the ankle and the leg, the logical sequence of the action will be lost and the power of the movement will lack total potential. The order of the sequence and how every segment of the body come into play are the keys to really bringing the best possible potential out of a practitioner's body. Correct technique is the result of a natural movement. If the technique is correctly practiced, the actions are harmonious, relaxed and powerful. The problem arises when people don't learn the right way and then go and teach incorrectly.

Q: You are an expert in kata and have been a world champion for many years. What is your perspective of kata training?

A: Kata should be kept as the original form that was developed. Kata represent the history of our art, and we can't change it as we please. Of course, the practitioner's style will affect the final result, [and you also have to consider that] the correct speed and timing in the movements — as well as the proper application of strength and muscle contraction and expansion — will change the outside part of the form. The practitioner will put his own flavor [into it], but he shouldn't alter the form to suit himself. Perfection in kata is something impossible to attain, but it is the goal we all should try to reach. It is an impossible goal, but that's why it is a life experience. The real challenge is in every time we do the movement and in every single time we repeat the kata. There is no goal in kata training. The goal is the training itself.

Q: Sensei, if you train in a traditional dojo with wooden floors, can that affect your performance in competition if the competition area features a mat?

A: If you don't train and get used to the particular surface, it may ruin your kata ... yes. If you are planning to compete in kata division, I would recommend that you train on the same kind of surface you are going to compete on. Just get used to it. If you don't compete, you don't have to worry about this. Just train diligently in the dojo, regardless the surface.

Q: Compared to other schools like goju-ryu or shito-ryu, it seems that the JKA does not pay as much attention to the bunkai of the kata. Why is that?

A: In order to understand kata, it is important that the practitioners understand the process and evolution of that particular form. The old masters used kata as a way of passing their knowledge and personal experiences to future generations. This is the main reason why a kata may have many variations. Bunkai is important in JKA shotokan, but there are some principles and ideas we all should remember. Traditional bunkai of the traditional kata, developed by our ancestors, is based on attacking methods used at the time they lived. We are now in the 21st century and even the way individuals attack you in the streets have changed. They have new technologies to abuse decent citizens. It is important to understand that we need to bring new perspective to old solutions for modern problems. Nakayama Sensei used kata as a training method for achieving technical perfection and bringing all the necessary attributes to the body of the practitioner. When looking at bunkai, we need to study the principles and try to apply them in a realistic environment. Self-defense does not always have to do with physical techniques. The study of bunkai, even if you will never use it in a self-defense situation, will help you to understand the techniques in kata. For the purpose of understanding the form, knowing the bunkai is extremely important. I personally believe that the old masters wanted us to participate in kata by using their knowledge as a sounding board for us to develop and research new and different possibilities that adapt to our time. We need to study and develop methods for applica-

Osaka

tions based on our own bodies and levels of understanding. I believe that it is here when we can find a link between kata and the personal expression in kumite. Knowing all shotokan kata without having the proper understanding and feeling for each form is useless. Personal expression of the art must be emphasized here.

Q: What do you mean by that?

A: In Budo, expression of an art can be interpreted as strength by some people, and at the same time, elegance by another. In essence, a genuine art such as karate will never be created until the artist is able to train his mind and body constantly and is able to acquire essential vigor to reach a stage of personal expression. In order to reach this stage, he must continually apply research and discipline.

Q: Do you consider kata an important part of karate training?

A: Definitely. All the strategies and techniques that a karate-ka needs for self-defense and fighting are contained in fundamental kata. It is important to differentiate between practicing kata and studying kata. At an advanced level, we need to investigate, research and probe the techniques we use.

Nakayama Sensei always said that heian kata makes the execution of advanced kata techniques very simple. I still think that way. Technical precision is critical. Focus on the intention of the movement and learn the proper timing, tempo and rhythm of the form. Keep maximum concentration while training and the correct attitude throughout the kata. The positive benefits of its [kata] training and practice are unquestionable.

Q: What is your opinion of makiwara training?

A: Makiwara training is necessary for real karate. If you want to develop

strong techniques, you need to train with the makiwara. Unfortunately, many people don't understand that its value is not based on developing calluses on your hands. Instead, the value is technique, focus, and proper kime. There is nothing like it to develop a strong body and a strong will.

Q: Why have we seen technical changes in the JKA during its history?

A: Karate techniques have not changed, but they have developed, which is different. The developments and modification of the techniques have been the product of a very intensive study. The only reason why these were done was to create a more efficient karate technique. They were not done for the idiosyncrasy of one particular individual. Unfortunately, I have seen basic karate techniques changed by some individual because of his inability to perform the [technique] correctly. [Of course] maybe he has been taught wrong, too. JKA karate tries to make the body stronger and the techniques more powerful. It is based on physics and principles of body mechanics. Shotokan is a system that is based on the expansion of the body and using the natural power of it to perform the techniques. The movements are big most of the time, and this can be used later in time to improve health and other physical benefits, too.

Q: Karate or karate-do?

A: For me, there is only one, and this is karate-do. But I'll try to answer your question. If you understand the art as karate-do, you'll practice it as a way of life. The training, the philosophy and the ethical values of the art will be present in all facets of your life. The dojo will be no different than your work place because the training is not only physical. On the contrary, if you see what you practice as karate, your training will be strictly physical and this will be pretty much as if you practice baseball, tennis or basketball. It is interesting to note that when someone approaches the practice of karate simply as a sport, this person will stop training as soon as another activity captures his attention. In karate, the idea is to beat others in competition or a fight. In karate-do, the goal is to overcome your own limitations and become one in spirit and body. It is important that the principle of shingi-ittai or mind and technique are together.

Q: How was the training under Nakayama Sensei?

A: I was fortunate to have trained under one of the most knowledgeable instructors in the history of karate. He always emphasized the importance of the basics. We did a lot of kihon, regardless of our rank and position.

Q: You traveled with Nakayama Sensei for many years, and he said you were an example of technical perfection.

A: I am proud of his words, and all I can say is that I have always tried my best. I don't consider my karate to be perfect in any way. If

fact, I think I'm very far from it. Many of my seniors are much better than me. Nakayama Sensei was a very kind man and maybe he said those words in an attempt to make me train harder because he saw many mistakes in my technique. I would like to say here that every karate practitioner must follow the principles of the technique and even if the outside "mold" doesn't look beautiful, his karate can be perfect because perfection is based on the proper use of the body and mechanical principles — not on the way the body looks.

Q: How do you see the influence of the sportive element in the art of karate?

A: I truly don't think sport competition has to interfere in the development of true karate-do. Competition is a part of the training and can be helpful if it is properly used. It is a phase of the art that teaches things that we can't learn in the dojo. It requires a different mental discipline and a different kind of self-control. This is the main reason why Nakayama Sensei began the competitions. But in karate-do we emphasize the complete process, the continued effort of becoming a better budoka. Competition has its place in karate, but its place is not in the regular basic training. Sometimes I get too worried because the emphasis these days is too much on tournaments and championships rather than in developing the important principles and ethics of karate as a way of life.

Q: What are the main differences you see between WKF and JKA competition?

A: In the JKA, we learn to not make a mistake because you will lose if

you do. Our approach to competition is based on Budo ... one strong attack, only one chance. This makes the matches less attractive for the spectators. On the other side, WKF rules allow more techniques, the competitor plays differently and there are more opportunities of recovering from going down in the score. If your opponent gets a point, you can always get it back. The style is lighter and maybe faster. Timing is important, but it is paramount in the JKA. There is more mental strategy involved. If you don't perfectly time the attack and the defense, you lose the match. Strength and concentration can be more relevant. I don't want to say what style is better. This is something that any practitioner needs to find out for himself. I personally like the idea of a karate practitioner establishing his base on the principle of the ikken-hisatsu, which is so important in the art. Olympic recognition for karate seems to be very important these days, but I'm concerned because I have seen judo lose control of the art when entered in the Olympics. It lost the principles of the founder, Jigoro Kano. Karate must keep its essence as a martial art and Budo.

Q: How does Budo apply to the art of karate-do?

A: The goal of Budo is to develop the practitioner as a warrior and as a human being. Some people think of a budoka as a warrior, and this is not correct in Budo, although it was correct in the old bujutsu because a practitioner needed to have extensive knowledge of fighting because he was facing enemies in the battlefield. Budo involves more than fighting, and in fact, learning fighting arts is not the main goal in Budo practice. The idea of Budo, as Nayakama Sensei described it, is "to gain deep knowledge of the [our] chosen art to perfect our character and see clearly in our own nature and existence." And karate-do can help you to do that.

Q: What we should do when we "hit the wall" in our training?

A: We all hit the wall sooner or later. Sometimes karate may be boring, but the true benefits are there for those who continue training. Sometimes we can get bored, but we need to keep going and training. Keep your training simple and focus until you feel better. In karate as in life, you must be capable of working through adversity and overcoming your weak-

nesses. Some people reach shodan, keep training and become godan and then they stop training! They go back to shodan because they didn't keep working and training. We must train all the time. Even if it is just a little. Students must train harder at higher levels. Not train less. Nakayama Sensei said that "karate is attained one step at a time and so is life. Train every day and try your best, and the truth will come to you."

Q: Should training change as the practitioner ages?

A: Of course! Karate has to be a reflection of who you are. And nobody is the same at 20 as he is at 50. Karate matures with age, and you karate must reflect your personal maturity as a human being. The natural body instinct slows down with age, but you have to keep training to revert this process back as much as you can. Train to develop focus and muscle control. These elements will be present during all of your years of karate, regardless of your age. Funakoshi Sensei always mentioned that karate should be used for perfection of character. The intelligent practitioner will change and adapt his training to his age. Specific injuries will affect how you'll train and practice when you get older. You must always practice physically and mentally. It must always be both ways.

Q: How has your perception of karate changed from the time you were a competitor to now that you don't compete?

A: I had a great teacher in Nakayama Sensei, so I always practice karate-do as though I were still competing when I was young. When you are

training for competition, you learn how to score and how to defeat the opponent. When you quit competition, the meaning of being strong reaches another level. You try to become strong and powerful to use your body properly for karate-do. You study your body and find out that going back to the basics is the secret. Karate technique will keep improving no matter what. And I hope future generations understand what they are doing so they can develop new technologies for training and [new] ways of using the body to perform karate better.

Q: Did you train with weapons in the JKA?

A: Karate is the art of the empty hand. We don't include weaponry training at the JKA, but it is true that Funakoshi Sensei practiced several weapons like sai, tonfa, bo, et cetera. Later on he focused more in karate-jutsu and followed the example of other similar forms of Budo. However, training in kobudo is something that anyone can do as a personal thing and for individual research. I believe weaponry training may be good for the student if he has the time and interest.

Q: What advice would you give karate practitioners for their personal training?

A: Proper mental training and understanding what you are doing is paramount to developing the right attitude so the essence of karate-do is not lost. Always focus on proper technique and make sure you understand what you are doing. Repeat the basics over and over. Repetition is the key. Try to feel and develop the proper control of your muscles when performing the technique. Concentrate on correct form and the natural movement. Correct the mistakes and add speed and power little by little. Then work on timing. The body must be built with proper training and this takes time, so don't expect results over night. Don't try to do too much too soon because there will be a loss of technique, and you'll never reach your true potential. Grow little by little and progressively. Training hard is the secret, but you must train hard within the structure of a correct and progressive training plan. Never stand still in karate. Always try to improve step by step. Finally, don't just train; you also have to think when you train.

Q: Sensei, you always try to develop new and better ways to execute karate techniques. Do you pass these discoveries on to the students?

A: That's a good question! Every discovery I make during my research is through personal experience. Students must learn how to see these elements in my technique when I'm teaching and copy them until they have a sense for them. Then, they should adapt these concepts to themselves and develop their own style of delivery of the technical principle.

Q: Do you mean that you keep them secret for yourself and the student must steal them from you?

A: That's a nice way of saying it.

Q: Osaka Sensei, do you have any final thoughts?

A: Be honest and sincere in your training. Use your maximum effort when you train and learn to understand your body and how it changes with age. Karate is based on hard training and sacrifice, but there is also joy and fun. Don't try to do anything that your brain doesn't understand, but understanding things that your body can't perform may be detrimental for a true karate practitioner. If you are a teacher, teach with love and a sense of warmth. Always try to help your students but make sure, as I said before, that you understand yourself. In karate, we say that you have to know yourself, your body and your mind before you can actually help others. Nakayama Sensei, before he died, was worried that karate practitioners were only in training for competition reasons and always thought that getting Olympic recognition shouldn't be our primary goal. He wanted us to understand the true way of martial arts and this is the way I'm following.

Osamu Ozawa

TEMPERED BY FIRE

BORN IN KOBE, JAPAN, OSAMU OZAWA BECAME, AT A YOUNG AGE, ENTRANCED WITH NOT JUST THE MARTIAL ARTS BUT ALSO WITH THE LIFE OF THE WARRIOR. AT AGE 17, HAVING ALREADY STUDIED WADO RYU KARATE-DO, HE LEFT KOBE FOR HOSEI UNIVERSITY WHERE HE BEGAN TRAINING UNDER GICHIN FUNAKOSHI. IN 1944, OZAWA WAS CALLED UP TO SERVE IN THE JAPANESE IMPERIAL NAVY AIR FLEET BUT HIS MILITARY CAREER ENDED IN A FLIGHT ACCIDENT THAT PUNCTURED ONE LUNG. UNTIL HIS DEATH ON APRIL 14TH, 1998, OZAWA SENSEI WAS THE HIGHEST-RANKED SHOTOKAN KARATE MASTER IN THE WESTERN HEMISPHERE. HE WAS AN EXTRAORDINARY MAN WHOSE LIFE WAS IN THE HANDS OF THE GODS FROM BEGINNING TO END.

Q: What was your family situation during your youth?

A: My family was not rich but we were well off.

Q: Did you live up to your parents expectations?

A: I don't think so. I guess my parents had a lot of dreams for me - I would grow and mature, attend the University, and enter the family firm. But I guess that was a dream destined not to be.

Q: How was life during pre-war times?

A: Life at that time was very disciplined. Life, pre-war, was very, very strict. It was a time of rising Japanese militancy in people minds. I remember that both judo and kendo were part of the educational system for

imparting the ways of the warrior to the young.

Q: What was your goal as a teenager?

A: I wanted to be a professional military man but my mother was disgusted with the idea. I went to a junior military school and applied. I took the test but I failed. It was very demanding physically and mentally. Out of every 100 applicants, one was selected.

Q: Because of your disappointment, did you give up?

A: Not at all! I remained undeterred in my goal and again, when I was 15, I tried to apply to a junior military academy sponsored by the Navy.

Q: Were your parents happy with that idea?

A: Of course not! My family was very disappointed with me. My mother was unhappy and my father didn't understand because he wanted me to attend the university to study business.

Q: How were people selected for karate classes at the university?

A: I remember that nearly 80 people signed up for the university karate team. Mr. Ito gave a short lecture on the history and traditions of karate and then an explanation of the art. He made us try the makiwara. I had trained before, and I had struck makiwara to toughen my hands. But many there had never seen the striking pole - then it was wound with tough rope. Mr. Ito commanded me to hit the makiwara 50 times with each hand. It didn't bother me but those who had never struck it were a different matter! Their hands were split and bleeding - some even cried.

Q: What did the seniors say?

A: Not too much. "Today is your day to decide - stay or go," they said. About 30 stayed. Over half indicated that they wanted to go. For those who stayed they announced that the training "was going to be different from then on; six days a week, six hours a day." The training became more severe than military discipline. In the military, superiors could beat subordinates with a bo, or order troop punishment but in Karate we would be left sitting in seiza for hours, forbidden to move. Being struck in the face was common punishment. The training was hard, terrible hard. It was about spiritual training...but technically...I don't know now. I have to confess that I was frightened: I didn't want to stay, but I was scared to quit.

Q: Why?

A: Because there was a formal ritual to say goodbye to all the members training in the dojo. It was a very formal occasion. The members were lined up according to seniority, from junior to senior. Then you approached them one by one. You said, "Goodbye," then the person would strike you in the face. I was really scared to quit!

Q: What's your opinion of Master Funakoshi?

A: Sensei was a very strong, very wise man. I don't think a day goes by that I do not think of him. I meditate in my dojo sitting before his photograph in the kamiza, and burn incense in his memory. Before the war, I don't really think we believed he was a great man. Sensei was very soft spoken; he would observe as seniors Obata, Hironishi and Tagaki supervised the training. Master Funakoshi would walk up and down the lines and stop and talk with every student and correct this or that. Sometimes at night I go to the dojo and practice my kata singing a poem written by Sensei Funakoshi that begins; "There is an island to the south, where there is a beautiful art. This is karate."

Q: How did the war affect Sensei Funakoshi's students?

A: It was a big change. A lot of classmates were being called up for military service and faces began to disappear from the dojo. Whenever anyone left, we had a farewell party. We would gather in a restaurant and wish farewell to our comrade. We would toast their fortunes. I remember that the training in the second year was not so unbearable as the first.

Q: Did they have a farewell party for you?

A: No, there wasn't time to hold a farewell party. Funny, but I was called up to serve in the Japanese Imperial Navy Air Fleet!

Q: You don't seem to like to talk much about the war.

A: Well, I think it is something that is best left in the past. I cannot

describe well what we felt. It was a time of purity - great emotional strength. We believed in our minds, in our hearts and souls, that we were to lay down our lives for the nation. It was very beautiful - but very hard to explain. I had a flight accident that punctured one lung. I spent six months in two different hospitals recovering. Physical injuries heal but the devastation done to Japan looked as if it could never be healed. Japan was a sea of rubble. In Tokyo, most of the people had no housing, not even huts or tents. Everything lay in ruin. Food, clothes, essentials - all were scarce.

Q: What was your personal situation those days?

A: My karate colleagues, the practitioners of the first great age of Japanese karate, had been scattered to the wind.

Q: Where was Sensei Funakoshi Sensei at that time?

A: He had gone to Kyushu in 1945, after the fall of Okinawa. He discovered that his wife was ill and dying. These were days of dark discovery. He did not return to Tokyo until about 1947. He looked very old when he returned from Kyushu. He had lost his wife, and many fine, wonderful karate students. I remember one, a much senior practitioner from Takushoku University. He had been the captain of the team and he was a very great student of Sensei's. We used to fear him because he was really powerful. In those days there was no tournament but after exchanging training, we would free spar. Sensei Funakoshi was very sad when he heard of this death.

Q: How were those sparring sessions?

A: It was not like a tournament. No rules, no protection. Just two men and a senior who called "Hajime!" And you fought until you couldn't fight anymore.

Q: How often did Sensei Funakoshi teach at the dojo?

A: He looked old but he remained healthy. Whenever we needed him, we went to pick him up. It was interesting because even if he looked old, when he changed into his uniform he was full of energy! Of course, he was not as active as before the war, but it was a truly honor to have him two or three times a month. There is no value that can be placed on having known him.

Q: When did the senior practitioners decide to organize the art?

A: It was around 1949. Seniors Obata, Tagaki, Nakayama, Fukui and Ito got together. They decided on inviting Sensei to be Instructor Emeritus. Senior Nakayama was given the duty of being the active Chief Instructor; the others assisting. A tiny office was set up in Ginza. The original dojo - the Shotokan - had been bombed during the war. There was no place to train and some wanted to rebuild the old Shotokan building. This is how the Japan Karate Association (JKA) was created. Later on, in 1949, we decided to create a national organization and Sensei Hidetaka Nishiyama was assigned the responsibilities of technical advisor.

Q: When was the reunification of Shotokan Karate completed?

A: I guess it was in 1952. But Master Funakoshi never wanted his karate to be called "Shotokan" - the Hall of Shoto. He always called his art "Japanese Karate," because it was of and for Japan. That is why there was a JKA and not a group called "Shotokan."

Q: At that time what was your opinion about the possibility of unifying all karate styles on a national basis?

A: There were some differences but not between the masters such as Yamaguchi, Funakoshi, Mabuni, et cetera. All those differences lay between the young students, and not the masters. I remember we managed to give a dinner for all the masters. Unfortunately, it was a dream that for whatever reasons, and there were many, failed to come about.

Hiroshi Shirai

BUDO WITHIN

HIROSHI SHIRAI WAS BORN ON 31 JULY 1937 IN NAGASAKI, JAPAN AND STARTED LEARNING KARATE IN 1956, THREE YEARS AFTER SEEING A PROMOTIONAL VIDEO OF THE JAPAN KARATE ASSOCIATION (JKA) AT KOMAZAWA UNIVERSITY, WHERE THE LEGENDARY SENSEI HIDETAKA NISHIYAMA WAS HIS TEACHER. ONCE HE BECAME INTERESTED IN COMPETITION IN 1962, HE WON BOTH THE KATA AND THE KUMITE CHAMPIONSHIPS OF THE JKA, BECOMING ONE OF THE FEW RECEIVING THE TITLE 'GRAND CHAMPION'.

AFTER A WORLD TRIP TO PROMOTE KARATE TOGETHER WITH SENSEI TAIJI KASE, SENSEI HIROKAZU KANAZAWA, AND SENSEI KEINOSUKE ENOEDA TO EUROPE, SOUTH AFRICA AND THE UNITED STATES OF AMERICA, HE SETTLED IN MILAN, ITALY IN 1965, WHERE UNDER HIS TUTELAGE THE ITALIAN KARATE FLOURISHED AND MANY TITLES WENT TO HIS STUDENTS.

SENSEI SHIRAI FEELS THAT THE SELF-DEFENSE (GOSHINDO) ASPECT OF KARATE HAS BEEN TOO MUCH IN THE SHADOW OF KUMITE AND KATA. ALTHOUGH HE PRACTICED KARATE FOR SELF-DEFENSE INITIALLY, HE FOCUSED ON KUMITE FOR A FEW YEARS UNTIL MOVING TO EUROPE. HE STARTED REFOCUSING ON SELF-DEFENSE AND ITS INCORPORATION IN THE PRACTICE OF SHOTOKAN KARATE, "DON'T TRAIN ONLY KARATE FOR COMPETITION SINCE THAT HAS A LIMITED LIFE. TRAIN FOR BUDO AND YOU WILL POSSESS TRULY EFFECTIVE COMBAT TECHNIQUES," HE SAYS.

Q: How was your beginning in karate training?

A: When I started karate, karate was mainly a self-defense method. It wasn't until later that competition was introduced and even then it was not highly emphasized. My interest in competition grew and I decided to pursue it more in the University and later in more advanced senior JKA

championships. I think this was a positive experience growing up but I also realized that I should not base all of my training in competition.

Q: How was your competition experience?

A: It was a good and rewarding journey. I had to face Sensei Enoeda several times and that was not easy! I think that competition is good if you try to learn from it. In my case, I had to develop ways and strategies of winning because most of the time I was facing seniors with more experience than me. I had to do a lot of observation and analysis in order to win.

Q: Who were the most influential Sensei during your early years?

A: Sensei Hidetaka Nishiyama and Sensei Taiji Kase. But I must say that they were not only influential during my early days but also during the rest of my life. They left a big mark in how I see, train and teach karate.

Q: How do you remember your training under Sensei Hidetaka Nishiyama?

A: I trained under his supervision [in the beginning] at Komazawa University. He was a very traditional teacher in all aspects, especially at that time before he decided to move to the United States of America. JKA karate is based on strong kihon and Sensei Nishiyama was very focused on us having a solid base. His training sessions were extremely hard and I want to emphasize the word "extremely". Very strong karate and very demanding physically. His classes used to be divided in three parts of one hour each; kihon, kumite and kata.

Q: What were the main points of his personal way of teaching karate?

A: In kihon he was very precise. He always emphasized the right mechanics, the right way of delivering the technique. Interestingly, although he had a great physical technique, he always told us to not copy his body movement but to reproduce the main mechanical principles with our own body. Don't copy your teacher, express those principles with your own body. Of course, we all wanted to punch and kick like Sensei Nishiyama because of his excellent technique so it was hard not to try "copy him", because he was a great example of the best Shotokan technique.

In kata, he focused on bringing the kihon together and in giving 'life' to that particular kata. Every movement was important. He emphasized a lot the transition between the main techniques of the kata and talked a lot about the "distance" or Maai between the techniques in kata.

Kumite was putting it all together. He had an amazing understanding of distance, ruled by the footwork, and the timing, ruled by the sense of rhythm. He used to say that if we can control distance and timing, the rest is easy. He had an unbelievable sense to feel the opponent's inner rhythm and breathing pattern.

Q: And Sensei Taiji Kase?

A: Although his physical appearance was rough, what really caught my attention was his open mind to training and different ways of doing things. He had all the JKA training and flavor to it but maybe because he came from the old dojo, he had something different than the rest. He was a very hard teacher but at the same time very charming and caring. He had a special kindness about him that transpired all over his teaching. He was very human, enjoy "human" things like good food, friends, company, family, etc. and he always wanted to stay out of all politics involved around karate. He didn't want to change the karategi for a pen and a desk. It simply wasn't him.

When he passed away, it was a very big loss for me. I was very close to him.

Q: What can you tell us about Sensei Kase's personal expression of kata and kumite?

A: His kumite was very budo oriented. He had the "killing" mentality when doing kumite. He agreed to sport competition because he knew the value of it as a practice tool and experience but his mind was budo not sport.

His kata represented all the karate principles but you had to be educated to "see" them. If you were simply looking at the external form, you were going to miss the important parts!

Q: How was the JKA Instructor's Training Course when you took part in it?

A: It was 1960 and there was a small group at the time. If I remember well, only four in my group. Sensei Nakayama was the main instructor. Sensei Nishyama, Sensei Kase and Sensei Sugiura too.

Q: How was the training? What is the most important thing that you remember?

A: Although it was very demanding for us physically as trainees, I think the main point was that you had to understand how other people, with other body types do karate. In order to do that, I had to learn about my body and how the principles applied to my body structure and type. Then, see how other people's karate [using the same principles] was expressed physically. In short I can say that it was like an "inner journey" for my own karate. I'd dare to say that if you don't understand your "personal" karate you can't make karate work personally for another individual. The understanding of others' karate starts with understanding your own.

Q: When did you decide to leave Japan and go overseas to teach?

A: I went with a JKA group which included Sensei Enoeda, Sensei Kase, and Sensei Kano on a world tour. Other teachers were already abroad. We visited several continents and most of us stayed in Europe although often traveled to America and South Africa for teaching too.

Q: What are the most relevant points and elements of karate training?

A: I know that some people may not understand now but time will open their eyes. The most important element of karate training is becoming a better human being. It is not the final goal to punch or kick or to learn how to hurt someone else. You need to go to the 'other side' and use karate for perfection of your own character like Sensei Funakoshi used to say. That is the main goal. Unfortunately when we are young, we don't see it and focus on other more external or physical aspects. The sooner you get to understand this and make it your guiding principle in karate training, the better karateka you will become.

Q: Sensei, would you please elaborate on how you developed "Goshindo" and what it really is?

A: Its original idea I had a long time ago, over four decades. I had the opportunity of learning kata directly from some of the best sensei but my mind kept going into the application of those kata movements, making them real. I knew I had to transcend from kata and normal kata bunkai to find the connection to use it in a very practical form. I studied kumite, kata, kihon, sport competition, self-defense, etc. to finally decipher a series of principles that took shape in the form of Goshindo. I went a little more into the Okinawa way of approaching karate which is different than the approach I learned all my life.

Q: So Goshindo deals with a more practical efficient way of applying Shotokan karate techniques, does it conflict with Shotokan training?

A: No, absolutely not. Goshindo means "The Way of Self Defense" but does not conflict with Shotokan at all. In fact I think that it helps Shotokan training and understanding in many ways. I have seen this in myself and in many of my students. My goal is to teach and preserve both. For me, they go hand in hand.

Q: How can the art of karate become a "way of life" for the practitioner?

A: I would say that things have changed a little bit. In the early days karate training was very hard physically, the main idea was to develop the spirit through an extremely demanding physical training. Spirit was first, then technique. It was a different time. Later on more and more knowledge was used to understand better ways of training and the post-war time passed. Then karate opened itself to many other areas of life. Other values became more relevant than the idea of "surviving". Karate is a means to develop self-defense and health; it is a good form of exercise, a valuable tool as a sport to communicate and grow socially and of course through hard training and dedication a tool to develop strong spirit. All these are karate and depending on the individual more emphasis will be done in one area than another. Karate has no limitations and is a very well-balanced tool for life if you know how to use it properly.

Q: Finally Sensei, what advice would you give to all karateka?

A: Think of yourself as a student at all times. Think always of training and developing your karate or martial art. Everyday. It is alright to think of yourself as a karateka, but on a bigger scale, also try to think of yourself as a martial artist, think outside of your method, look for other ideas, expand your horizons and be open to other forms of moving your body and applying technique. There is no shortcut in karate, all is based on hard training and dedication. Make a real effort to follow the Dojo Kun in your life and above all, never give up.

Shunsuke Takahashi

UNDIVIDED PAST

IT WAS IN 1972, THAT TAKAHASHI SHIHAN DECIDED TO MOVE TO AUSTRALIA, BRINGING HIS WIFE AND CHILDREN, TO SETTLE IN BRISBANE FOR TWO YEARS, TEACHING KARATE AND ESTABLISHING A TECHNICAL AND ORGANIZATIONAL CORE OF MEMBERS TO ADVANCE THE AUSTRALIAN SHOTOKAN KARATE ASSOCIATION, LATER TO BECOME THE JAPAN KARATE ASSOCIATION OF AUSTRALIA, AND AS OF 2009, TO BECOME THE TRADITIONAL SHOTOKAN KARATE-DO FEDERATION OF AUSTRALIA, TSKFA, AS WE KNOW IT TODAY. IT WAS THAT YEAR SENSEI TAKAHASHI BROKE AWAY FROM JKA (AUSTRALIA) TO FORM THE TSKF AUSTRALIA (TRADITIONAL SHOTOKAN KARATE-DO FEDERATION).

IN THIS DAY AND AGE, A PERMANENT COMMITMENT OF MORE THAN FOUR DECADES TO ANYTHING, WHETHER IT BE A MARRIAGE, PARTNERSHIP, OR JOB, IS VERY RARE. OVER THIS PAST PERIOD OF 40 YEARS, SENSEI TAKAHASHI HAS BEEN RESPONSIBLE FOR THE EXPANSION OF TRADITIONAL STYLE SHOTOKAN KARATE IN AUSTRALIA. HE HAS ALSO ARRANGED MANY EXCHANGES BETWEEN JAPANESE AND AUSTRALIAN UNIVERSITIES, AND PRIVATELY FOR INDIVIDUAL JAPANESE STUDENTS TO ATTEND AUSTRALIAN HIGH SCHOOLS AND VICE VERSA. IT IS UNDER SHIHAN TAKAHASHI GUIDANCE, THAT ALL PRACTITIONERS ARE WELCOMED AND ACCEPTED IN HIS ORGANIZATION, SIMPLY THROUGH A MUTUAL LOVE OF KARATE.

Shotokan Legends

Q: How did you decided to train in karate ad how it was your first contact with the art?

A: I was 18 years old I entered Komazawa University I met an old friend from high school, who convinced me to join the karate club there. That was the first time I ever saw karate and I decided to start immediately. During my time at the University I was practicing karate all the time. Right there, the karate club at Komazawa University was very famous in Japan. The instructors then were Shihan Nishiyama, Shihan Shirai, Shihan Itaya, Shihan Ohishi and Shihan Mizuno. There were so many great instructors at my university that I wanted to take advantage of the situation and therefore I decided to dedicate my life to karate-do when I was a third-year student at Komazawa University.

I think I was very fortunate of having these great karate teachers at my University.

Q: What did you do right after graduation at Komazawa University and how you decided to go outside of Japan to teach?

A: After I graduated from university I did not have no doubts that what I had to do was to enter the JKA Instructor School. I was also asked to teach karate at Komazawa University for Physical Education. I accepted the offer and the position with only one condition: that my commitment to the JKA Instructor School had first priority.

I always had a desire to teach karate abroad, as other instructors did, but back then it was also the "unwritten law" that most graduates had to go abroad and spread karate. When Shihan Nakayama told me that an instructor was needed in Australia, don't forget that I had just graduated from the school, I decided without any doubt in my mind to go to there. I chose Brisbane as the main city because Mr. Mike Connolly, had established the Australian JKA and the karate club at Komazawa University belongs to the JKA, so it was a logical decision.

Today, I am still teaching karate as a full-time instructor, but my primary purpose is to introduce Japanese martial arts, karate-do, as one of the forms of Japanese cultures.

Q: Sensei, you were the JKA representative in Australia for over three decades years. What goals did you set when you took that role?

A: In JKA karate, the fundamental approach to master karate is established in the three essential components: basic movements [kihon], kata and kumite. There are 25 kata. Kumite has the "ippon" rule, and the JKA had it first karate tournament in the world based on these rules that Shihan Nakayama developed based on other activities like Kendo, I believe. I think that all practitioners of karate should be open to the world and compete against anyone in the world. This will bring the level up.

I remember that in the beginning the people used to think that karate training was similar to the ones shown in the action movies. It has changed completely because practitioners of karate understand now that the three fundamentals pillars and encompasses the development of the human spirit as well.

Q: Where do you see the art of karate going in the future?

A: Things are changing in our society and that is normal. Karate perception as a method of communication in our society has to change too. I think that the young practitioners of karate are hoping that karate will be an Olympic Games sport one day and are quite sure it will happen. This may be positive and also negative…it all depends on how the people responsible handle the situation. In karate there are four dominating styles, shotokan, shito ryu, goju ryu and wado ryu ; they will not be changed and will be passed on to the future in the right way and with their own philosophy and principles.

Nevertheless, I believe that karate-do is only one regardless of how you do the technique. The spirit and the essence…it is the same for all of us.

Q: Is it very different the way karate is practiced outside Japan when compared to the training in Japan?

A: There should be no difference between world karate-do and Japanese karate-do, as long as practitioners train and practice karate sincerely with the right heart.

The ways of thinking are due to the different nationalities, of course, different. And that may affect the perception of the art. Countries all over the world recognize have invited high-level karate instructors from Japan (whatever the style may be) and try to understand correct karate-do and Japanese culture. And that's the correct way to learn, develop and pass karate to the next generations.

I hope top martial arts teacher agree with me in this point.

Q: What do you think that it is the most difficult aspect for the student to develop or achieve?

A: I should say the "naturalness" of the body. It is normal to become rigid and move like "karate" but after years of training the body should move differently. Yes, it is karate but it doesn't "look" hard or rigid. In both kata and kumite, this is an important. It is very hard to see karatekas moving with a true "naturalness" in their actions. Basically it is like the principle is "there" but the body doesn't look like the rigid mold we used to have in our beginnings. In short…your body is "expressing" a karate principle but your body doesn't necessarily has to "look" like the basic or primitive karate we know. Karate should be very relaxed and flexible art. You can see this principle in other great teachers…unfortunately some of them are not with us anymore.

Q: What are your personal thoughts about karate?

A: During all these years of training, I had the opportunity of knowing and meeting a lot of people and some of them have become very close friends. All the people around me have been my teachers in other ways. They are what I like to call "my assets".

In karate training, when done seriously, you may get hurt, but at the same time you can develop certain areas of yourself due to that kind of training.

I think that through the serious training you learn how to have compassion for others, even though you may get hurt.

Any martial art is fine. I am not talking about karate now. The aim of all martial arts training is to seek perfection of character.

Q: How much time and effort should a student be prepared to put into learning karate and what will they get out of it?

A: The most common reason why people become involved in karate is for health and fitness. I think instructors should train as frequently and hard as they can. The important thing is to continue training. Many people stop training. I think that if you continue training you will find other motivations for karate. You will find ways that will improve your karate without necessarily being karate. Recently, more people have started karate after watching a karate competition, since there are now more opportunities to watch tournaments. They begin the training because they want to win a competition. And that is good because it brings them to the art of karate. In that case they have to train very hard, depending on the size of the competition. You have to train more than others and you have to think about karate all the time — by that I mean how to improve your techniques, study the psychology of opponents and learn to control your own thoughts. That's why I think that competition is good because it forces you to improve and get better...always trying to improve.

From a traditional point of view, it is polite manners to train hard before you fight in competition because it shows respect for your opponents, it means that you take them seriously. Train hard and often. If you decide to train for karate without any kind of challenge like a competition, only your personal development as individual then constant training is paramount. In fact, nothing changes... it is important to continue training no matter what. It is easy to slack off and a true martial artist should make sure doesn't fall into this trap.

Shotokan Legends

Q: So you are not against competition...

A: Sport competition has a big part in our society. It brings the excitement and attention of the young people and it is up to us – the instructors – to eventually teach them the traditional values of "do" and Budo. Karate is karate but we need to understand our modern society and see how we can use the art as a tool for the education and moral development of the individual. This is important for our society. Important principles are being lost in this modern times and karate can be used to teach these principles to the younger generations. Traditional karate is not about how we punch and kick or we do this or that movement in kata but about the kind of ethical and moral values that we preserve as budoka.

Q: Sensei, what do you think is the deepest fear of any human being?

A: That's a tough question. As a budoka, I know that Samurai had to learn to be liberated from death, and they trained for that. Therefore, I should say that facing our own death may be the most difficult thing; knowing that all can be coming to an end. Everything we did, do, felt or feel. Western and Eastern religions deal with this topic differently but the important point here is to find a way tat is meaningful to you and follow it. That it will be what gives meaning to your existence. For me personally, the key is to have a sense of direction, a mission, knowing that your life is here to accomplish something. That gives a 'meaning' for everything else.

Q: What happens when we reach a point and we can't progress anymore?

A: The point when we "can't" progress anymore does not exit. I will explain. Sometimes we can get to a point where our technique doesn't seem to improve but that doesn't mean that we can't improve. The body has its limitations and when that occurs – depending of the level of the practitioner – we need to find ways to break that wall. The answer may be to change the way we train or change the way we do karate. It may be a "break through" in your life as karateka. You have to look into yourself and try to find the reason why things are not going and evolving in the same way and direction than before. It is about introspection. Then it comes the mental aspect of it...if you endure and keep training regardless of what you think...your are getting better at a different level. Special training like "gasshuku" is designed to train the

mind through exhausting physical sessions. The body is a tool for reaching a higher mental level.

Q: Sensei, any final words of advice?

A: Do your best, always. Only when you do your best you don't have to worry about future insecurities about who you are. You will be in peace with yourself no matter what the overcome may be. Like a Samurai...do your best in the fight...to live or die is not relevant...since you already have reached the goal of a full personal accomplishment by giving your best.

Masahiko Tanaka

THE LEGEND

THIS MAN TOOK THE WORLD OF KARATE WITH HIS DYNAMIC AND POWERFUL TECHNIQUES. EXTRAORDINARILY FAST AND AGILE, TANAKA SENSEI IS ONE OF THE MOST IMPRESSIVE AND DEMANDING INSTRUCTORS UNDER WHICH ANY KARATE PRACTITIONER CAN TRAIN. FORMED AT THE FAMOUS HORNET'S NEST AT THE KENSHUSEI IN THE JKA HEADQUARTERS, MASAHIKO TANAKA BECAME A LEGEND TO ALL HIS CONTEMPORARIES WITH HIS UNIQUE AND CHARISMATIC PERSONALITY, PERFECTLY CONTROLLED POWER AND FLUID FLEXIBILITY OF MOVEMENT. WHEN ENTERED IN COMPETITION, HE WON EVERY POSSIBLE TITLE. WHEN COACHING THE JAPAN NATIONAL TEAM, HE DID THE SAME. HIS ACT AND WORDS ARE A TRUE INSPIRATION, AND HE IS A LIVING EXAMPLE OF KARATE PHILOSOPHY. "THERE ARE TWO ASPECTS TO KARATE TRAINING," HE SAYS. "THE TECHNIQUE OF THE BODY AND THE WAY OF THE MIND. THE MENTAL TRAINING CENTERS ON THE DEVELOPMENT OF ZANCHIN AND THE ABILITY TO CONCENTRATE FULLY ON THE OPPONENT, WHICH [BOTH COMBINE TO] POINT YOUR CONSCIOUSNESS TOWARDS THE HARA." WORDS OF WISDOM FROM ONE OF THE BEST KARATE MASTERS IN THE WORLD.

Q: Sensei, tell us about your youth.

A: I have always been a loner. My family was constantly moving, and I didn't have any opportunity to make friends and stay with them for a long period of time. I would pack my knapsack and go hiking into the mountains alone. I believe this influenced me greatly. I chose rugby at my

school because it seemed like it was the toughest activity, and I wanted to prove that I was a man. This experience was all happiness for me. If I wasn't bleeding or scraped, I would feel unhappy with myself, but I did well. In fact, I can say that all my karate power comes from those sprints during my rugby years because everything was ankles, knees and hips. Rugby helped to mold my legs in those early years.

Q: What university did you attend?

A: I went to Nihon University. I studied economics in the footsteps of my father who died when I was 19. That was a very important turning point in my life because everything changed [at that point]. I decided to switch courses. Not only did I begin to study veterinary medicine, but I also studied to become an expert in forestry. I dreamt about having a farm in South America.

Q: How did you got involved in karate?

A: A friend of mine at the university took me to a karate dojo. Yaguchi Sensei was the teacher there. I joined, but I never told my mother that I did. I didn't want her to worry about me learning how to fight! Later on, someone saw me fight and invited me to participate in the Kanto Area Championship. My team took first place.

Q: When you graduated, why didn't you pursue your dream of going to South America?

A: Well, karate was really important to me already. It was my life. I was a san-dan at the time, and I really wanted to take the courses for kenshusei [student instructor] at the JKA Headquarters. They refused my request because there weren't enough funds to support a student instructor at the time. However, if I could support myself, they said that I would be allowed to enter the course. Of course, I started to look for any kind of job that would allow me to pay my bills, and it didn't matter to me what kind of work it was. I was everything from a river man to a real estate agent. For a year I transported logs along canals. When doing this, you have to actually ride the logs, so I thought of it as a training for my legs. Gradually, as my balance improved, I fell into the water less and less.

Q: Did the JKA send you abroad?

A: Yes, I was sent to Denmark in 1975 for approximately a year, but I kept training so I could compete in the World Karate Championships that were held that year in Los Angeles, California. I used some of the Danish karateka to prepare myself for that tournament, and I found out later on that they weren't enjoying the training with me at all. It turns out that they thought I was very hard with them and with myself, but that was the only way I knew how to get better ... training as hard as I can.

Q: What happened in the Championship?

A: I won the world title. In the final, I had to face Oishi Takeshi Sensei, and he was one of the best in the world. His nickname was "Mr. Lightning" because he was so fast, and he was the kumite champion the previous four years. To be honest, the rest of the fighters were also very strong and dangerous. There were never any easy competitors ... unless someone made an error. One fighter was always very hard to beat, at least for me. His name was Norihiko Iida. In fact, I lost seven times to him in competition matches. Only once, the eighth time, could I beat him.

Q: When you weren't fighting Japanese opponents, what kind of approach did you use?

A: I did have a favorite strategy when facing foreign opponents. Despite their size and strength, most of them had a weakness in their initial speed and in between their waza. I would wait for such an opening to occur so I could score. I was very successful at it.

Q: You came out of competition retirement in 1986 and entered the 29th JKA Championship. Why?

A: It was a good challenge for me. I was 45 years old, and I knew I presented a challenge to all the young fighters. It was a tough challenge for me, too! I was defeated in the quarterfinals. I was a little disappointed, but I wanted to prove myself that I could contest the young champions in competition ... not just in the dojo. I did this for my own satisfaction. I love to fight and that urge was with me for some time. Now that I have it out of my system, I don't get upset about the outcome of a fight. The ultimate aim of karate lies not in victory or defeat.

Q: What does karate represent to you?

A: Karate is an art, and art is — more than anything — an expression. When you see a kata performed well, you realize that immediately. As artists, we all strive for perfection. In our case, we should strive for perfection in technique, even though we will never achieve it. A lot of high-ranking instructors have expressed their concerns about how many karate dojo around the world have become competition minded. Yes, it is true that I have competed many times, but competition was always down on the list of my priorities when it came to the true values of karate.

Karate is a martial art and a way of life, not only a physical activity that has a sportive side to it. Master Funakoshi said karate should be used as a tool to develop and perfect one's character ... both physically and mentally. When we talk about karate as a way of life, we open the possibility of many interpretations. It is interesting that, regardless of how people understand it, there are some fundamental truths to it that don't change. Through many years of intense training under our teachers, we learn the basics of both the technical and spiritual side of the art. We follow our sensei, and by watching and listening to him, we reach a high level of skill and understanding. So, in some sort of way, we are following the way of life that has been handed down through the years. Now it is up to us to find our own way or put it together in a personal format that applies to our life. The quest is now to make it our own. It is important to respect and give credit to the teachers, because without them, our spiritual growth probably would never come about. And without their guidance in training, we wouldn't be who we are today.

Q: Sensei, why is it so important to keep our heels flat on the ground when we do techniques like gyaku-tsuki but not when we spar?

A: This is very simple question to answer. In the JKA, we worked hard to develop a form of karate that uses the human body in the best possible way when it comes to utilizing all muscles and joints in the body to generate power. It is a very simple concept, but it is a difficult task to achieve. Keeping the heel down when performing kihon teaches the body to use all the power from the ground and get the right feeling of the movement. We strive to keep it down while doing kata, kihon, makiwara, et cetera because it is the best way to develop the feeling for body power. Once you have the correct technique and feeling for how the body must move and absorb the impact, you can do it any way you want. By lifting the heel up when punching in combat, you get an extra few inches that can be useful in a free fight. You can also put more body torque in the action, if necessary. This is something often seen in competition, due to obvious reasons. You can't teach this to a beginner because he doesn't have the right body feel for the technique. In the past, old masters never did any kind of competition, and that is why we always see pictures of them with the back heel flat.

Q: So you generate more power with the heel down than with the heel up?

A: No. You can generate the same amount of power in both cases. But this only works when you have the right body feel, a sense of the technique and all the lines of power in your body are in perfect coordination. For instance, when punching, always keep your shoulder and chest relaxed. You should only tense these muscles at the moment of impact. The kime should be over in a split second and not stay tense after the technique has been thrown. All these elements are important to understand. Things like kime, zanchin and hara don't come without hard training and dedication. The secret is the body. There are no other secrets in karate.

Q: How would you describe "JKA Shotokan"?

A: Very simple. It's a straight down-the-line karate that places emphasis on good form, speed and kime. Is not that what any karate should be? JKA Shotokan is more a method or approach to karate than a separate style. Unfortunately, many people don't understand this.

Q: Shotokan is a very straight-line method of karate, isn't it?

A: What is the shortest distance between two points? The straight line is always the simplest path to reach your target, but I guess I understand what you are implying in your question. When you are young, the strong, straight-line approach to combat is more suitable because of the physical characteristics of the individual. Unconsciously, young people rely more on strength, so running over the opponent when you have a powerful

technique seems to be the best way. It is when your body and interpretation of the art changes — and this usually happens when you get older — that you realize other venues of dealing with a powerful attack. At a senior level, to be linear is not enough. In the fundamentals of JKA karate, we work on making the technique better. This includes punches and kicks. Every single punch and every single block and kick must be fast, powerful and precise, and they should have kime and power. These are the tools the artist must use. Considering this, it is not difficult to incorporate softer approaches to use the "tools" because the elements are already there. You may add a circular motion to the way your body moves, but when you punch, block or kick … you do it with power and determination.

Q: Do you see karate as a fighting art for self-defense?

A: I believe it is fair to say that not all karateka have confidence in their ability to fight in a real self-defense situation, but those using the "do" aspect of the art in their lives should, at least, have a total different and level-headed approach to these kinds of encounters. Foresee where the problem may arise and avoid it before it happens. Karate is not just a sport or a physical activity; it is a martial art and a way of life. A way of life is always part of us in every minute of our existence.

Q: Sensei, these days we can see many different karate organizations around the world. What is your opinion of this?

A: It is all politics and personal interest. Period. Many people want to make money with karate, even if they are not fully qualified to do it. Associations and federations are the same. For me it is more rewarding to study the art, follow your teacher and try to be the best human being you can. This is traditional Budo, and this is what I believe. If karate training teaches us anything, it teaches us that the truth is always harder to take and less attractive than we would like.

Q: Why do some practitioners modify and create different methods of training?

A: Young practitioners try to develop new methods of doing things without first mastering the old. Their foundation is not good and not strong enough to build other new things on top. I think that true traditional karate will [eventually] be lost if there aren't any instructors or students who adhere to the traditional methods and values of karate and Budo. Unfortunately, students want to learn everything fast; therefore, instructors have to teach more than the student can chew, because otherwise he will leave the school and then the instructor will have financial problems. The traditional training method of doing a high number of repetitions for kihon techniques is boring for the new generations. They don't want to repeat the same punch or kick 1,000 times. You can't treat the new students the way we were taught in the past. Yes, it is true that there are more scientific approaches to training, but what happens to the spirit of karate? Punching 1,000 times trains the spirit — not only technique. I know it is boring, but the spirit needs this kind of training. If you don't like training like this, you'll be missing an important part of who you are because you'll never understand the other side of yourself. Karate must be followed the way it is, and you cannot try to change it. When you get into your car to go to work, you follow the street, right? You don't create new streets or simply go ahead because you don't like curves! You follow the streets. That's the way karate is and the way it should be practiced.

Q: Do you recommend special training sessions like gasshuku and kangeiko?

A: I do. Your techniques get better and your spirit gets stronger. The JKA instructor's course is a constant special training program. You need to push your body to the limit and then use the spirit to reach further. If you don't put yourself at your very limit, how do you know how far can you go? How do you know how strong you are and how far your spirit will take you?

Q: Sensei, one of your special techniques is the use of the lead leg to score on your opponent's attack. How did you develop this?

A: This is not my tokui waza, but I did use it in competition very much. It is basically an interception movement, and it is performed with the lead leg. Most of the time people use a roundhouse kick in this capacity, and it is called saya mae mawashi geri. The idea is to stop the opponent in his tracks. It is a very tricky movement because you have to coordinate the timing of the opponent's entry with your own action. You don't retreat with your back foot. You bring your lead leg toward you and snap the kick. To generate power, you need a strong ankle on your supporting leg and the ability to snap your hip out so you can put all of your power behind the kick. Don't forget. Your opponent is charging you, and he is bringing force and momentum behind him.

Q: Are modern practitioners focusing too much on the martial aspect of karate and forgetting the element of art?

A: It is possible that this is happening. Karate was created and developed as a self-defense method. Funakoshi Sensei saw the flaws in trying to keep a warrior mentality in times of peace and developed a new approach to the art. Fighting has always been and always will be an important part of karate because that is where the true spirit of Budo is absorbed. Therefore, karate-do is an art because it allows us to reach higher levels of existence as human beings. It is also an art because the students need to learn the principles, work hard and develop their own way of expressing karate through their bodies. Art is not something that you develop by simply copying others. I can copy a Picasso's painting, but it doesn't make me an artist. To be an artist, and every karateka should be one, we need to learn how to express — in our own words — what we have learnt from our teacher. If the art is to survive, this is the only way.

Q: Injuries are part of the game if a practitioner trains hard. What are your thoughts on that?

A: Well, injuries are a risk for anyone doing any kind of physical activity. Karate, because it involves fighting between two or more individuals, can be dangerous because of a lack of control or technical ability [someone may have]. What is interesting to me is that most of the injuries that long-time practitioners suffer result from the wrong technique — not from fighting! If you don't understand how to use and relax your body properly, you may experience problems in your joints and lower back when you get older. You must learn not only how to make karate natural to you but also how to strengthen your body without stressing it more than necessary. Wrong technique brings a lot of injuries.

Q: Does modern society influence the way new generation of practitioners look at the art?

A: Definitely. In modern society, things are obtained instantly. Everything is about now. Fast food, fast cars, e-mail, et cetera. This is good because it allows us to do things in less time and with less effort, but karate-do has nothing to do with this. In fact, for a complete understanding of what karate implies as an art of Budo, we need to look in the opposite direction. Funakoshi Sensei clearly explained that the goal of karate is perfection of character. Therefore, we have to look at it as a lifetime training and philosophy that involves the body, the mind and also the spirit. In life, the goals that are worth keeping are the ones that take time and effort to achieve. Those things are not achieved quickly and require sincere dedication and good character.

Q: What final advice would you like to give to the practitioners?

A: They should all think about this. If you are training in karate as a simple physical activity, you will derive less benefit as you get older. And there is a very simple test that you can do to determine this. If you are getting less [benefit], then you are not following the right way of karate. This is not the way of the art. Karate training is a mirror of life, and the way you live your life must go hand in hand with the way your train. Your mind must grow as your muscles when you are young and strong. Don't neglect one side of your training because you are too busy trying to improve the other. No matter who you are, what your skill level is or how much you progress, you'll realize, generally after 40, that regardless of how many times you train and repeat the movements, the techniques won't improve. They will get slower as you grow older, and they will get weaker. Are you ready to put all the time, effort, sweat and blood during your young years only to find out that everything you have worked for is gradually becoming less effective? Well, remember that balance is the key. And by balancing both side of the coin [physical and spiritual], you'll find the answer.

Katsuhiro Tsuyama

CHANGING LIVES

SENSEI TSUYAMA IS SYNONYMOUS WITH THE ART OF KARATE. ONE OF THE LEADING MEN IN THE "JAPAN KARATE-DO FEDERATION", HE HAS A RICH AND PROUD HERITAGE SPANNING OVER DECADES OF DEDICATED AND DISCIPLINED TRAINING. AS IMPRESSIVE AS HIS KARATE CREDENTIALS ARE, HOWEVER, WHAT SETS SENSEI TSUYAMA APART IS HIS UNCANNY ABILITY TO RELATE TO AND UNDERSTAND PEOPLE FROM ALL RACES, CULTURES AND BACKGROUNDS. HE BECAME ONE OF THE MOST SUCCESSFUL TRAINERS AND COACHES IN THE HISTORY OF SPORT KARATE, AND HE HAS COACHED AND TRAINED A LONG LIST OF INTERNATIONAL CHAMPIONS. FOR HIM, SPIRIT AND HEART ARE THE MOST IMPORTANT ATTRIBUTES IN KARATE TRAINING; "IN ORDER TO BE THE BEST," SENSEI TSUYAMA SAYS FIRMLY, "YOU MUST HAVE THE WARRIOR'S SPIRIT AND THE WARRIOR'S HEART."

Q: Sensei Tsuyama, you are highly regarded teacher and coach in the world of Karate, is Shotokan your main style?

A: Yes, Shotokan is my main style and Karate is the art I dedicated my life to.

Q: How do you remember yourself in the early days of your training?

A: Well, as a youngster you always try to show and do your best physically. The mental and spiritual aspect is not really inside of you yet but the hard Budo training will eventually make you realize that there is more to Karate than simply punching and kicking and winning competitions. I

think tat my training was very natural from the very beginning. I knew what I was attracted to Karate and also what to expect of its training... obviously as a young man. My understanding of Karate evolved as I grew as human being and as my Karate matured too I saw other important elements that were not there when I started.

Training was very rigid and very hard. A lot of repetitions!

Q: Sensei you travel a lot around the world, what is the most important lesson that you have learn from teaching all over the globe?

A: I learned a lot from meeting people from all over the world and this developed my Karate style.

It made me realize that looking at the big picture not matter how big we think we are...we are very small. This changed my attitude and made me continue training and learn further from every single person I meet. People from different countries have different cultural backgrounds, different characters and different languages that affect how we see things but deep down we are all human. Karate makes no distinction between people and levels everybody up!

Q: How good is the repetition training in the karateka's development?

A: I think that repetition training is the best way to make the body understand the proper way of delivering a technique. I'd like to differentiate between someone tat is young and someone that is in his 50s or 60s. When you are young you need to do hundreds of repetitions in each training session. Repeating a 'gyaku tsuki' twenty times in a class simply is not going to cut it in the early phases of training. You need to do 200, 300 or

1,000 reverse punches per training session. The same applies for the other basic punching techniques and the kicks. Don't waste you time with fancy things hat won't contribute to your progress in the later years of your Karate training.

Q: How that changes when you get older?

A: When you get older I assume that you already have a solid technique and therefore doing 1,000 repetitions of the same technique in a training session doesn't have the same effect. Let me explain an important point; when you do 1,000 punches the idea is to force the body to learn the 'right way' without intellectualize the physical action. But the time you punch your 500 punch the body is naturally forced to save energy by itself and use the right mechanism to make the technique correct. By keep doing this kind of training the body leans by itself. That is the reason why you should do it when you are young and the joint can take that type of training. Once you know how to use the body properly… it is about quality and not necessarily quantity in the amount of repetitions.

Q: Do you think participate in sport competitions is important?

A: Sport competition is a very important aspect of the development of every karateka. I understand that some people may think it is not, but today's world is different and the sportive aspect 'opens' the doors for a deeper understanding of other relevant values that are necessary in our society. The old times were about war and fighting for your life. Nowadays we can practice sport kumite and develop our skill in combat and at the same time to have a good sportive experience that will make us grow as human beings and karateka. It is important though that winning is not the reason why we do it. Winning is important of course but we should look at competition as a whole experience. Sport competition kumite is different than dojo kumite for many reasons.

Q: Would you mind to elaborate?

A: When you spar in the dojo you know your opponents, you pretty much know their timing, their favorite techniques, their personalities, etc…but when you go to a competition and especially a national or inter-

Shotokan Legends

national competition, you don't know the guy that your are going to fight. He is there with the same determination and passion to win that you have. He is not going to be 'nice' and take the win home. You don't have 5 or 6 minutes to figure out his timing, rhythm, technical tempo, etc…In a matter of 30 seconds or less you have to know 'who he is' and how you are going to defeat him. Therefore, sport competition allows you to develop the ability to decipher and read an opponent in a very short time. This is something that you simply don't get by sparring in the dojo. Here I am not talking about what kind of rules are being used in that competition. That's irrelevant now.

Q: Does the rules affect how to approach a match?

A: Of course. If you are in a "Shobu Ippon" match is different that if it is a "Sanbon". Rules kind of determine how you are going to approach the match but this doesn't change the aspects I talked before. You still don't know your opponent, you don't know how he is going to play his cards and what kind of strategy he has prepared to deal with you. Your game plan is partially dictated by the rules. It is important to know how to use the rules for your own advantage as a competitor.

Q: Do you feel that you still have more to learn?

A: Definitely. I look at Karate as an extension of life. In life you don't stop growing and learning new things. I believe that we always have something new to learn – I don't understand those who claim otherwise. I like to read new books and watch videos whenever I can to absorb more information. That helps me to improve my technical level and better understand how the different aspects and elements of the art and sport work together. I think it is very important to compete as much as possible because the art of Karate is evolving and there is always a new twist for an old technique. Competing gives you a sparring edge that is impossible to have otherwise.

Q: Sensei, you are very strict about rank and titles in Martial Arts and specifically Karate. Why it bothers you when people claim a rank that doesn't match with their knowledge and skill?

A: They are a fraud for the rest of the people who really trained and dedicated their lives to Karate and Martial Arts. You have people who have trained very hard for decades to become who they are in Karate or any other style, then these other individuals are showing off their ranks and titles that they've got through the back door because or friendship or money. They should be embarrassed. But the one that should be embarrassed the most are those teachers whom gave that rank and title! They don't understand what Martial Arts and Karate training really means. The teachers are the ones to blame, the students, are just ignorant.

Q: How do you achieve relaxation?

A: Number one is proper breathing. You need to keep your breathing pattern under control. The timing of the breath has to be steady and consistent under any circumstances. You also need to be confident of your technical ability. No confidence, no calmness. No calmness and you'll begin to gasp for air like crazy. In order to have confidence in your technique, you need to have proper training in the fundamentals so they become automatic reflexes. Only then can you be relaxed in a match.

Q: What are the most important qualities of a successful competitor?

A: First and foremost, you have to be brave enough to expose yourself to the world. It is easy to talk about what you could do, but quite another thing to put it all on the line and step into that mat in front of everyone. You have to have a little bit of fearlessness and a lot of heart to make it through the tough moments. You have to be able to take your falls like a warrior and your wins like a champion. You have to have a well-rounded arsenal. You have to be courageous and intelligent with a sort of calmness of mind during hectic situations.

It's important to train hard, be healthy and do the right things. Mentally, it's important for your soul to choose between the spirit and the flesh. The

Shotokan Legends

flesh is immediate gratification such as having a good time. There's too much corruption in flesh. That is why the world is so dangerous. The spirit chooses wise things that are solid and stay forever. For some people, it's hard to stay on course, but as Karate practitioners we need to make sure we behave properly regardless if we win or we lose.

Q: What are the actual qualities that make a good Coach?

A: I think that you have to be very patient with everyone. You have to know how to divide the competitors that you are coaching. Some guys you can't press hard, because they are just doing it for a hobby and for fun. Other guys train to be elite competitors and they are professional Karate teachers– so these guys you can push harder. But you can't treat everyone the same. I think the methodology you use to teach is very important. You have to stress the basics and always keep going back to the basics. The simple things are very hard to teach and to learn. You have to visualize every student. You also need to be able of adapting and changing to the change of rules and training methods.

Q: So change is good?

A: People are afraid of changes but they're usually for the better. Intelligent people get used to change more quickly than others. It does upset them initially but they accept and embrace it.

Q: Do you think that the diet and nutrion plays an important part of the athlete?

A: Absolutely! I think that diet is very important, not just for a competition but for you entire life. You are what you eat. The way you eat is connected to your success. As a karateka you eat, you train, and then you rest. Everything is connected. If you train, train, train, and then afterwards go get unhealthy food and then sleep until 2 p.m. and then try to train again, you've never going to be at your full potential. You have to have the right diet. You have to mix the right amounts of protein, carbs, and fiber.

Q: What is your approach when you coach elite competitors?

A: Over the years, I have learned that you can't change people that much from how they naturally are. You can't turn a leopard into a lion. What you have to do is to take what they do best, improve on it and find their weakest points. Then you can help them find alternatives so the weak point gets stronger. I can't tell you to fight the way I want or I would because you are not me and you are not like the rest of the competitors of the team. You have your own style so I have to take your characteristics and make you better. To do that, I don't need that much time, because I am not trying to reinvent the wheel; I am just trying to improve it. To be able to fight, you need to stay within your style of doing things. I won't try to change it; I'll just make the right adjustments. I have a lot of experience in Karate competition and people know that I talk from personal knowledge – not from something that I have just heard or read about.

Q: Finally, what do you think is your role now as a teacher in Karate?

A: I have to explain clearly the principles of techniques of the art in a way that people can understand. I enjoy training competitors and teaching people. It is important to develop instructors who can pass on the knowledge correctly. I see teaching and coaching as an art within an art. You have something inside you, which you know, and your goal is to get another person to know what you know and do their best. For me this is an art.

Yutaka Yaguchi

A CUT ABOVE

Sensei Yaguchi was born on Kyushu Island during the fall of 1932. He grew up going to school in Hiroshima and later attended Nihon University in Tokyo, majoring in Marine Biology. While training karate, he participated in a number of sports, including competitive swimming. After Graduating from Collage, Yutaka Yaguchi worked for an engineering firm. After few months, he left the job and enrolled in the second class of JKA Instructor Training Program. He tested under Master Funakoshi, the founder of Shotokan Karate, for his first and second degree black belts.

Sensei Yaguchi remained in Tokyo after graduating from the Instructor Training Program and taught for the JKA. In 1965, he left Japan and traveled to the United States first visiting Los Angeles and then Denver, Colorado. In 1966, he returned to Los Angeles where he stayed for 6 years. He then moved to Denver where he still resides and has his school today.

As one of the first graduates of the JKA Instructors Training Program, he has played an important role in the growth of karate in America and the internationalization of the Shotokan style around the world.

Shotokan Legends

Q: When and how you decided to visit the U.S. for teaching?

A: I was requested by Nakayama Sensei to come to the U.S. to teach so I didn't have much to say. I was a young 5th Dan at the time and when Nakayama Sensei asked me, I accepted, packed my bags and move to America.

Q: How it was your first impression of the U.S.?

A: In the beginning I had my doubts but Nakayama Sensei told me to express myself honestly. Master Nishiyama and Master Okazaki were already here in the U.S. so to some extent that made things a little easier since people knew a little bit about the art of karate. They had already opened the doors for a young generation and I was pleased to see that in the U.S. people already knew about Martial Arts and the true spirit of Budo.

Q: You have a very special relationship with Sensei Okazaki and Sensei Kanazawa, what can you tell us about it?

A: Yes, both Okazaki Sensei and Kanazawa Sensei have been a very important part of who I am today as karate-ka. They always were there when I did 'hit a wall' or got frustrated because of something. They went to those phases before so they knew what it was going on inside of my mind. They knew how to let me struggle and when it was the right moment to give me the tools to get out of that frustration. They never gave me the solution to my problems directly but pointed me in the right direction to find the solution by myself. I have found this approach extremely valuable in life because when you are teaching your students, the truth is...there is a limited amount of things that can be taught, but when you teach them to find the answers by themselves is when you see them growing on their own. And that is what a good teacher does with his students.

Q: When did you meet for the first time Nakayama Sensei?

A: It was around 1951 when I was in College. He was my main instructor but Okazaki Sensei and Sigura Sensei also taught me when Nakayama Sensei was not around.

Q: Did you meet Funakoshi Gichin?

A: Yes, he was alive when I started but I only saw him in testing and special events.

Q: How would you describe Sensei Nakayama's karate?

A: He was a short person, so he based his own karate in developing strong blocks to protect himself. But he never thought of a block as a simple defense. For him, a block was an attack, and aggressive action in mind. A block was not simply a block for him. There are offensive element in all blocking techniques and those he always emphasized. He had a very special ability to know his own body and to work on small details to improve his technique. I think this ability made him one of the best teachers in the world because he could spot any mistake in the student's form or technique in order to correct them.

Q: Do you see the practice of karate as a sport?

A: Karate involves more than simply sport. Therefore it is important to fully understand the meaning of every part which constitutes the complete art. Kata is in many ways a repository of old masters experiences and knowledge. They formatted those techniques and developed the katas we do today because of many reasons. Kata is not only self-defense. There are many other aspects intrinsic to its practice. To begin with, kata teaches body mechanics in sequences. Body mechanics are the final level of mastery when it comes to free sparring or kumite. The ability to use your body in perfect coordination and at will is the sign of a master. Well, kata training develops this important aspect. There are many elements inside of the principle of proper body mechanics and all of them can be found in kata. The problem is many people don't see this and they think kata is just a group of techniques put together by old karate-ka. But when you know how to look at the different segments or sections of any kata, you'll see that the true value in developing your body is in there. Different sections develop different karate principles that are the key to master the are of karate-do.

Q: What is that a karate-ka should never forget?

A: It is important to always keep the 'beginner's mind' because it reminds us that nobody knows it all. For instance, when I was young there were times when I felt very confident of my skills and knowledge and I thought " I was getting there." Well, ten or fifteen years later, you look

back and realize that you still had a lot to learn! So it is important for any martial arts practitioner to be sure that the knowledge they have at any given moment is correct and solid but don't allow their heads to get big because by doing it they will be closing the doors of knowledge and their improvement will be none.

Q: Do you see any down falls in the current approach of karate as sport?

A: There is nothing wrong with training the sport aspect of karate and becoming a champion. This is good because it pushes the practitioners to train more and harder in order to achieve their goals. Sport is good…it is not a bad thing. The problem arises when the practitioner only see karate as a sport; when winning or losing is the only thing it matters; when his or her training is based only in winning that tournament. Then, the practitioner's mind is focused in the wrong reason to practice karate. We need to learn how to put in the right perspective the sport aspect of karate without forgetting the true values of the art. For instance, respect is one of the most important lesson in Budo. When you beat you opponent in competition, you should show respect. How you do that? Well, go back to the line after scoring and stand there in 'yoi.' Show respect to your opponent by not jumping and screaming around the mat. If you lose, show respect by accepting the defeated as a warrior. Don't get upset, don't complain or protest to the referee – who maybe even made a mistake in calling a point – and show proper etiquette and Budo manners. This behavior is permissible in football, tennis or other sports but not in karate-do. Basic and important things like these are there to reminds us that karate can be used as a sport but at the end we should not forget that the foundation of karate is Budo and Budo implies etiquette and proper manners. Happiness in life doesn't come from external things. In karate, the mastery of the art doesn't come form winning or losing tournaments.

Q: So what do you think are the advantages of participating in karate tournaments?

A: Well, to begin with competition always brings pressure and it is under pressure the human beings bring the best we have. In other sports we see how athletes run faster and they are stronger. Competition will keep bringing the athletic level up for years to come and that is good. But once again...what an Olympic medallist does after retires? Karate is for life...sport just for a few years.

Q: Sensei, we are witnessing these days an alteration and modification of some of the movements in kata to better fit the kata competition "requirements." What is your opinion about modify or alter the timing of kata movements to 'look' more impressive in front of the judges?

A: Karate kata are not gymnastics. There is no need to alter the tempo or rhythm of the kata to impress judges. Every movement has its speed, timing and cadence so altering those to win a competition it means that instead of winning you should lose! What is happening now, is many competitors slow down movements to make their stances and forms visible for a longer period of time in front of the judges but this is not to perform the kata correct. If I slow down the movement for judges be able of 'see' my stances then I am performing the kata wrong. If the movement is fast, then the stance should be perfect within this short period of time... and judges should be trained to see that.

Q: What Sensei Nakayama represented to the world of karate?

A: He was a very special person. He knew where karate was and where he wanted to take the art. He listened to everybody and took into consideration all ideas and points of view but at the same time he knew what it was best for the art of karate. I learn many things from him and how to work on my patience was one of them. He taught me how not to get excited about things and be patient so I could see what is the best way to

Shotokan Legends

deal with problems and situations. In many ways, when I look myself into a mirror I see things of Nakayama Sensei in me. Sometimes I act or behave in a certain way and then I remember how Nakayama Sensei used to behave and they are similar. In a way, I am happy that some of the lessons he taught me are still with me.

Q: You always stress the importance of kihon, how would you recommend approaching the training of the basics?

A: Let's start saying that running the dojo up and down doing basic techniques it is not necessarily training kihon. It seems so but it may not. The right way of practicing kihon is to constantly test and be aware of the body in every single movement; Is that leg correct? Are the hips moving properly? is my body vertical

in the technique?, etc... We need to maintain a constant examination of all the technical points when doing the basics. Just because you punch 1,000 times it doesn't mean you are doing it right. Just because you do one more punch, it doesn't mean that punch is better than the one before....unless you do something to make it better. Repetition doesn't bring technical perfection. Only correct repetition does it. It has to be focused in body and spirit.

Q: What is the quality you consider to be the most important in a karate-ka?

A: I would recommend to develop patience. I did have very little when I was young and throughout the years I was taught by my teachers and by life itself, that patience is an important tool for anything you do. Good things don't come overnight. They take time, and even if you think now it is the right time for something...it may not be. Patience is not only important for karate but for any endeavor in life. Parents need patience with their kids, teachers with their students, brother with sisters and vice versa, etc...

Q: How we should adapt our training when we get older and develop injuries that prevent us from doing certain things?

A: Karate is karate. Kihon is kihon; kata is kata and kumite is kumite. What I mean by this is that you don't do a different gyaku-tsuki or mae-geri when you are 20 years old than when you are 50. The reverse punch is the reverse punch and the front kick is the front kick. You simply keep doing it. Now, because of age, we need to adapt the training program to our specifics and not think we can train with the same intensity when we are 60 years old than when we were in our 20s. Also we need to listen to our body and work around the injuries we may have. There is no need to keep doing things that will make our body injuries worse. We should learn how to work around these things.

Q: What you think is the most important aspect of training when you reach the 50s or 60s?

A: Assuming you already have a good technique...which that's the way it supposed to be, you should focus on your physical conditioning. A healthy body is always ready to train. I believe stretching is good, muscle conditioning too, proper limberness and correct breathing are also important.

Q: Any final word, Sensei?

A: Yes, I'd like to say that karate is a long term activity. We are here because all the efforts of Funakoshi and Nakayama Sensei and we should make sure our conduct and manners are the proper ones to preserve the legacy and teachings of these two great masters. They were humble individuals. Humbleness is not a weakness but s strength we all should nurture inside us. Karate is for the development of the human being.

Mikio Yahara

THE UNCONQUERABLE SPIRIT

Yahara Sensei was born on April 4, 1947, in the Ehime prefecture. After graduating from Kokushikan University, he became Kenshusei, or junior instructor, in the Japan Karate Association. He rampaged through the world, monopolizing the high rankings in many tournaments, establishing legendary fame. Known for his leopard-like carriage, beautiful jumping techniques and adaptations, his unique karate style fascinated karateka all over the world.

In April 2000, to further develop his idea of karate, Yahara Sensei established the Karatenomichi World Federation, and the concept behind the Federation was simple: The essence of karate is technical, and that is exactly where karate starts. For example, the nature of his karate entails several key elements, including the necessity to strive persistently [toward goals] despite the general current trend towards sportive aspects in the karate world; to attain ippon technique or efficiency in the execution of the killing blow concept, and to stake one's life on the offensive and defensive actions inside a split second. Yahara Sensei's karate techniques, having been formed during countless fighting scenes, make use of the maximum possibilities of human muscles and the maximum possible movement of the joints. The point is to focus all the potential energy of the body into the fists or feet during the briefest of moments. The theory behind these techniques is — without a doubt — an eye opener, even to karateka who have performed many years of arduous practice.

Shotokan Legends

Q: The name of your organization is the "Karatenomichi World Federation". Is there any difference between karatenomichi and shotokan? And, do you teach shotokan karate or is it more like another style of karate?

A: Shotokan was the original style. The simple thing I teach is that karate is changing, and it is possible that it could disappear. I know karate as a martial art, but now it seems [more] like dancing. I would like to return to the original karate ... to its sources. Budo karate, as far as I am concerned, is a situation in which I may finish my opponent definitively by one killing blow. My work basically consists in forming ways and methods to increase my technical level to the perfection I require and that is one blow should be enough to cause an opponent's defeat.

Q: How did you develop the Karatenomichi World Federation as an organization?

A: First of all, it's a true Budo karate that has very effective techniques, and the purpose of the organization is to teach people the kumite methods that I referred to earlier. I want to teach my students so well that they are capable of winning any competition, and then I want them to travel worldwide. I also want people to know and learn my techniques and understand my aim for perfection. Sports karate is very popular now and many people consider karate a game. These people usually forget about karate immediately after competition. If necessary, I would like my students to be able to use karate in real life, but I don't want them to treat it like it was strictly a game.

Q: Sensei, does competition help competitors to understand the essence of Budo?

A: I am against the type of competition that promotes the development of game karate. I frequently have debates and conversations with representatives of other organizations to defend my opinion about karate, and it is possible that my actions remind them of true karate.

Q: What is your perception of the art?

A: Many people don't understand my karate. You have to be spiritually strong because karate must be spiritually strong, too. Then the correct technique will grow from it. I have seen some people who think they are strong, but the truth is they are bigheaded. If you ask me — even after many years of training — I will tell you that I still don't know karate. I look for perfection in what I do, but I still have a long road ahead. Technique comes to some students quickly and to others slowly. But if they keep training hard and follow the principle of nichi nichi no keko (train harder over and over again), they will be alright.

Q: You were highly ranked in many tournaments and you were also the world and JKA champion many times. What victory do you remember most?

A: Certainly, I, as well as many other people, remember those tournaments. The most important moments that remain in my memory are those times in which I realized that my opponent wasn't able to control the situation and his skill wasn't as perfect as mine. Everyone applauded when I used the techniques that amazed my opponent and made him nonplused. Perhaps, these moments are the ones that I remember most of all.

Q: Is physical or spiritual victory more important for you? And did you ever feel moral satisfaction in spite of defeat?

A: Is it possible to be happy after suffering a defeat? When a strong person loses, he doesn't feel any satisfaction, and he will never find both spiritual and psychological victory. However, victory and spiritual satisfaction could come later, because your defeat stimulates new feats. You try to improve your skill, and as a result, you win. In this case, you will understand that the victory is the result of your last defeat.

Q: The chairman of the Karatenomichi World Federation is internationally renowned fashion designer Yohji Yamamoto. Could you please tell us why this person came into the world of karate?

A: Actually, it is not as difficult to answer your question as you would expect. I think that there are two reasons. The first reason is psychological. The world of Mr. Yohji Yahamoto is a magnificent world with a brilliant atmosphere and amazing surroundings. Of course, this atmosphere dims the enthusiasm. Photographers, cameras, beautiful people and clothes have a very strong influence on his emotional condition because he is part of this world. Karate allows him to restrain himself and allows him to follow the spiritual way, which is defined by conscience. Karate is the deterrent that gives him a chance to remain himself. The second reason is physical. Mr. Yamamoto's world creates a sedentary way of life, and it does not have a good effect on his health. Weak muscles are not good for man. Due to his karate practice, he now is in good physical condition. I think that Mr. Yamamoto has the Budo consciousness that only a true samurai could have. Mr. Yamamoto has practiced karate with me for about 10 years, and he is very zealous while training. He came into shotokan due to our friendship, and we have been friends more than 10 years.

Q: There are many books about Zen Buddhism and Budo philosophy. Is there any connection between karate and Zen?

A: Recently, many people have turned to Zen, and there are many books about this; however, it is a fake. Why? Of course, Zen could be indicated in a fight. But what is the sense of Zen? If two opponents had a knife, it would be too easy if they just killed each other. In this case, it would be an ordinary murder. Both of the opponents would die, and they would be absolutely tranquil, because there is no difference for each opponent. But there is a significant problem. Each adversary keeps wondering what will occur in case of a mistake? Maybe someone will be wounded. The body becomes enslaved and the mind just thinks about fear. This fear disturbs the use of your actual power. Kumite teaches us to stay tranquil. If you follow the Zen way, you will have the emptiness in your mind while doing kumite. Fear and thought disappear from your mind, and you don't feel the fear. In this moment, you are able to demonstrate your true power ...

the power that is available only to you. No emotions, no thoughts about past and future. This is Zen. That is why people who write books about Zen Buddhism in the martial arts without experiencing serious fighting or mortal combat are liars.

Q: What is the philosophy of karate?

A: Karate has no philosophy. Some people think that the tradition of karate came from Buddhism and karate has a connection with the absolute, space and universe, but I don't believe in that. My philosophy is to knock my opponent out with one technique. One finishing blow!

Q: Do you have any time for rest?

A: Karate is the rest in my life. You know I am very busy, because I have my own business, as well as karate. [This arrangement] keeps my mind busy but often creates tension because I always have to think about some deals. Of course, this can have a negative influence on my sleep and mind. While training, my body feels tremendous stress, but this enables me to step closer to the art of karate. My body relaxes after training, and I can sleep. By falling asleep after a grueling training session, I am collecting and re-charging my power for a new day ... to make it as useful as possible.

Q: Besides karate, what do you like?

A: I like music very much. I like Tchaikovsky. I am very tired after training, and music helps me to relax. I think that music is even necessary for me. I listen to music when I am resting and when I am driving.

Q: I understand that you like to drive fast and once experienced a terrible accident.

A: Yes, I like speed very much. I even do some road events. Some time ago I was in an unbelievable road event. I was driving a Porsche, which is my favorite car, and my speedometer indicated that I was going 250 kilometers per hour. The speed limit of my car was 280 kilometers per hour, and I tried to reach that speed. The car in front of me wasn't going that fast, so I went around him. While I was in the passing lane, I noticed another car coming toward me at about 100 kilometers per hour. If there had been a head-on collision, it would have been a terrible accident.

Thankfully, and probably due my reactions as a skilled karateka, I avoided the oncoming car by swerving toward the curb. I made this decision instantaneously; otherwise, we would have slammed into each other with a combined speed of 350 kilometers per hour! I remember how my car turned over, and I remember all my movements and actions at this time. At the time, it all seemed like slow motion. The only thing I thought to protect was my head. I did everything to receive as little damage as possible. The car was so destroyed that it could not be restored. Fortunately, I was OK.

Q: Sensei, do you like to read in your free time?

A: Yes, I like to read very much. Usually I read books about the samurai and how they bravely passed away as a result of hara-kiri (ritual suicide). It is very important for me, and I will tell you about this without any embellishment. Three of my friends have died in such a way and the last one occurred in December 2003. The most courageous way to die from hara-kiri is the crisscross. [Using a sword], you go from left to right and then bottom to top. This gives you the hieroglyph "ju," and that means 10. Maybe you know the famous Japanese writer Yukio Mishima; perhaps you even read his books. He was my student. We trained together for one and half a years. He was much older than me. When he was 45, I was 24. One week before his passing we were training together. After training, we were in the traditional Japanese bath or furo. His behavior was normal, he laughed and nobody — even I — suspected that he was going to leave this life. Something like this is a very important decision, and I am sure that one week prior to his death he certainly knew that he would do it. I very much respect him for it, and I believe that he was a really great person. It's even documented how it happened. It began when he entered the commander's office at the Japan Defense Agency. And let me state right now. No one, including those who suspected something might be wrong, had time to stop him. He and his friend, Masakatsu Morita, went into the room and locked the door. He was with a friend because the code of the samurai requires that a friend, colleague or student — someone he trusts — chop the head off after the suicide. Having opened his stomach with his blade, he felt an inhuman pain. In the meantime, Morita held a sword in

his hands, and his hands shivered because of excitement or inexperience. Mishima became angry and started to shout at him, "Let's do it — faster!" After that, he [Morita] struck, but he missed and split part of Mishima's skull. Mishima then screamed even more loudly, "You are fool! What are you waiting for? Let's do it quickly!" The second impact of the sword of Morita fell onto Mishima's shoulder. Only after the third attempt had he completed the task [beheaded him]. Subsequently, the police rushed into the office. Please trust me. These events are true and fixed in the police report. I do not want to scare you; I just want to say that this person I believe had a strong spirit.

Q: Why did Mr. Yukio Mishima commit suicide?

A: The purpose was rather great. By then he was already a well-known writer, and he knew that people would speak widely and frequently about his death. Shortly before his death, Mishima made a political declaration from a balcony of the same building. By his death, he wanted to draw the public's attention to new Japanese orders and laws. He was very much against them, and he wanted people to protest these. Certainly, he achieved this purpose.

Q: Do you practice any other kind of Budo except karate?

A: Yes, I practice iaido. I like the spirit of this martial art. One single sword blow results in the death of the opponent.

Q: What is love for you?

A: I do not know how to answer, and this is actually a very difficult question. If I were to say something, I'd say that love is the impossibility of

personal happiness in loneliness. What I mean is that it would be necessary to give everything [you have] completely up and make sure that your sweetheart has everything and is happy [to really experience love]. And, of course, you'd have to be happy with this result. In addition to that, you must be ready for everything, even death. I'm not saying that you should look for such things, but you should be ready for anything that life may send your way.

Q: You are a strong advocate for makiwara training. Why?

A: The makiwara is not only a tool to be used for conditioning, but when used correctly, it makes the body strong, especially the hips and hara areas. Makiwara training brings control to the technique. Traditional karate training places great emphasis upon the mind, and makiwara training helps this, because in many ways, it is the basis of the art.

Q: Do you recommend cross-training in different arts?

A: In the beginning, it is good for a student to concentrate on a few things that he can develop strongly. I don't like to give students too many things to concentrate on. Not aikido one day, the next karate, judo and then something else! That is not good. Unfortunately, some students think this is the correct way because they want too much too soon, and there is nothing the instructor can do about it. Their minds are diffused over too many ideas. That's why it is very important to train the mind of the student in the right direction. If the student has "no mind" in training, he will get into these kinds of situations and will make incorrect decisions. Hard, physical training helps to develop the right mind for karate. And technique isn't the only important thing; you must also make good, true karate.

Q: What is missing in some forms of sport competition today?

A: The way we always competed was very Budo-oriented. We always looked for the "kill," but I understand your question. Since the advent and growth of freestyle karate, the main goal in many dojo around the world is simply competition. Unfortunately, many associations that regulate the competition rules allow participants to do strange things. For instance, punching with good and strong positioning and scoring with a simple touch is one of those. Also, contestants lack zanchin. They concentrate more on what the referee will say than on their opponent. They should look at the opponent and not the referee. Forget the referee! Many students around the world never learn this serious approach to kumite karate, and the art becomes a simple sport. This approach brings a lack of confidence to the students simply due to the fact that they haven't been trained properly. They must be trained to kill with one blow, but they also have to learn how to control their power and techniques.

Q: Would you like to wish something to the karate practitioners?

A: Everybody should ask himself the following question: "What is the most important thing for me in karate?" I think that we all should practice karate with the same spirit, mood and ideas. Likely, people who practice karate with very similar ideas have identical inquiries, needs and purposes. The name of our organization — Karatenomichi — means "Way of karate, way to karate, way due to karate." Perhaps this also is the way in which we walk the karate path together, and we should meet many people on this way. Somewhere this way could become wider and somewhere it could become narrower. The most important thing that I want to pass on to you all is that you should never forget about the source of karate, its basic functions and purposes. If you ignore this and do not diligently execute all techniques, you will absolutely walk the other way, which is very far from the karate that I try to bring to your country and to your life. Control your ego properly because the true enemy is inside yourself, and this is the toughest opponent to beat.

DOJO KUN

BY TERUYUKI OKAZAKI

1. Jinkaku kansei ni tsutomuru koto

SEEK PERFECTION OF CHARACTER.

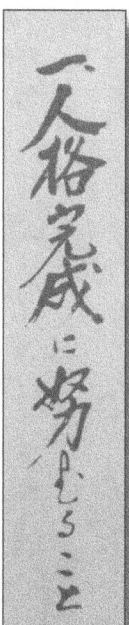

This is the ultimate goal of karate; it is the main reason why we train. The other four principles of the dojo kun, as well as the entire nijyu kun, all tell us what it means to seek perfection of character—how we can go about pursuing this most important objective. But to strive to improve, to always try to become a better human being – that is the most important thing! That's how we can bring peace to the world through karate – by making better human beings through training. That was the main goal of Master Funaskoshi – to help bring peace to the world.

It's okay to make mistakes – we are human beings after all. But we must always try to improve. Training develops the body, through physical exercise, and the mind as well, through the focus we need, to concentrate on techniques. But it also develops our spirit, because we must try hard, we must challenge ourselves when we train. This is how training develops character.

To seek perfection of character means we should never stop learning, and never stop training. It is good to set goals, but as soon as we accomplish them, it is important to set our sights on the next goal, to try to improve. There is no one ultimate goal we can achieve so we can say, "Okay, that's it, I don't have to improve." That's why I always say, it's good to get another rank, or it's good to do well at a tournament. But then we have to try to get better. Karate is about making better human beings.

2. Makoto no michi o mamoru koto

BE FAITHFUL

To be faithful means to be sincere in everything you do. Here we are talking about making a total effort, all the time, in whatever you do.

To be faithful of course means that you have to be true to other people, to your obligations—but it also means you have to be true to yourself. And to do so means you have to do your best in everything you do.

When you are faithful to yourself, others will have faith in you. This creates mutual trust between people. Being faithful to yourself is essential to realizing the first goal of being the best person you can be.

3. Doryoku no seishin o yashinau koto

ENDEAVOR

Try hard at everything you do. No matter what you are doing, whether it's training, working, having a relationship—give it one hundred percent. To do anything else is to cheat yourself and others. If you don't endeavor to do your best, you are not being faithful to yourself and others, and you are not seeking perfection of character.

4. Reigi o omonzuru koto

RESPECT OTHERS

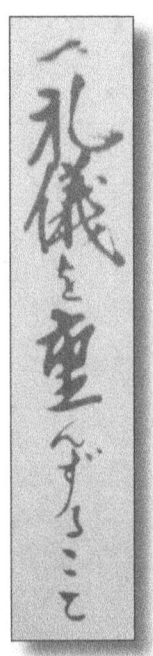

A true martial artist always shows respect to other people. And it is something you ought to feel in your heart. Showing respect is a sign of humility, and humility is necessary for an open mind. If your mind is not open, you cannot learn; you cannot grow. Remember that you can always learn something from every person you meet. Likewise, every person you encounter is a possible opponent of some kind, and that opponent can pose a threat to you, physical or otherwise. In either case, if you respect everyone, you will more clearly see things for what they are, and you will be able to get the most of every experience.

5. Keki no yu o imashimuru koto

REFRAIN FROM VIOLENT BEHAVIOR

This is a reminder to keep calm inside. Control yourself at all times, from within. Conflict within is a form of violence. It leads to violent actions, which is something you should try to avoid at all costs. A martial artist should always be in control, and that begins with an inner calmness, with peace of mind. If you are forced to defend yourself as a last resort, then it is all right to do so. But you will only be successful defending yourself when you maintain a calm, clear mind. Then you will be able to use karate techniques to protect yourself. When you have a clear mind, a karate technique will truly be your reaction of last resort.

Karate's Finest Masters Teach

KARATE MASTERS Vol.1 (Revised Edition)
By Jose M. Fraguas

Through conversations with many historical figures such as Osamu Ozawa, Teruo Hayashi, Kenzo Mabuni, Masatoshi Nakayama, and numerous current world-class masters such as Hirokazu Kanazawa, Fumio Demura, Takayuki Mikami, Teruyuki Okazaki, Morio Higaonna, Hidetaka Nishiyama, James Yabe, Tak Kubota, Bill Dometrich, Dan Ivan, and Stan Schmidt, the many threads of karate learning, lore, and legend are woven together to present an integrated and complete view of the empty-handed art of fighting, philosophy, and self-defense. Containing information that has not appeared anywhere else, the interviews contain intriguing thoughts, fascinating personal details, hidden history, and revealing philosophies.
#110 – 7 x 10 – 350 pages
ISBN: 978-1-933901-22-0

KARATE MASTERS Vol. 2
By Jose M. Fraguas

The second volume of the series offers a new repertoire of historical figures, such as Mas Oyama, Kyoshi Yamazaki. Masahiko Tanaka, Eihachi Ota, Yukiyoshi Marutani, Randall Hassell, Keinosuke Enoeda, Richard Kim, Shinpo Matayoshi, Tsutomu Ohshima, Yoshiaki Ajari, Goshi Yamaguchi, and other world-recognized professional martial artists. In this volume, new interviews with the world's top karate masters have been gathered to present an integrated and complete view of the empty-handed art of fighting, philosophy, and self-defense.
111 – 7 x 10 – 350 pages
ISBN: 978-1-933901-20-9

TO ORDER VISIT: www.empirebooks.com

Budo Greatest Lessons

KARATE MASTERS Vol.3
By Jose M. Fraguas

Including twenty-three exclusive interviews with legendary masters, such as Gogen "The Cat" Yamaguchi, Teruo Chinen, Edmond Otis, Akio Minakami, Jiro Ohtsuka, Shojiro Koyama, Ryusho Sakagami, Katsutaka Tanaka, Anthony Mirakian, Tetsuhiko Asai, Mikio Yahara, and other karate giants, this volume contains intriguing thoughts, fascinating personal details, hidden histories, and inspiring philosophies, as each master reveals his true love for the art and a deep understanding of every facet associated with the practice and spirit of the Japanese art of Karate-do as a way of life. This invaluable reference book is a "must have" addition to your personal library.
112 – 7 x 10 – 350 pages
ISBN: 978-1-933901-04-6

KARATE MASTERS Vol.4
By Jose M. Fraguas

After the acclaimed success of the first three volumes of Karate Masters, the author proudly presents "Karate Masters 4", with a new repertoire of historical figures, such as Yutaka Yaguchi, Hiroyasu Fujishima, Takeshi Uchiage, Kenneth Funakoshi, Kunio Murayama, Shoji Nishimura, Hiroshi Okazaki, Gene Tibon, Les Safar, Koss Yokota, Richard Amos, Taku Nakasaka, and other world-recognized Karate masters like George E. Mattson, Joe Carbonara, Tony Annesi, etc…. In this fourth volume, new interviews with the world's top Karate masters have been gathered to present an integrated and complete view of the empty-handed art of fighting, philosophy, and self-defense. Containing information that has not appeared anywhere else, the interviews contain intriguing thoughts, fascinating personal details, hidden history, and revealing philosophies as each master reveals his true love for the art and a deep understanding of every facet associated with the practice and spirit of the Japanese art of Karate-do as a way of life. It's a detailed reference work, and a "must have" addition to your personal library.
#133 – 7 x 10 – 370 pages
ISBN: 978-1-933901-49-7

TO ORDER VISIT: www.empirebooks.com

Karate's Finest Masters Teach

KARATE MASTERS Vol.5
By Jose M. Fraguas

After the acclaimed success of the "Karate Masters" series, the author presents "Karate Masters" Volume 5. With a new repertoire of historical figures, such as Hideo Ochi, Yoshimi Inoue, Sadaaki Sakagami, Masaru Miura, Genzo Iwata,, Katsuhiro Tsuyama, Yasuyoshi Saito, Nobuaki Kanazawa, Jerry Figgiani and legendary Okinawa masters like Kensei Taba, Takeshi Tamaki, Masahiko Tokashiki and Toshihiro Oshiro, amongst others, the many threads of traditional karate learning, lore, and legend are woven together. In this final volume, new interviews have been gathered to present an integrated and complete view of the empty-handed art of fighting, philosophy, and self-defense. This volume contains intriguing thoughts, fascinating personal details, hidden histories, and inspiring philosophies, as each master reveals his true love for the art and a deep understanding of every facet associated with the practice and spirit of the Japanese and Okinawan art of Karate-do as a way of life. It's a detailed reference work, and a "must have" addition to your personal library.

#134 – $45 – 7 x 10 – 400 pages
ISBN: 978-1-933901-53-4

KARATE WISDOM
By Jose M. Fraguas

After the acclaimed success of the "Karate Masters" Drawing from his personal experience with legendary Karate masters, the author presents for the first time in martial arts literature a single volume providing hundreds of quotations from the greatest Karate masters in history. Divided into eight chapters for easier comprehension, this work will give you many insightful words of help and wisdom for your martial arts journey. A classic collection of inspiring knowledge in philosophy, tradition, training, combat, kata, and weaponry as taught and developed by masters like Gichin Funakoshi, Gogen Yamaguchi, Mas Oyama, Kenwa Mabuni, Masatoshi Nakayama, and other Karate legends. Let this book inspire and guide you in your martial arts training and life..

#113 - 6 x 9 – 320 pages
ISBN: 978-1-933901-09-1

TO ORDER VISIT: www.empirebooks.com

Budo Greatest Lessons

SHOTOKAN MASTERS IN THEIR OWN WORDS
By Jose M. Fraguas

A rare and definitive book featuring the Japanese masters of the most popular style of Karate in the world. This outstanding compilation gathers the best Japanese Shotokan masters in one comprehensive volume; in their own words, they explain the philosophy, training and spirit of the art. Legendary masters of the teachings of Grandmaster and founder Gichin Funakoshi, like Tsutomu Ohshima, Masatoshi Nakayama, Taiji Kase, Hidetaka Nishiyama, Teruyuki Okazaki, Takayuki Mikami, Hirokazu Kanazawa, Keinosuke Enoeda and others contemporaries, openly talk about their struggles and training in the art of the "empty hand." This excellent book provides fascinating insights into the true lives and times of the masters of Shotokan Karate.
#121 – 6 x 9 – 160 pages
ISBN: 978-1-933901-15-2

COMBAT KARATE
By Jose M. Fraguas

The methods of the world's greatest karate fighters have been gathered together into this incredible volume to demonstrate the most closely-guarded secrets of sport competition, bare-knuckle fighting, and life-or-death street combat! The highly-technical and effective methods of karate's most dangerous masters are revealed for the first time in a single spectacular book! In addition to presenting numerous "how-to" techniques, each master reveals fascinating hidden aspects of karate-do, going back to the combat essentials developed in Okinawa, where unarmed peasants used the art of the "open hand" to defeat heavily-armed bandits and armored invaders!
Combat Karate is a must-have training aid for all those who wish to return to the true roots of karate and who desire to further their understanding of the practical applications of karate-do methods and techniques in both self-defense and competition. This book provides a greater understanding of karate's combat secrets and reveals its devastating fighting methods to the world!
129 – 7 x 10 - 350 pages approx.
ISBN: 978-1-933901-50-3

TO ORDER VISIT: www.empirebooks.com

NOTES

松濤館

NOTES

松濤館

NOTES

www.ingramcontent.com/pod-product-compliance
Lightning Source LLC
Chambersburg PA
CBHW081346080526
44588CB00016B/2389